I0234547

BEHEMOTH:

The History of the Causes

of

the Civil Wars of England,

and

the Councils and Artifices by which
They Were Carried on from the
Year 1640 to the Year 1660.

---

by THOMAS HOBBES of Malmesbury

LONDON
Hounskull Publishing
2018

HOUNSKULL PUBLISHING
BM Hounskull Publishing
London WC1N 3XX

Behemoth originally published in 1681
First edition edited by Ferdinand Tönnies published in 1889

First Hounskull edition published 2018
Second printing with corrections published June 2018

ISBN 978-1-910893-00-5

British Library Cataloguing-in-Publication Data:
A catalogue record for this book is available from the British Library.

*To the Right Honourable

SIR HENRY BENNET, BARON OF ARLINGTON.

My Lord,

I present your Lordship with four short dialogues concerning the memorable civil war in his Majesty's dominions from 1640 to 1660. The first contains the seed of it, certain opinions in divinity and politics. The second hath the growth of it in declarations, remonstrances, and other writings between the King and Parliament published. The two last are a very short epitome of the war itself, drawn out of Mr. Heath's chronicle. There can be nothing more instructive towards loyalty and justice than will be the memory, while it lasts, of that war. Your Lordship may do with it what you please. I petition not to have it published. But I pray your Lordship not to desist to be favourable as you have been, to me that am,

My Lord,

Your Lordship's most humble
and obliged servant,

THOMAS HOBBES.*

Table of Contents

The Bookseller to the Reader (1682 Edition)

My duty, as well to the public as to the memory of Mr. Hobbes, has obliged me to procure with my utmost diligence, that these tracts should come forth with the most correct exactness.

I am compelled by the force of truth to declare, how much the world and the memory of Mr. Hobbes have been abused by the several spurious editions of the History of the Civil Wars; wherein, by various and unskilful transcriptions, are committed above a thousand faults, and in above a hundred places whole lines left out, as I can make appear.

I must confess Mr. Hobbes, upon some considerations, was averse to the publishing thereof; but since it is impossible to suppress it, no book being more commonly sold by all booksellers, I hope I need not fear the offence of any man by doing right to the world and this work, which I now publish from the original manuscript, done by his own amanuensis, and given me by himself above twelve years since.

To this I have joined the treatise against Archbishop Bramhall, to prevent the like prejudice, which must certainly have fallen on it, there being so many false copies abroad, if not thus prevented; as also the Discourse of Heresy, from a more correct copy; and have likewise annexed his Physical Problems, as they were translated by himself and presented to his Majesty, with the epistle prefixed, in the year 1662, at the same time they came forth in Latin.

These things premised, there remains nothing but to wish for myself good sale, to the buyer much pleasure and satisfaction.

Your humble servant,

WILLIAM CROOKE

Foreword (1889 Edition)

Of Hobbes's *Behemoth*, or (as it was commonly called) the *Dialogue of the Civil Wars of England*, though written probably a few years after the Restoration, there was no genuine edition during the author's lifetime, which lasted until 1679. But three years later his old publisher, William Crooke, issued a volume entitled, *Tracts of Mr. Th. H. of Malmsbury*, containing in the first place the treatise entitled *Behemoth*, which is followed by three other pieces, and introduced by the following remarks: "My duty, as well to the Public as to the memory of Mr. Hobbs, has obliged me to procure, with my utmost diligence, that these Tracts should come forth with the most correct exactness. I am compelled by the force of Truth to declare, how much both the world and the name of Mr. Hobbs have been abused by the several spurious editions of the 'History of the Civil Wars,' wherein, by various and unskilful transcriptions, are committed above a thousand faults, and in above a hundred places whole lines left out, as I can make appear. I must confess Mr. Hobbs, upon some considerations, was averse to the publishing thereof; but since it is impossible to suppress it, no book being more commonly sold by all booksellers, I hope I need not fear the offence of any man, by doing right to the world and this work, which I now publish from the original manuscript, done by his own amanuensis, and given me by himself above twelve years since," &c. In the meantime, Mr. Crooke had been printing a letter by Hobbes, written to him shortly before the philosopher's death, and relating to the same affair, which in part explains, in part modifies, his foregoing statements. This letter he prefixed to his new edition of Hobbes's apology for his own life and character, in 1680 (*Considerations upon the reputation, loyalty, manners, and religion of Thomas Hobbes of Malmsbury written by himself by way of letter to a learned person*), inserting it in the following "advertisement to the readers": "I do here present you with a piece of Mr. Hobbes's writing, which is not published from an imperfect MS., as his 'Dialogue of the Civil Wars of England' was (by some that had got accidentally a copy of it) absolutely against his consent, as you may see by some passages out of some of his letters to me which I have here inserted. In his letter of June, 1679, he saith: I would fain have published my 'Dialogue of the Civil Wars of England' long ago, and to that end I presented it to his Majesty; and some days after, when I thought he had read it, I humbly besought him to let me print it; but his Majesty (though he heard me graciously, yet he) flatly refused to have it published. Therefore I brought away the book, and gave you leave to take a copy of it; which, when you had done, I gave the original to an honourable and learned friend, who about a year after died. The king knows better, and is more concerned in publishing of books than I am: therefore I dare not venture to appear in the business, lest it should offend him. Therefore I pray you not to meddle in the business. Rather than to be thought any way to further or countenance the printing, I would be content to lose twenty times the value of what you can expect to gain by it," &c. To this now may be added the following unprinted passage from a letter, which was addressed at a still later date (August 19, 1679) by the aged philosopher to his friend John Aubrey (the end of it being inserted in Aubrey's Sketch of Hobbes's Life, published in "Letters from the Bodleian," vol. ii., *ubi vid.* p. 614), running thus: "I have been told that my book of the civil war is come abroad, and am sorry for it, especially because I could not get his Majesty to license it, not because it is ill printed or has a foolish title set to it, for I believe that any ingenious man may understand the wickedness of that time, notwithstanding the errors of the press." (*Bodl. MS., Wood E.*, 4.)

Now, though it is true that Crooke's edition was very much improved as compared with the spurious ones, yet it was not made from the original copy, which I believe myself to have discovered and made use of now for the first time. The copy of which I speak is a beautifully written MS., preserved in St. John's College, Oxford; and upon this, as a matter of course, the present new edition, after a careful collation, has been founded, and may justly be said to stand in the same relation to the text as hitherto known,[1] which this one had to the unauthorized pamphlets above mentioned. For not only are there in this edition a very great number of places corrected, but also many deficient passages have been supplied. Amongst the latter there were some, erased with great care in the MS. itself, which I had great trouble in deciphering, though with very few exceptions I succeeded in so doing. I have not hesitated to insert these passages into the text, since they were evidently suppressed, not for reasons connected with the style and composition of the work, but as containing statements of opinion too strong to be made known, even through the medium of a manuscript copy; as will be better understood from the purport of the foregoing letters. The value of the cor-

1 It was said already with good reason (notwithstanding the publisher's assurance) by Mr. Anthony à Wood (or Mr. Aubrey) to contain many faults [*Athence Oxon*, vol. ii. col. 1213, ed. Bliss]; and the same text has been reprinted, first in the *Moral and Political Works of T. H.*, 1750, then in a collection of *Select tracts relating to the civil wars in England in the reign of King Charles the First, by writers who lived in the time of those wars, and were witnesses of the events which they describe. Edited by Francis Maseres, London*, 1815 (in this reprint there are a few alterations from conjecture). And, lastly, in Molesworth's edition, *English Works*, vol. vi., which I have compared here in the first place with the MS.

rections and additions made in this edition will in part be seen from the notes at the foot of the page, in which the more important of them are indicated.[2]

As to the book itself, it will give not a little pleasure to any thinking reader, being, in the words of Warburton, "full of shrewd remarks;" and it may be recommended as of high interest to the historical student as well as to the philosopher and politician. For, "in spite of his estrangement from the world around him, Hobbes continues to possess an increasing historical importance. Men and things change, but ideas expressed in words and in writing can soar above this change, and exercise an influence over the most distant epochs" (Leopold von Ranke, *History of England*, Engl. trans., vol. iii. p. 576). And in confirmation of this view it may not be amiss also to quote the words by which a former editor (Mr. Maseres) justifies the republication of "Behemoth."

"As Mr. Hobbes," he says (vol. ii. p. 657), "was a man of great ability and learning, and well acquainted with the history and forms of government of many different nations, both ancient and modern; and was also, as I believe, a very honest man and a great lover of truth; and as he lived through the two reigns of King James the First and King Charles

2 The words and passages which were never printed before, and amongst them the Epistle dedicatory, have been marked by *asteriscs* at the beginning and the end of them; and the sentences which were erased in the MS., by parentheses *[. . . .]* also. In the foot-notes I would chiefly draw attention to a number of corrections which are inserted in the MS. by the author's own hand.

the First, and through the Interregnum after King Charles's death to the Restoration of King Charles the Second, and through the next following eighteen years; and as he was, for the most part, resident in England during the ten years immediately preceding the civil war, and had conversed with several of the most eminent persons who afterwards were engaged in it, both on the king's side and that of the Parliament—I thought he was a writer singularly fit to be consulted and cited as a witness of the several events and transactions in those preceding years of King Charles's reign, which might justly be considered as the causes of the unhappy contest," &c.

It will be needful, perhaps, to give an explanation of the aged philosopher's complaint, quoted above (p. viii), as to the 'foolish title' prefixed to previous editions of the present work. The fact is that the words, "or the Long Parliament," now inserted according to the MS., had been left out in those editions, and consequently the meaning of the principal title (*viz.* Behemoth) failed to be suggested to the reader's mind; which meaning, as will now be sufficiently evident, implies a relation of contrast to the better known Leviathan, as representing the idea of a lawful government.

F. T.

HUSUM (SCHLESWIG-HOLSTEIN),
March, 1889.

Note on the Text (2018 Edition)

cholarly editions of a classic, non-fiction text like the present tend to be expensive or difficult to obtain, and come printed in tightly packed print, which make them difficult to read; while both the latter and modern non-scholarly reprints tend to neglect the aesthetic dimension of a book. The purpose of this edition, therefore, is to offer an aesthetically pleasing, easy to read source text that has some of the aids of scholarly editions.

The text of the present volume is based on the text of the edition published in 1889 by Simpkin, Marshall, and Co., which was edited from the original manuscript by Ferdinand Tönnies. To that, a comprehensive index, editorial footnotes, and six appendices have been added. An identifier has been applied to the editorial footnotes for this edition so as to distinguish them from Tönnies'.

BEHEMOTH

Dialogue I

A. If in time, as in place, there were degrees of high and low, I verily believe that the highest of time would be that which passed between the years of 1640 and 1660. For he that thence, as from the Devil's Mountain, should have looked upon the world and observed the actions of men, especially in England, might have had a prospect of all kinds of injustice, and of all kinds of folly, that the world could afford, and how they were produced by their *dams* hypocrisy and self-conceit, whereof the one is double iniquity, and the other double folly.

B. I should be glad to behold that prospect. You that have lived in that time and in that part of your age, wherein men used to see best into good and evil, I pray you to set me (that could not then see so well) upon the same mountain, by the relation of the actions you then saw, and of their causes, pretensions, justice, order, artifice, and event.

A. In the year 1640, the government of England was monarchical; and the King that reigned, Charles, the first of that name, holding the sovereignty, by right of a descent continued above six hundred years, and from a much longer descent King of Scotland, and from the time of his ancestor Henry II., King of Ireland; a man that wanted no virtue, either of body or mind, nor endeavoured anything more than to discharge his duty towards God, in the well governing of his subjects.

B. How could he then miscarry, having in every county so many trained soldiers, as would, put together, have made an army of 60,000 men, and divers magazines of ammunition in places fortified?

A. If those soldiers had been, as they and all other of his subjects ought to have been, at his Majesty's command, the peace and happiness of the three kingdoms had continued as it was left by King James. But the people were corrupted generally, and disobedient persons esteemed the best patriots.

B. But sure there were men enough, besides those that were ill-affected, to have made an army sufficient to have kept the people from uniting into a body able to oppose him.

A. Truly, I think, if the King had had money, he might have had soldiers enough in England. For there were very few of the common people that cared much for either of the causes, but would have taken any side for pay or plunder. But the King's treasury was very low, and his enemies, that pretended the people's ease from taxes, and other specious things, had the command of the purses of the city of London, and of most cities and corporate towns in England, and of many particular persons besides.

B. But how came the people to be so corrupted? And what kind of people were they that could so seduce them?

A. The seducers were of divers sorts. One sort were ministers; ministers, as they called themselves, of Christ; and sometimes, in their sermons to the people, God's ambassadors; pretending to have a right from God to govern every one his parish and their assembly the whole nation.

Secondly, there were a very great number, though not comparable to the other, which, notwithstanding that the Pope's power in England, both temporal and ecclesiastical, had been by Act of Parliament abolished, did still retain a belief that we ought to be governed by the Pope, whom they pretended to be the vicar of Christ, and, in the right of Christ, to be the governor of all Christian people. And these were known by the name of Papists; as the ministers I mentioned before, were commonly called Presbyterians.

Thirdly, there were not a few, who in the beginning of the troubles were not discovered, but shortly after declared themselves for a liberty in religion, and those of different opinions one from another. Some of them, because they would have all congregations free and independent upon one another, were called Independents. Others that held baptism to infants, and such as understood not into what they are baptized, to be ineffectual, were called therefore Anabaptists. Others that held that Christ's kingdom was at this time to begin upon the earth, were called Fifth-monarchy-men;[1] besides divers other sects, as Quakers, Adamites, &c., whose names and peculiar doctrines I do not well remember. And these were the enemies which arose against his Majesty from the private interpretation of the Scripture, exposed to every man's scanning in his mother-tongue.

Fourthly, there were an exceeding great number of men of the better sort, that had been so educated, as that in their youth having read the books written by famous men of the ancient Grecian and Roman commonwealths concerning their polity and great actions; in which books the popular government was extolled by the glorious name of liberty, and monarchy disgraced by the name of tyranny; they became thereby in love with their forms of government. And out of these men were chosen the greatest part of the House of Commons, or if they were not the greatest part, yet, by advantage of

1 The Fifth Monarchy Men, an extreme Puritan sect, took their name from a prophecy in the Book of Daniel, which stated that the kingdom of Christ would be preceded by four monarchies, the Babylonian, the Persian, the Macedonian, and the Roman. Since all of these were already passed, members of the sect believed that their prophesied thousand-year kingdom was upon them. Led by led by Thomas Harrison, they came to be active during the Interregnum, between 1649 and 1660. —Ed.

their eloquence, were always able to sway the rest.

Fifthly, the city of London and other great towns of trade, having in admiration the great prosperity of the Low Countries after they had revolted from their monarch, the King of Spain,[2] were inclined to think that the like change of government here, would to them produce the like prosperity.

Sixthly, there were a very great number that had either wasted their fortunes, or thought them too mean for the good parts which they thought were in themselves; and more there were, that had able bodies, but saw no means how honestly to get their bread. These longed for a war, and hoped to maintain themselves hereafter by the lucky choosing of a party to side with, and consequently did for the most part serve under them that had greatest plenty of money.

Lastly, the people in general were so ignorant of their duty, as that not one perhaps of ten thousand knew what right any man had to command him, or what necessity there was of King or Commonwealth, for which he was to part with his money against his will; but thought himself to be so much master of whatsoever he possessed, that it could not be taken from him upon any pretence of common safety without his own consent. King, they thought, was but a title of the highest honour, which gentleman, knight, baron, earl, duke, were but steps to ascend to, with the help of riches; they had no rule of equity, but precedents and custom;

2 Philip IV. —Ed.

and he was thought wisest and fittest to be chosen for a Parliament that was most averse to the granting of subsidies or other public payments.

B. In such a constitution of people, methinks, the King is already ousted of his government, so as they needed not have taken arms for it. For I cannot imagine how the King should come by any means to resist them.

A. There was indeed very great difficulty in the business. But of that point you will be better informed in the pursuit of this narration.

B. But I desire to know first, the several grounds of the pretences, both of the Pope[3] and of the Presbyterians, by which they claim a right to govern us, as they do, in chief: and after that, from whence, and when, crept in the pretences of that Long Parliament, for a democracy.

A. As for the Papists, they challenge this right from a text in Deut. xvii. 12, and other like texts, according to the old Latin translation in these words: *And he that out of pride shall refuse to obey the commandment of that priest, which shall at that time minister before the Lord thy God, that man shall by the sentence of the judge be put to death.* And because, as the Jews were the people of God then, so is all Christendom the people of God now, they infer from thence, that the Pope, whom they pretend to be the high-priest of all Christian peo-

3 The reigning Pope at this time was Urban VIII. He was succeeded in 1644 by Innoncent X, who was succeeded in 1655 by Alexander VII. —Ed.

ple, ought also to be obeyed in all his decrees by all Christians, upon pain of death. Again, whereas in the New Testament (Matt. xxviii. 18-20) Christ saith: *All power is given unto me in heaven and in earth; go therefore and teach all nations, and baptize them in the name of the Father, and of the Son, and of the Holy Ghost, and teach them to observe all these things which I have commanded you*: from thence they infer, that the command of the apostles was to be obeyed, and by consequence the nations were bound to be governed by them, and especially by the prince of the apostles, St. Peter, and by his successors, the Popes of Rome.

B. For the text in the Old Testament, I do not see how the commandment of God to the Jews, to obey their priests, can be interpreted to have the like force in the case of other nations Christian, more than upon nations unchristian (for all the world are God's people); unless we also grant, that a king cannot of an infidel be made Christian, without making himself subject to the laws of that apostle, or priest, or minister, that shall convert him. The Jews were a peculiar people of God, a sacerdotal kingdom, and bound to no other law but what first Moses, and afterwards every high-priest, did go and receive immediately from the mouth of God in Mount Sinai, in the tabernacle of the ark, and in the *sanctum sanctorum* of the temple. And for the text in St. Matthew, I know the words in the Gospel are not *go teach*, but *go, make disciples*; and that there is a great difference between a subject and a disciple, and between teaching and commanding. And if such texts as these must be so interpreted, why do not Christian kings lay down their titles of majesty and sovereignty, and call themselves the Pope's lieutenants? But the doctors of the Romish Church seem to decline that title of absolute power in their distinction of power spiritual and temporal; but this distinction I do not very well understand.

A. By spiritual power they mean the power to determine points of faith, and to be judges, in the inner court of conscience, of moral duties, and a power to punish those men, that obey not their precepts, by ecclesiastical censure, that is, by excommunication. And this power, they say, the Pope hath immediately from Christ, without dependence on any king or sovereign assembly, whose subjects they be that stand excommunicate. But for the power temporal, which consists in judging and punishing those actions that are done against the civil laws, they say, they do not pretend to it directly, but only indirectly, that is to say, so far forth as such actions tend to the hindrance or advancement of religion and good manners, which they mean when they say in *ordine ad spiritualia*.

B. What power then is left to Kings and other civil sovereigns, which the Pope may not pretend to be his in *ordine ad spiritualia*?

A. None, or very little. [And this power not only the Pope pretends to in all Christendom; but most bishops also, in their several dioceses, jure divino, that is, immediately from Christ, without deriving it from the Pope.][4]

B. But what if a man refuse obedience to this pretended power of the Pope and his bishops? What harm can excommunication do him, especially if he be the subject of another sovereign?

A. Very great harm. For by the Pope's or bishop's signification of it to the civil power, he shall be punished sufficiently.

B. He were in an ill case then, that adventured to write or speak in defence of the civil power, that must be punished by him whose rights he defended, like Uzza, that was slain because he would needs, unbidden, put forth his hand to keep the ark from falling.[5] But if a whole nation should revolt from the Pope at once, what effect could excommunication have upon the nation?

A. Why, they should have no more mass said, at least by any of the Pope's priests. Besides, the Pope would have no more to do with them, but cast them off, and so they would be in the same case

4 *The sentence:* "And this power . . . from the Pope", *though erased in the MS. by Hobbes' own hand, is not wanting in the text of Edd., where it has:* "some of his bishops", *instead of* 'most bishops'.

5 The men of Kirjath-jearim had placed the Ark of the Covenant in the house of Abinadab. When David then sought to bring the bring the Ark to Jerusalem, Uzzah and his brother Ahio put in on a cart, pulled by oxen, and began making their way. At one point, however, the oxen stumbled, and Uzzah steadied the Ark with his hand, in violation of a divine injunction against touching divine objects. For this he was immediately killed. —Ed.

as if a nation should be cast off by their king, and left to be governed by themselves, or whom they would.

B. This would not be taken so much for a punishment to the people, as to the King; and therefore when a Pope excommunicates a whole nation, methinks he rather excommunicates himself than them. But I pray you tell me, what were the rights the Pope pretended to in the kingdoms of other princes?

A. First, an exemption of all priests, friars, and monks, in criminal causes, from the cognizance of civil judges. Secondly, collation of benefices on whom he pleased, native or stranger, and exaction of tenths, first fruits, and other payments. Thirdly, appeals to Rome in all causes where the Church could pretend to be concerned. Fourthly, to be the supreme judge concerning lawfulness of marriage, that is, concerning the hereditary succession of Kings, and to have the cognizance of all causes concerning adultery and fornication.

B. Good! A monopoly of women.

A. Fifthly, a power of absolving subjects of their duties, and of their oaths of fidelity to their lawful sovereigns, when the Pope should think fit for the extirpation of heresy.

B. This power of absolving subjects of their obedience, as also that other of being judge of manners and doctrine, is as absolute a sovereignty as is possible to be; and consequently there must be two kingdoms in one and the same nation, and no man be able to know which of his masters he must obey.

A. For my part, I should rather obey that master that had the right of making laws and of inflicting punishments, than him that pretendeth only to a right of making canons (that is to say rules) and no right of co-action, or otherwise punishing, but by ex-communication.

B. But the Pope pretends also that his canons are laws; and for punishing, can there be greater than excommunication; supposing it true, as the Pope saith it is, that he that dies excommunicate is damned? Which supposition, it seems, you believe not; else you would rather have chosen to obey the Pope, that would cast your body and soul into hell, than the King, that can only kill the body.

A. You say true. For it were very uncharitable in me to believe that all Englishmen, except a few Papists, that have been born and called heretics ever since the Reformation of Religion in England, should be damned.

B. But for those that die excommunicate in the Church of England at this day, do you not think them also damned?

A. Doubtless, he that dies in sin without repentance is damned, and he that is excommunicate for disobedience to the King's laws, either spiritual or temporal, is excommunicate for sin; and therefore, if he die excommunicate and without desire of reconciliation, he dies impenitent. You see what follows. But to die in disobedience to the precepts and doctrines of those men that have no authority or jurisdiction over us, is quite another case, and bringeth no such danger with it.

B. But what is this heresy, which the Church of Rome so cruelly persecutes, as to depose Kings that do not, when they are bidden, turn all heretics out of their dominions?

A. Heresy is a word which, when it is used without passion, signifies a private opinion. So the different sects of the old philosophers, Academians, Peripatetics, Epicureans, Stoics, &c., were called heresies. But in the Christian Church, there was in the signification of that word, comprehended a sinful opposition to him, that was chief judge of doctrines in order to the salvation of men's souls; and consequently heresy may be said to bear the same relation to the power spiritual, that rebellion doth to the power temporal, and is suitable to be persecuted by him that will pre-serve a power spiritual and dominion of men's consciences.

B. It would be very well (because we are all of us permitted to read the Holy Scriptures, and bound to make them the rule of our actions, both public and private) that heresy were by some law defined, and the particular opinions set forth, for which a man were to be condemned and punished as a heretic; for else, not only men of mean capacity, but even the wisest and devoutest Christian, may fall into heresy without any will to oppose the Church; for the Scriptures are hard, and the interpretations different of different men.

A. The meaning of the word heresy is by law declared in an Act of Parliament in the first year of Queen Elizabeth; wherein it is ordained, that the persons who had by the Queen's letters-patent the authority spiritual, meaning the High Commission, *shall not have authority to adjudge any matter or cause to be heresy, but only such as heretofore have been adjudged to be heresy by the authority of the canonical Scriptures, or by the first four general Councils, or by any other general Council, where the same was declared heresy by the express and plain words of the said canonical Scriptures, or such as hereafter shall be adjudged heresy by the high court of Parliament of this realm, with the assent of the clergy in their convocation.*[6]

B. It seems therefore, if there arise any new error that hath not yet been declared heresy (and many such may arise), it cannot be judged heresy without a Parliament. For how foul soever the er-

6 Hobbes refers to the Act of Supremacy 1558, which received royal assent in 1559. The wording of the original text includes the following: 'shall hereafter by letters patents under the great seal of England give authority to have or execute any jurisdiction, power, or authority spiritual, or to visit, reform, order, or correct any errors, heresies, schisms, abuses, or enormities by virtue of this act, shall not in any wise have authority or power to order, determine, or adjudge any matter or cause to be heresy but only such as heretofore have been determined, ordered, or adjudged to be heresy by the authority of the canonical Scriptures, or by the first four general councils or any of them, or any other general council wherein the same was declared heresy by the express and plain words of the said canonical Scriptures, or such as hereafter shall be ordered, judged, or determined to be heresy by the high court of parliament of this realm, with the assent of the clergy in their convocation'. —Ed.

ror be, it cannot have been declared heresy neither in the Scriptures nor in the Councils; because it was never before heard of. And consequently there can be no error, unless it fall within the compass of blasphemy against God or treason against the King, for which a man can in equity be punished. Besides, who can tell what is declared by the Scripture, which every man is allowed to read and interpret to himself? Nay more, what Protestant, either of the laity or clergy, if every general Council can be a competent judge of heresy, is not already condemned? For divers Councils have declared a great many of our doctrines to be heresy, and that, as they pretend, upon the authority of the Scriptures.

A. What are those points, that the first four general Councils have declared heresy?

B. The first general Council, held at Nicæa,[7] declared all to be heresy which was contrary to the Nicene Creed, upon occasion of the heresy of Arius, which was the denying the divinity of Christ. The second general Council, held at Constantinople, declared heresy the doctrine of Macedonius;[8] which was that the Holy Ghost was created. The third Council, assembled at Ephesus, condemned the doctrine of Nestorius, that there were two persons in Christ.[9] The fourth, held at Chalce-

---

7 Convoked by Emperor Constantine I, it was held in 325. —Ed.

8 Macedonius I of Constantinople was bishop between 324 and 346, and again between 351 and 360. Convoked by Emperor Constantius II, the Council was held in 360. —Ed.

9 Nestorius (386 – 350) was Patriarch of Constantinople be-

don, condemned the error of Eutyches, that there was but one nature in Christ.[10] I know of no other points condemned in these four Councils, but such as concern church-government, or the same doctrines taught by other men in other words. And these Councils were all called by the Emperors, and by them their decrees confirmed at the petition of the Councils themselves.

A. I see by this, that both the calling of the Council, and the confirmation of their doctrine and church-government, had no obligatory force but from the authority of the Emperor. How comes it then to pass, that they take upon them now a legislative power, and say their canons are laws? That text, *all power is given to me in heaven and earth*, had the same force then as it hath now, and conferred a legislative power on the Councils, not only over Christian men, but *also* over all nations in the world.

B. They say no; for the power they pretend to is derived from this, that when a king was converted from Gentilism to Christianism, he did by that very submission to the bishop that converted him, sub-

---

tween 428 and 431. Convoked by Emperor Theodosius II of the Byzantine Empire, the Council was held in 431. —Ed.

10 Eutyches (c. 380 – c. 456), a presbyter and archimandrite at Constantinople, had vehemently opposed Nestorianism at the Council of Ephesus, yet his condemnation of the latter as a heresy led him to an equally extreme, although opposite view, which caused him to be denounced as a heretic himself. The Council of Chalcedon, convoked by Emperor Marcian of the Byzantine Empire, was held in 451. —Ed.

mit to the bishop's government and became one of his sheep; which right therefore he could not have over any nation that was not Christian.

A. Did Sylvester (which was Pope of Rome in the time of Constantine the Great, converted by him) tell the Emperor, his new disciple, beforehand, that if he became a Christian he must be the Pope's subject?

B. I believe not. For it is likely enough, if he had told him so plainly, or but made him suspect it, he would either have been no Christian at all, or but a counterfeit one.

A. But if he did not tell him so, and that plainly, it was foul play, not only in a priest, but in any Christian. And for this derivation of their right from the Emperor's consent, it proceeds only from this, that they dare not challenge a legislative power, nor call their *canons laws* in any kingdom in Christendom, further than the kings make them so. But in Peru, when Atabalipa was King,[11] the friar told him, that Christ being King of all the world, had given the disposing of all the kingdoms therein to the Pope, and that the Pope had given Peru to the Roman Emperor Charles the Fifth, and required Atabalipa to resign it; and for refusing it, seized upon his person by the Spanish army there present, and murdered him. You see by this how much they claim, when they have power to make it good.

11 Better known as Atahualpa (1502 – 1533), the latter reigned between 1525 and 1533. —Ed.

B. When began the Popes to take this authority upon them first?

A. After the inundation of the northern people had overflowed the western parts of the empire, and possessed themselves of Italy, the people of the city of Rome submitted themselves, as well in temporals as spirituals, to their bishop; and then first was the Pope a temporal prince, and stood no more in so great fear of the Emperors, which lived far off at Constantinople. In this time it was that the Pope began, by pretence of his power spiritual, to encroach upon the temporal rights of all other princes of the west; and so continued gaining upon them, till his power was at the highest in that three hundred years, or thereabout, which passed between the eighth and eleventh century, that is, between Pope Leo the Third and Pope Innocent the Third.[12] For in this time Pope Zachary the First[13] deposed Chilperic,[14] then King of France, and gave the kingdom to one of his subjects, Pepin;[15] and Pepin took from the Lombards a great part of their territory and gave it to the Church. Shortly after, the Lombards having recovered their es-

12 Technically correct, if measuring from when the respective Popes began their reign, but they each reigned mostly during the century following: Leo III reigned from 795 until his death in 816, and Innocent III between 1198 and 1216. —Ed.

13 Pope Zachary (679 – 752), reigned from 741 until his death. —Ed.

14 Chilperic III (717 – 754) was King of the Franks from 743 until 751. —Ed.

15 Pepin the Short (714 – 768), son of Charles Martel (686 – 741) and grandfather of Charlemagne (742 – 814). —Ed.

tate, Charles the Great retook it, and gave it to the Church again; and Pope Leo the Third made Charles Emperor.

B. But what right did the Pope then pretend for the creating of an Emperor?

A. He pretended the right of being Christ's vicar; and what Christ could give, his vicar might give; and you know that Christ was King of all the world.

B. Yes, as God; and so he gives all the kingdoms of the world, which nevertheless proceed from the consent of people, either for fear or hope.

A. But this gift of the empire was in a more special manner, in such a manner as Moses had the government of Israel given him; or rather as Joshua had it given him, to go in and out before the people as the high-priest should direct him. And so the empire was understood to be given him, on condition to be directed by the Pope. For when the Pope invested him with the regal ornaments, the people all cried out *Deus dat*, that is to say, *it is God that gives it; and the Emperor was contented so to take it*. And from that time, all or most of the Christian Kings do put into their titles the words *Dei gratia*, that is, *by the gift of God*; and their successors use still to receive the crown and sceptre from a bishop.

B. It is certainly a very good custom, for Kings to be put in mind by whose gift they reign; but it cannot from that custom be inferred that they receive the kingdom by mediation of the Pope, or by any other clergy; for the Popes themselves received the Papacy from the Emperor. The first that ever was elected Bishop of Rome after Emperors were Christians, and without the Emperor's consent, excused himself by letters to the Emperor with this: that the people and clergy of Rome forced him to take it upon him, and prayed the Emperor to confirm it, which the Emperor did; but with reprehension of their proceedings, and the prohibition of the like for the time to come. The Emperor was Lotharius, and the Pope Calixtus the First.[16]

A. You see by this the Emperor never acknowledged this gift of God was the gift of the Pope, but maintained that the Popedom was the gift of the Emperor. But in process of time, by the negligence of the Emperors (for the greatness of Kings makes them that they cannot easily descend into the obscure and narrow mines of an ambitious clergy), they found means to make the people believe, there was a power in the Pope and clergy, which they ought to submit unto, rather than to the commands of their own Kings, whensoever it should come into controversy: and to that end devised and decreed many new articles of faith, to the diminution of the authority of Kings, and to the disjunction of them and their subjects, and to a closer adherence of their subjects to the Church of Rome; articles either not at all found in, or not well founded upon the Scriptures; *as first, that it should not be lawful for a priest to marry.*

16 Calixtus was Pope from 218 until 222, while Lothair I was Holy Roman Emperor from 817 until 855. —Ed.

B. What influence could that have upon the power of Kings?

A. Do you not see, that by this the King must of necessity either want the priesthood, and therewith a great part of the reverence due to him from the most religious part of his subjects, or else want lawful heirs to succeed him? by which means, being not taken for the head of the Church, he was sure, in any controversy between him and the Pope, that his people would be against him.

B. Is not a Christian King as much a bishop now, as the heathen Kings were of old? for among them *episcopus* was a name common to all Kings. Is not he a bishop now, to whom God hath committed the charge of all the souls of his subjects, both of the laity and the clergy? And though he be in relation to our Saviour, who is the chief pastor, but a sheep, yet, compared to his own subjects, they are all sheep, both laic and cleric, and he only shepherd. And seeing a Christian bishop is but a Christian endued with power to govern the clergy, it follows that every Christian king is not only a bishop, but an arch-bishop, and his whole dominion his diocese. And though it were granted, that imposition of hands is necessary from a priest; yet, seeing Kings have the government of the clergy, that are his subjects even before baptism; the baptism itself, wherein he is received as a Christian, is a sufficient imposition of hands, so that whereas before he was a bishop, now he is a Christian bishop.

A. For my part I agree with you: this prohibition

of marriage to priests came in about the time of Pope Gregory the Seventh,[17] and William the First, King of England;[18] by which means the Pope had in England, what with secular and what with regular priests, a great many lusty bachelors at his service.

Secondly, *that auricular confession to a priest was necessary to salvation*. It is true that, before that time, confession to a priest was usual, and performed for the most part by him that confessed, in writing. But that use was taken away about the time of King Edward III.,[19] and priests commanded to take confessions from the mouth of the confitent: and men did generally believe, that without confession and absolution before their departure out of the world, they could not be saved; and having absolution from a priest, that they could not be damned. You understand by this, how much every man would stand in awe of the Pope and clergy, more than they would of the King; and what inconvenience it is to a state for their subjects to confess their secret thoughts to spies.

B. Yes, as much as eternal torture is more terrible than death, so much they would fear the clergy more than the King.

A. And though perhaps the Roman clergy will not maintain that a priest hath power to remit sins absolutely, but only with a condition of repent-

17 Gregory VII (1015 – 1085) was Pope from 1073 until his death.

18 William the Conqueror (1028 – 1087). —Ed.

19 Edward III (1312 – 1377) was King of England from 1327 until his death. —Ed.

ance, yet the people were never so instructed by them; but were left to believe, that whensoever they had absolution, their precedent sins were all discharged, when their penance, which they took for repentance, was performed. Within the same time began the article of transubstantiation. For it had been disputed a long time before, in what manner a man did eat the body of our Saviour Jesus Christ, as being a point very difficult for a man to conceive and imagine clearly; but now it was made very clear, namely, that the bread was transubstantiated into Christ's body, and so was become no more bread, but flesh.

B. It seems then that Christ had many bodies, and was in as many places at once, as there were communicants. I think the priests then were so wanton, as to insult upon the dulness, not only of common people, but also of kings and their councillors.

A. I am now in a narration, not in a disputation; and therefore I would have you to consider at this time nothing else, but what effect this doctrine would work upon kings and their subjects, in relation to the clergy, who only were able of a piece of bread to make our Saviour's body, and thereby at the hour of death to save their souls.

B. For my part, it would have an effect on me, to make me think them gods, and to stand in awe of them as of God himself, if he were visibly present.

A. Besides these, and other articles tending to the upholding of the Pope's authority, they had many fine points in their ecclesiastical polity, conducing to the same end; of which I will mention only such as were established within the same time. For then it was the order came up of preaching friars, that wandered up and down, with power to preach in what congregation they pleased, and were sure enough to instil into the people nothing that might lessen the obedience to the Church of Rome; but, on the contrary, whatsoever might give advantage to it against the civil power. Besides, they privately insinuated themselves with women and men of weak judgment, confirming their adherence to the Pope, and urging them, in the time of their sickness, to be beneficial to the Church[20] by contribution of money, or building religious houses, or pious works and necessary for the remission of their sins.

B. I do not remember that I have read of any kingdom or state in the world, where liberty was given to any private man to call the people together, and make orations to them frequently, or at all, without first making the state acquainted, except only in Christendom. I believe the heathen Kings foresaw, that a few such orators would be able to make a great sedition. Moses did indeed command to read the Scriptures and expound them in the Synagogues every Sabbath-day. But the Scriptures then were nothing else but the laws of the nation, delivered unto them by Moses himself. And I believe it would do no hurt, if the laws of England

20 beneficial to it—*corr. H.*

also were often read and expounded in the several congregations of Englishmen, at times appointed, that they may know what to do; for they know already what to believe.

A. I think that neither the preaching of friars nor monks, nor of parochial priests, tended to teach men what, but whom to believe. For the power of the mighty hath no foundation but in the opinion and belief of the people. And the end which the Pope had in multiplying sermons, was no other but to prop and enlarge his own authority over all Christian Kings and States.

Within the same time, that is, between the time of the Emperor Charles the Great and of King Edward the Third of England, began their second polity; which was, to bring religion into an art, and thereby to maintain all the decrees of the Roman Church, by disputation, not only from the Scriptures, but also from the philosophy of Aristotle, both moral and natural. And to that end the Pope exhorted the said Emperor by letter, to erect schools of all kinds of literature; and from thence began the institution of universities; for not long after, the universities began in Paris and in Oxford.[21] It is true, that there were schools in England before that time, in several places, for the instruction of children in the Latin tongue, that is to say, in the tongue of the Church. But for an university of learning, there was none erected till that

21 The University of Paris was founded in 1150; the University of Oxford in 1096. —Ed.

time; though it be not unlikely there might be then some that taught philosophy, logic, and other arts, in divers monasteries, the monks having little else to do but to study. After some colleges were built to that purpose, it was not long time before many more were added to them, by the devotion of princes and bishops, and other wealthy men: and the discipline therein was confirmed by the Popes that then were; and abundance of scholars sent thither by their friends to study, as to a place from whence the way was open and easy to preferment both in Church and Commonwealth. The profit that the Church of Rome expected from them, and in effect received, was the maintenance of the Pope's doctrine, and of his authority over kings and their subjects, by school-divines; who, striving to make good many points of faith incomprehensible, and calling in the philosophy of Aristotle to their assistance, wrote great books of school-divinity, which no man else, nor they themselves, are able to understand; as any man may perceive that shall consider the writings of Peter Lombard,[22] or Scotus[23]

22 Peter Lombard (1096 – 1160) was a scholastic theologian and, during his final year, Bishop of Paris; he authored the *Four Books of Sentences*, a systematic compilation of theology, written around 1150, which became a standard textbook. —Ed.

23 John Duns, or Duns Scotus (1266 – 1308), began his commentaries, which contain nearly all the views and philosophical arguments for which he is known, around 1300, while still at the University of Oxford; they were still unfinished when he arrived at the University of Paris in 1302, when he began giving lectures on Peter Lombard, but was expelled later in the same academic year, his commentaries still unfinished. —Ed.

that wrote commentaries upon him, or of Suarez,[24] or any other school-divine of later times. Which kind of learning nevertheless hath been much admired by two sorts of men, otherwise prudent enough; the one of which sorts were those that were already devoted and really affectionate to the Roman Church; for they believed the doctrine before, but admired the arguments because they understood them not, and yet found the conclusions to their mind. The other sort were negligent men, that had rather admire with others, than take the pains to examine. So that all sorts of people were fully resolved, that both the doctrine was true, and the Pope's authority no more than was due to him.

B. I see that a Christian king, or state, how well soever provided he be of money and arms, where the Church of Rome hath such authority, will have but a hard match of it, for want of men. For their subjects will hardly be drawn into the field and fight with courage against their consciences.

A. It is true that great rebellions have been raised by Church-men in the Pope's quarrel against kings, as in England against King John,[25] and in France

24 Francisco Suárez (1548 – 1617) was a Spanish philosopher and scholastic theologian, chiefly known for his work on metaphysics and the philosophy of law. —Ed.

25 The Norman and Angevin kings had exercised power over the Church within their territories, but, from 1040, a procrocess of change begun, instigated by the Pope, who had desired a more centralised rule from Rome. Structures had been put in place that ran parallel and independent from the lay power, the principles behind which had become well accepted by the Church in

against King Henry IV.[26] Wherein the Kings had a more considerable part on their sides, than the Pope had on his; and shall always have so, if they

---

England by 1140. By the time of King John, the King's authority regarding appointments was being brought into question. The death of the Archbishop of Canterbury, Hubert Walter, in 1205 gave John opportunity to experience this. He favoured John de Gray as Walter's successor, but the cathedral chapter at Canterbury claimed exclusive right to elect the aforementioned, and they favoured the chapter's sub-prior, Reginald. The matter was taken to Rome, where Pope Innocent III rejected both choices in favour of a third, Stephen Langton, who was consecrated in spite of John's objections. John then punished the Church by barring Langton's entry into England and seizing the Archbishopric's lands, along with other Papal possessions. The Pope responded by placing an interdict on England, prohibiting clergy from conducting religious services, with some exceptions. John retaliated with more land seizures and the arrest of illicit clerical concubines. The Pope finally excommunicated John in 1209. However, the threat of invasion from France, which John feared was being planned on the Pope's behalf, caused him opt for a negotiated reconciliation. He surrendered the Kingdom of England to the Papacy in exchange for a feudal service of 1000 Marks, and agreed to recompense the Church for the lost income. Amazingly, there was little reaction from John's subjects, and, in the end, he gained more than the Pope, for the latter became a loyal ally, deterred France from invading, and conveniently forgot about John's debt after the latter stopped paying a year after their agreement. —Ed.

26 When Henry IV succeeded his predecessor in 1572, Henry III, he faced opposition from the Catholic League, which was supported, among others, by Pope Sixtus V, on account of his religion. The League committed to the eradication of Huguenot Protestants. Henry IV, a Huguenot, kept his faith for a while, but, eventually, thought it best to convert to Roman Catholicism, thus allowing him to be crowned, finally, in 1594. He subsequently issued the Edict of Nantes in 1598, which granted the Huguenots substantial rights in France. —Ed.

have money. For there are but few whose consciences are so tender as to refuse money when they want it. But the great mischief done to kings upon pretence of religion is, when the Pope gives power to one king to invade another.

B. I wonder how King Henry the Eighth could then so utterly extinguish the authority of the Pope in England, and that without any rebellion at home, or any invasion from abroad.

A. First, the priests, monks, and friars, being in the height of their power, were now for the most part grown insolent and licentious; and thereby the force of their arguments was now taken away by the scandal of their lives, which the gentry and men of good education easily perceived: and the Parliament consisting of such persons, was therefore willing to take away their power: and generally the common people, which from a long custom had been in love with Parliaments, were not displeased therewith. Secondly, the doctrine of Luther beginning a little before, was now by a great many men of the greatest judgment so well received, as that there was no hope to restore the Pope to his power by rebellion. Thirdly, the revenue of abbeys and all other religious houses, falling thereby into the King's hands, and by him being disposed of to the most eminent gentlemen in every county, could not but make them do their best to confirm themselves in the possession of them. Fourthly, King Henry was of a nature quick and severe in the punishing of such as should be the first to oppose his designs. Lastly, as to invasion from abroad, in case the Pope had given the kingdom to another prince, it had been in vain; for England is another manner of kingdom than Navarre. Besides, the French and Spanish forces were employed at that time one against another: and though they had been at leisure, they would have found perhaps no better success than the Spaniards found afterwards in 1588. Nevertheless, notwithstanding the insolence, avarice, and hypocrisy of the then clergy, and notwithstanding the doctrine of Luther, if the Pope had not provoked the King by endeavouring to cross his marriage with his second wife, his authority might have remained in England till there had risen some other quarrel.

B. Did not the bishops, that then were, and had taken an oath, wherein was, amongst other things, that they should defend and maintain the Regal Rights of St. Peter (the words are, *Regalia Sancti Petri*, which nevertheless some have said are *regulas Sancti Petri*, that is to say, St. Peter's Rules or Doctrine; and that the clergy afterward did read it, being perhaps written in short-hand, by a mistake to the Pope's advantage *regalia*): did not, I say, the bishops oppose that Act of Parliament against the Pope, and against the taking of the oath of supremacy?

A. No, I do not find the bishops did many of them oppose the King; for having no power without him, it had been great imprudence to provoke his anger. There was besides a controversy in those times between the Pope and the bishops, most of which did maintain that they exercised their jurisdiction episcopal in the right of God, as immediately as the Pope himself did exercise the same over the whole Church. And because they saw that by this Act of the King's in Parliament they were to hold their power no more of the Pope, and never thought of holding it of the King, they were perhaps better content to let that Act of Parliament pass. In the reign of King Edward VI.[27] the doctrine of Luther had taken so great root in England, that they threw out also a great many of the Pope's new articles of faith; which Queen Mary[28] succeeding him restored again, together with all that had been abolished by Henry VIII., saving (that which could not be restored) the religious houses; and the bishops and clergy of King Edward were partly burnt for heretics, partly fled, and partly recanted. And they that fled betook themselves to those places beyond sea, where the reformed religion was either protected or not persecuted; who, after the decease of Queen Mary, returned again to favour and preferment under Queen Elizabeth, that restored the religion of her brother King Edward. And so it hath continued till this day, excepting the interruption made in this late rebellion of the presbyterians and other democratical men. But though the Romish religion were now cast out by the law, yet there were abundance of people, and many of them of the nobility, that still retained the religion

27 Edward VI (1537 – 1553) reigned from 1547 until his death. —Ed.

28 Reigned from 1553 until her death in 1558. —Ed.

of their ancestors, who as they were not much molested in points of conscience, so they were not by their own inclination very troublesome to the civil government; but by the secret practice of the Jesuits and other emissaries of the Roman Church, they were made less quiet than they ought to have been; and some of them to venture on the most horrid act that ever had been heard of before, I mean the Gunpowder Treason. And upon that account, the Papists of England have been looked upon as men that would not be sorry for any disorders here that might possibly make way to the restoring of the Pope's authority. And therefore I named them for one of the distempers of the state of England in the time of our late King Charles.

B. I see that Monsieur Mornay du Plessis, and Dr. Morton, Bishop of Durham, writing of the progress of the Pope's power, and intituling their books, one of them, "The Mystery of Iniquity," the other, "The Grand Imposture," were both in the right.[29] For I believe there was never such another cheat in the world, and I wonder that the Kings

29 Thomas Morton (1564 – 1659), who served as Bishop of Chester (1616 – 1619, of Lichfield and Coventry (1619 – 1632), and of Durham (1632 – 1659) wrote violently and polemically against Papism. His text, *The Grand Imposture,* was published in 1626, with a second, revised edition appearing in 1628. Philippe de Mornay (1549 – 1623)'s *The Mystery of Inquity* was a polemical history of the Pontifical authority, published in 1611, which was later best remembered chiefly for its frontispice. According to Edward Smedley, in this frontispice 'a huge pile of Babel, typifying the Papal sway, rears its gigantic summit to the skies; but its foundation is a frail wooden plat-

and States of Christendom never perceived it.

A. It is manifest they did perceive it. How else durst they make war, *as they have done*, against the Pope, and some of them take him out of Rome itself and carry him away prisoner? But if they would have freed themselves from his tyranny, they should have agreed together, and made themselves every one, as Henry VIII. did, head of the Church within their own respective dominions. But not agreeing, they let his power continue, every one hoping to make use of it, when there should be cause, against his neighbour.

B. Now, as to that other distemper by Presbyterians, how came their power to be so great, being of themselves, for the most part, but so many poor scholars?

A. This controversy between the Papist and the Reformed Churches could not choose but make every man, to the best of his power, examine by the Scriptures, which of them was in the right; and to that end they were translated into vulgar languages; whereas before, the translation of them was not allowed, nor any man to read them but such as had express license so to do. For the Pope did concern-

---

form, benath which the activity of a man coarsely habited has already kindled a fire. On the opposite side, a Jesuit, in a contemplative attitude, is regarding the stupendous height of the tower, of whose approaching downfall he is warned by the following distich: '*Falleris æternam qui suspicis ebrius arcem: Subruta succensis mox corruet ima tigillis*'. *History of the Reformed Religion in France* (London: J. G. and F. Rivington, 1834) 3:103-104. —Ed.

ing the Scriptures the same that Moses did concerning Mount Sinai. Moses suffered no man to go up to it to hear God speak or gaze upon him, but such as he himself took with him; and the Pope suffered none to speak with God in the Scriptures, that had not some part of the Pope's spirit in him, for which he might be trusted.

B. Certainly Moses did therein very wisely, and according to God's own commandment.

A. No doubt of it, and the event itself hath made it appear so. For after the Bible was translated into English, every man, nay, every boy and wench, that could read English, thought they spoke with God Almighty, and understood what he said, when by a certain number of chapters a day they had read the Scriptures once or twice over. *And so* the reverence and obedience due to the Reformed Church here, and to the bishops and pastors therein, was cast off; and every man became a judge of religion, and an interpreter of the Scriptures to himself.

B. Did not the Church of England intend it should be so? What other end could they have in recommending the Bible to me, if they did not mean I should make it the rule of my actions? Else they might have kept it, though open to themselves, to me sealed up in Hebrew, Greek, and Latin, and fed me out of it in such measure as had been requisite for the salvation of my soul and the Church's peace.

A. I confess this licence of interpreting the Scripture was the cause of so many several sects, as having lain hid till the beginning of the late

King's reign, did then appear to the disturbance of the commonwealth. But to return to the story. Those persons that fled for religion in the time of Queen Mary, resided, for the most part, in places where the Reformed religion was professed and governed by an assembly of ministers; who also were not a little made use of (for want of better statesmen), in points of civil government. Which pleased so much the English and Scotch Protestants that lived amongst them, that at their return they wished there were the same honour and reverence given to the ministry in their own countries. *And* in Scotland (King James being then young) soon (with the help of some of the powerful nobility) they brought it to pass. Also they that returned into England in the beginning of the reign of Queen Elizabeth, endeavoured the same here, but could never effect it till this last rebellion, nor without the aid of the Scots. And it was no sooner effected, but they were defeated again by the other sects, which, by the preaching of the Presbyterians and private interpretation of Scripture, were grown numerous.

B. I know indeed that in the beginning of the late war, the power of the Presbyterians was so very great, that, not only the citizens of London were almost all of them at their devotion, but also the greatest part of all other cities and market-towns of England. But you have not yet told me by what art and what degrees they became so strong.

A. It was not their own art alone that did it, but

they had the concurrence of a great many gentlemen, that did no less desire a popular government in the civil state than these ministers did in the Church. And as these did in the pulpit draw the people to their opinions, and to a dislike of the Church-government, Canons, and Common-prayerbook, so did the other make them in love with democracy by their harangues in the Parliament, and by their discourses and communication with people in the country, continually extolling liberty and inveighing against tyranny, leaving the people to collect of themselves that this tyranny was the present government of the state. And as the Presbyterians brought with them into their churches their divinity from the universities, so did many of the gentlemen bring their politics from thence into the Parliament; but neither of them did this very boldly during the time of Queen Elizabeth. And though it be not likely that all of them did it out of malice, but many of them out of error, yet certainly the chief leaders were ambitious ministers and ambitious gentlemen; the ministers envying the authority of bishops, whom they thought less learned; and the gentlemen envying the privy-council and principal courtiers, whom they thought less wise than themselves. For it is a hard matter for men, who do all think highly of their own wits, when they have also acquired the learning of the university, to be persuaded that they want any ability requisite for the government of a commonwealth, especially having read the glorious histories and the sententious politics of the ancient popular governments of the Greeks and Romans, amongst whom kings were hated and branded with the name of tyrants, and popular government (though no tyrant was ever so cruel as a popular assembly) passed by the name of liberty. The Presbyterian ministers, in the beginning of the reign of Queen Elizabeth, did not (because they durst not) publicly *and plainly* preach against the discipline of the Church. But not long after, by the favour perhaps of some great courtier, they went abroad preaching in most of the market-towns of England, as the preaching friars had formerly done, upon working-days in the morning; in which sermons, these and others of the same tenets, that had charge of souls, both by the manner and matter of their preaching, applied themselves wholly to the winning of the people to a liking of their doctrines and good opinion of their persons.

And first, for the manner of their preaching; they so framed their countenance and gesture at their entrance into the pulpit, and their pronunciation both in their prayer and sermon, and used the Scripture phrase (whether understood by the people or not), as that no tragedian in the world could have acted the part of a right godly man better than these did; insomuch as a man unacquainted with such art, could never suspect any ambitious plot in them to raise sedition against the state, as they then had designed; or doubt that the vehemence of their voice (for the same words with the usual pronunciation had been of little force) and forcedness of their gesture and looks, could arise from anything else but zeal to the service of God. And by this art they came into such credit, that numbers of men used to go forth of their own parishes and towns on working-days, leaving their calling, and on Sundays leaving their own churches, to hear them preach in other places, and to despise their own and all other preachers that acted not so well as they. And as for those ministers that did not usually preach, but instead of sermons did read to the people such homilies as the Church had appointed, they esteemed and called them *dumb dogs*.

Secondly, for the matter of their sermons, because the anger of the people in the late Roman usurpation was then fresh, they saw there could be nothing more gracious with them than to preach against such other points of the Romish religion as the bishops had not yet condemned; that so receding further from popery than they did, they might with glory to themselves leave a suspicion on the bishops, as men not yet well purged from idolatry.

Thirdly, before their sermons, their prayer was or seemed to be extempore, which they pretended to be dictated by the spirit of God within them, and many of the people believed or seemed to believe it. For any man might see, that had judgment, that they did not take care beforehand what they should say in their prayers. And from hence came a dislike of the *common-prayer-book*, which is a set form, premeditated, that men might see to what they were to say *Amen*.

Fourthly, they did never in their sermons, or but lightly, inveigh against the lucrative vices of men of trade or handicraft; such as are feigning, lying, cozening, hypocrisy, or other uncharitableness, except want of charity to their pastors and to the faithful: which was a great ease to the generality of citizens and the inhabitants of market-towns, and no little profit to themselves.

Fifthly, by preaching up an opinion that men were to be assured of their salvation by the testimony of their own private spirit, meaning the Holy Ghost dwelling within them. And from this opinion the people that found in themselves a sufficient hatred towards the Papists, and an ability to repeat the sermons of these men at their coming home, made no doubt but that they had all that was necessary, how fraudulently and spitefully soever they behaved themselves to their neighbours that were not reckoned amongst the Saints, and sometimes to those also.

Sixthly, they did, indeed, with great earnestness and severity, inveigh often against two sins, carnal lusts and vain swearing; which, without question, was very well done. But the common people were thereby inclined to believe, that nothing else was sin, but that which was forbidden in the third and seventh commandments (for few men do understand by the name of lust any other concupiscence, than that which is forbidden in that seventh commandment; for men are not ordinarily said to lust after another man's cattle, or other goods or possessions): and therefore never made much scruple of the acts of fraud and malice, but endeavoured to keep themselves from uncleanness only, or at least from the scandal of it. And, whereas they did, both in their sermons and writings, maintain and inculcate, that the very first motions of the mind, that is to say, the delight men and women took in the sight of one another's form, though they checked the proceeding thereof so that it never grew up to be a design, was nevertheless a sin, they brought young men into desperation and to think themselves damned, because they could not (which no man can, and is contrary to the constitution of nature) behold a delightful object without delight. And by this means they became confessors to such as were thus troubled in conscience, and were obeyed by them as their spiritual doctors in all cases of conscience.

B. Yet divers of them did preach frequently against oppression.

A. It is true, I had forgot that; but it was before such as were free enough from it; I mean the common people, who would easily believe themselves oppressed, but never oppressors. And therefore you may reckon this among their artifices, to make the people believe they were oppressed by the King, or perhaps by the bishops, or both; and incline the meaner sort to their party afterwards, when there should be occasion. But this was but sparingly done in the time of Queen Elizabeth, whose fear and jealousy they were afraid of. Nor had they as yet any great power in the Parliament-house, whereby to call in question her prerogative by petitions of right and other devices, as they did afterwards, when democratical gentlemen had received them into their counsels for the design of changing the government from monarchical to popular, which they called liberty.

B. Who would think that such horrible designs as these could so easily and so long remain covered with the cloak of godliness? For that they were most impious hypocrites, is manifest enough by the war their proceedings ended in, and by the impious acts in that war committed. But when began first to appear in Parliament the attempt of popular government, and by whom?

A. As to the time of attempting the change of government from monarchical to democratical, we must distinguish. They did not challenge the sovereignty in plain terms, and by that name, till they had slain the King; nor the rights thereof altogether by particular heads, till the King was driven from London by tumults raised in that city against him, and retired for the security of his person to York; where he had not been many days, when they sent unto him nineteen propositions, whereof above a dozen were demands of several powers, essential parts of the power sovereign. But before that time they had demanded some of them in a petition which they called a Petition of Right;[30] which nevertheless the King had granted them in a former Parliament, though he deprived himself thereby, not only of the power to levy money without their consent, but also of his ordinary revenue by custom of tonnage and poundage, and of the liberty to put into custody such men as he thought likely to disturb the peace and raise sedition in the kingdom. As for the men that did this, it is enough to say they were members of the last Parliament, and of some other Parliaments in the beginning of King Charles and the end of King James his reign; to name them all is not necessary, further than the story shall require. Most of them were members of the House of Commons; some few also, of the Lords; but all, such as had a great opinion of their

30 Passed on 7 June 1628, the petition came in response to various measures taken by Charles in his efforts to secure funds from Parliament for the continued conduct of the Thirty Year War, which he had inherited from his father, James, along with the throne. These measures included the raising of funds through forced loans (taxes not approved by Parliament); the imprisonment without charges or trial of those refusing to pay; and the declaration of martial law, which, at the time, meant the suspension of the rule of law in favour of summary judgments by local military commanders, albeit in accordance to certain rules. The latter had been declared by previous monarchs, such as Elizabeth I, but Charles lacked her popularity, Parliamentary support, and perceived justification. The petition requested no payment of taxes without an act of Parliament; no imprisonment, except under the law and not without charges being shown; *habeas corpus* for everyone; no forced billeting of soldiers, and restrictions on the use of martial law. —Ed.

sufficiency in politics, which they thought was not sufficiently taken notice of by the King.

B. How could the Parliament, when the King had a great navy, and a great number of trained soldiers, and all the magazines of ammunition in his power, be able to begin the war?

A. The King had these things indeed in his right; but that signifies little, when they that had the custody of the navy and magazines, and with them all the trained soldiers, and in a manner all his subjects, were by the preaching of Presbyterian ministers, and the seditious whisperings of false and ignorant politicians, made his enemies; and when the King could have no money but what the Parliament should give him, which you may be sure should not be enough to maintain his regal power, which they intended to take from him. And yet, I think, they never would have ventured into the field, but for that unlucky business of imposing upon the Scots, who were all Presbyterians, our book of Common-prayer. For I believe the English would never have taken well that the Parliament should make war upon the King, upon any provocation, unless it were in their own defence, in case the King should first make war upon them; and, therefore, it behoved them to provoke the King, that he might do something that might look like hostility.

It happened in the year 1637, that the King, by the advice, as it was thought, of the Archbishop of Canterbury, sent down a book of Common-prayer into Scotland, not differing in substance from ours, nor much in words besides the putting of the word Presbyter for that of Minister, commanding it to be used (for conformity with this kingdom) by the ministers there, for an ordinary form of Divine service. This being read in the church at Edinburgh, caused such a tumult there, that he that read it had much ado to escape with his life; and gave occasion to the greatest part of the nobility and others to enter, by their own authority, into a Covenant amongst themselves, which impudently they called a *Covenant with God*, to put down episcopacy, without consulting with the King: which they presently did, animated thereto by their own confidence, or by assurance from some of the democratical Englishmen that in former Parliaments had been the greatest opposers of the King's interests, that the King would not be able to raise an army to chastise them without calling a Parliament, which would be sure to favour them. For the thing which those democraticals chiefly then aimed at, was to force the King to call a Parliament, which he had not done for ten years before, as having found no help, but hindrance to his designs in the Parliaments he had formerly called. Howsoever, contrary to their expectation, by the help of his better-affected subjects of the nobility and gentry, he made a shift to raise a sufficient army to have reduced the Scots to their former obedience, if it had proceeded to battle. And with this army he marched himself into Scotland; where the

Scotch army was also brought into the field against him, as if they meant to fight. But then the Scotch sent to the King for leave to treat by commissioners on both sides; and the King, willing to avoid the destruction of his own subjects, condescended to it. The issue was peace;[31] and the King thereupon went to Edinburgh, and passed an Act of Parliament there to their satisfaction.

B. Did he not then confirm episcopacy?

A. No, but yielded to the abolishing of it: but by this means the English were crossed in their hope of a Parliament. But the said democraticals, formerly opposers of the King's interest, ceased not to endeavour still to put the two nations into a war; to the end the King might buy the Parliament's help at no less a price than sovereignty itself.

B. But what was the cause that the gentry and nobility of Scotland were so averse from the episcopacy? For I can hardly believe that their consciences were extraordinarily tender, nor that they were so very great divines, as to know what was the true Church-discipline established by our Saviour and his Apostles; nor yet so much in love with their ministers, as to be over-ruled by them in the government either ecclesiastical or civil. For in their lives they were just as other men are, pursuers of their own interests and preferments, wherein they were not more opposed by the bishops than by their Presbyterian ministers.

A. Truly I do not know; I cannot enter into oth-

31 The Treaty of Berwick was signed on 19 June 1639. —Ed.

er men's thoughts, farther than I am led by the consideration of human nature in general. But upon this consideration I see first, that men of ancient wealth and nobility are not apt to brook, that poor scholars should (as they must, when they are made bishops) be their fellows. Secondly, that from the emulation of glory between the nations, they might be willing to see this nation afflicted by civil war, and might hope, by aiding the rebels here, to acquire some power over the English, at least so far as to establish here the Presbyterian discipline; which was also one of the points they afterwards openly demanded. Lastly, they might hope for, in the war, some great sum of money, as a reward of their assistance, besides great booty, which they afterwards obtained. But whatsoever was the cause of their hatred to bishops, the pulling of them down was not all they aimed at: if it had, now that episcopacy was abolished by act of Parliament, they would have rested satisfied, which they did not. For after the King was returned to London, the English Presbyterians and democraticals, by whose favour they had put down bishops in Scotland, thought it reason to have the assistance of the Scotch for the pulling down of bishops in England. And in order thereunto, they might perhaps deal with the Scots secretly, to rest unsatisfied with that pacification, which they were before contented with. Howsoever it was, not long after the King was returned to London, they sent up to some of their friends at court a certain paper, containing, as they pretended, the articles of the said pacification; a false and scandalous paper, which was by the King's command burnt, as I have heard, publicly. And so both parties returned to the same condition they were in, when the King went down with his army.

B. And so there was a great deal of money cast away to no purpose. But you have not told me who was general of that army.

A. I told you the King was there in person. He that commanded under him was the Earl of Arundel, a man that wanted not either valour or judgment. But to proceed to battle or to treaty, was not in his power, but in the King's.

B. He was a man of a most noble and loyal family, and whose ancestor had formerly given a great overthrow to the Scots, in their own country; and in all likelihood he might have given them the like now, if they had fought.

A. He might indeed: but it had been but a kind of superstition to have made him general upon that account, though many generals heretofore have been chosen for the good luck of their ancestors in like occasions. In the long war between Athens and Sparta, a general of the Athenians[32] by sea won many victories against the Spartans; for which cause, after his death, they chose his son [33]for general with ill success. The Romans that conquered Carthage by the valour and conduct of Sci-

32 Phormio. —Ed.

33 Asopius. —Ed.

pio,[34] when they were to make war again in Africa against Cæsar, chose another Scipio[35] for general; a man valiant and wise enough, but that perished in the employment. And to come home to our own nation, the Earl of Essex[36] made a fortunate expedition to Cadiz;[37] but his son, sent afterwards to the same place, could do nothing. It is but a foolish superstition to hope that God has entailed success in war upon a name or family.

---

34 Scipio Aemilianus (185–129 BC). —Ed.

35 Metellus Scipio (c. 100/98 BCE – 46 BCE). —Ed.

36 Robert Devereux, 3rd Earl of Essex (1591 – 1646) was the son of Robert Devereux, 2nd Earl of Essex, Elizabeth's I favourite, and of Frances Walsingham, only daughter of Sir Frances Walsingham, Elizabeth I's Secretary of State. —Ed.

37 Robert Devereux, 2nd Earl of Essex, had successfully raided Cadiz in 1596, costing the Spanish 5 million ducats and contributing to the bankruptcy of Spain's royal treasury later that year. The Spanish treasury recovered quickly and Spain and England ended the war with the Treaty of London in 1604. In November 1625, however, a second expedition was launched to capture the city, partly as an exercise to restore the prestige of the Elizabethan Era, and the 3rd Earl of Essex was sent along, as a vice-admiral and as a colonel, with less fortunate results. Sir Edward Cecil, the commander of the expedition, not only failed to take the city, which Philip II had since robustly fortified, but, after allowing his men to drink from the wine vats in local houses, was forced to retreat, leaving a 1000 of them behind, who, fully armed but drunk, were captured by the Spanish army upon arrival and put to the sword. As the outcome was embarrassing for both Charles and his favourite, the Duke of Buckingham (whose responsibility it had been to make sure the ships were well supplied), the King opted not to inquire into the matter. —Ed.

B. After the pacification broken, what succeeded next?

A. The King sent Duke Hamilton[38] with commission and instructions into Scotland, to call a Parliament there, and to use all the means he could otherwise; but all was to no purpose. For the Scots were now resolved to raise an army and to enter into England, to deliver, as they pretended, their grievances to his majesty in a petition; because the King, they said, being in the hands of evil councillors, they could not otherwise obtain their right. But the truth is, they were animated to it by the democratical and Presbyterian English, with a promise of reward and hope of plunder. Some have said, that Duke Hamilton also did rather encourage them to, than deter them from, the expedition; as hoping by the disorder of the two kingdoms, to bring to pass that which he had formerly been accused to endeavour, to make himself King of Scotland. But I take this to have been a very uncharitable censure, upon so little ground to judge so hardly of a man, that afterwards lost his life in seeking to procure the liberty of the King his master.—This resolution of the Scots to enter England being known, the King wanting money to raise an army against them, was now, as his enemies here wished, constrained to call a parliament, to meet at Westminster the 13th day of April, 1640.

B. Methinks a Parliament of England, if upon

38 James Hamilton, 1st Duke of Hamilton (1606 – 1649), Charles' chief advisor in Scottish affairs. —Ed.

any occasion, should furnish the King with money now, in a war against the Scots, out of an inveterate disaffection to that nation that had always anciently taken part with their enemies the French, and which always esteemed the glory of England for an abatement of their own.

A. It is indeed commonly seen that neighbour nations envy one another's honour, and that the less potent bears the greater malice; but that hinders them not from agreeing in those things which their common ambition leads them to. And therefore the King found not the more, but the less help from this Parliament: and most of the members thereof, in their ordinary discourses, seemed to wonder why the King should make a war upon Scotland; and in that Parliament sometimes called them *their brethren the Scots.* But instead of taking the King's business, which was the raising of money, into their consideration, they fell upon the redressing of grievances, and especially such ways of levying money as in the late intermission of Parliaments the King had been forced to use; such as were ship-money, for knighthood, and such other vails (as one may call them) of the regal office, which lawyers had found justifiable by the ancient records of the kingdom. Besides, they fell upon the actions of divers ministers of state, though done by the King's own command and warrant. Insomuch, that before they were to come to the business for which they were called, the money which was necessary for this war (if they had given any, as they never meant to do) had come too late. It is true, there was mention of a sum of money to be given the King, by way of bargain, for the relinquishing of his right to ship-money, and some other of his prerogatives, but so seldom, and without determining any sum, that it was in vain for the King to hope for any success; and therefore upon the 5th of May following he dissolved it.

B. Where then had the King money to raise and pay his army?

A. He was forced the second time to make use of the nobility and gentry, who contributed some more, some less, according to the greatness of their estates; but amongst them all they made up a very sufficient army.

B. It seems then that the same men, that crossed his business in the Parliament, now out of Parliament advanced it all they could. What was the reason of that?

A. The greatest part of the Lords in Parliament, and of the gentry throughout England, were more affected to monarchy than to a popular government, but so as not to endure to hear of the King's absolute power; which made them in time of Parliament easily to condescend to abridge it, and bring the government to a mixed monarchy, as they called it; wherein the absolute sovereignty should be divided between the King, the House of Lords, and the House of Commons.

B. But how, if they cannot agree?

A. I think they never thought of that; but I am

sure they never meant the sovereignty should be wholly either in one or both the houses. Besides, they were loath to desert the King, when he was invaded by foreigners; for the Scotch were esteemed by them as a foreign nation.

B. It is strange to me, that England and Scotland being but one island, and their language almost the same, and being governed by one King, should be thought foreigners to one another.—The Romans were masters of many nations, and to oblige them the more to obey the edicts and laws sent unto them from the city of Rome, they thought fit to make them all Romans; and out of divers nations, as Spain, Germany, Italy, and France, to advance some, that they thought worthy, even to be senators of Rome, and to give every one of the common people the privileges of the city of Rome, by which they were protected from the contumelies of other nations where they resided. Why were not the Scotch and English united in like manner into one people?

A. King James at his first coming to the crown of England did endeavour it, but could not prevail. But for all that, I believe the Scots have now as many privileges in England as any nation had in Rome, of those which were so as you say made Romans. For they are all naturalized, and have right to buy land in England to themselves and their heirs.

B. It is true of them, that were born in Scotland after the time that King James was in possession of the kingdom of England.

A. There be very few now that were born before. But why have they a better right that were born after, than they that were born before?

B. Because they were born subjects to the King of England, and the rest not.

A. Were not the rest born subjects to King James? And was not the King of England?

B. Yes, but not then.

A. I understand not the subtilty of that distinction. But upon what law is that distinction grounded? Is there any statute to that purpose?

B. I cannot tell; I think not; but it is grounded upon equity.

A. I see little equity in this: that those nations that are bound to equal obedience to the same King, should not have equal privileges. And now seeing there be so very few born before King James's coming in, what greater privilege had those ingrafted Romans by their naturalization in the state of Rome, or in the state of England the English themselves, more than the Scots?

B. Those Romans, when any of them were in Rome, had their voice in the making of laws.

A. And the Scots have their Parliaments, wherein their assent is required to the laws there made, which is as good. Have not many of the provinces of France their several parliaments and several constitutions? And yet they are all equally natural subjects of the King of France. And therefore for my part I think they were mistaken, both English and Scots, in calling one another foreigners.

Howsoever that be, the King had a very sufficient army, wherewith he marched towards Scotland; and by the time he was come to York, the Scotch army was drawn up to the frontiers and ready to march into England; which also they presently did; giving out all the way, that their march should be without damage to the country, and that their errand was only to deliver a petition to the King, for the redress of many pretended injuries they had received from such of the court, whose counsel the King most followed. So they passed through Northumberland quietly, till they came to a ford in the river of Tyne, a little above Newcastle, where they found some little opposition, from a party of the King's army sent thither to stop them; whom the Scots easily mastered; and as soon as they were over, seized upon Newcastle, and coming further on, upon the city of Durham; and sent to the King to desire a treaty, which was granted; and the commissioners on both sides met at Ripon. The conclusion was, that all should be referred to the Parliament, which the King should call to meet at Westminster on the 3rd of November following, being in the same year 1640; and thereupon the King returned to London.

B. So the armies were disbanded?

A. No; the Scotch army was to be defrayed by the counties of Northumberland and Durham, and the King was to pay his own, till the disbanding of both should be agreed upon in Parliament.

B. So in effect both the armies were maintained

at the King's charge, and the whole controversy to be decided by a Parliament almost wholly Presbyterian, and as partial to the Scotch as themselves could have wished.

A. And yet for all this they durst not presently make war upon the King: there was so much yet left of reverence to him in the hearts of the people, as to have made them odious, if they had declared what they intended. They must have some colour or other to make it believed that the King made war first upon the Parliament. And besides, they had not yet sufficiently disgraced him and his actions in sermons and pamphlets, nor removed from about him those they thought could best counsel him. Therefore they resolved to proceed with him like skilful hunters; first to single him out, by men disposed in all parts to drive him into the open field *with their noise,* and then in case he should but seem to turn head, to call that a making of war against the Parliament.

And first they called in question such as had either preached or written in defence of any of those rights, which, belonging to the Crown, they meant to usurp, and take from the King to themselves: whereupon some few preachers and writers were imprisoned.[39] The King not protecting these, they proceeded to call in question some of the King's own actions in his ministers, whereof they imprisoned some, and some went beyond sea. And where-

39 *After* "imprisoned" *follows in Edd.* "or forced to fly". *These words have been erased in the MS. by the amanuensis.*

as certain persons, having endeavoured by books and sermons to raise sedition, and committed other crimes of high nature, had therefore been censured by the King's council in the Star-chamber, and imprisoned; the Parliament by their own authority, to try, it seems, how the King and the people would take it (for their persons were inconsiderable), ordered their setting at liberty; which was accordingly done, with great applause of the people, that flocked about them in London, in manner of a triumph. This being done, without resistance, *they called in question* the King's right to ship-money—

B. Ship-money! what's that?

A. The Kings of England, for the defence of the sea, had power to tax all the counties of England, whether they were maritime or not, for the building and furnishing of ships; which tax the King had then lately found cause to impose, and the Parliament exclaimed against it as an oppression. And by one of their members that had been taxed but 20s. (mark the oppression; a Parliament-man of 500*l*. a year, land-taxed at 20s.!) they were forced to bring it to a trial at law, he refused payment, and was cast. Again, when all the judges of Westminster were demanded their opinions concerning the legality of it, of twelve that there were, it was judged legal by ten; for which though they were not punished, they were affrighted by the Parliament.

B. What did the Parliament mean, when they did exclaim against it as illegal? Did they mean it was against statute-law, or against the judgments of lawyers given heretofore, which are commonly called reports; or did they mean it was against equity, which I take to be the same with the law of nature?

A. It is a hard matter, or rather impossible, to know what other men mean, especially if they be crafty; but sure I am, equity was not their ground for this pretence of immunity from contributing to the King but at their own pleasure. For when they have laid the burthen of defending the whole kingdom, and governing it, upon any person whatsoever, there is very little equity he should depend on others for the means of performing it; or if he do, they are his Sovereign, not he theirs. And as for the common law contained in reports, they have no force but what the King gives them. Besides, it were unreasonable, that a corrupt or foolish judge's unjust sentence should by any time, how long soever, obtain the authority and force of a law. But amongst Statute Laws there is one, called *Magna Charta*, or the *Great Charter of the liberties of Englishmen*, in which there is one article, wherein a King heretofore hath granted that no man shall be distrained, that is, have his goods taken from him, otherwise than by the law of the land.

B. Is not that a sufficient ground for their purpose?

A. No; that leaves us in the same doubt, which you think it clears. For where was that law of the land then? Did they mean another *Magna Charta,* that was made by some King more ancient yet? No; that statute was made, not to exempt any man from payments to the public, but for securing every man from such as abused the King's power, by surreptitiously obtaining the King's warrants, to the oppressing of those against whom he had any suit in law. But it was conducing to the ends of some rebellious spirits in this Parliament, to have it interpreted in the wrong sense, and suitable enough to the understanding of the rest, or most part of them, to let it pass.

B. You make the members of that Parliament very simple men; and yet the people chose them for the wisest of the land.

A. If craft be wisdom, they were wise enough. But wise, as I define it, is he that knows how to bring his business to pass (without the assistance of knavery and ignoble shifts) by the sole strength of his good contrivance. A fool may win from a better gamester, by the advantage of false dice, and packing of cards.

B. According to your definition, there be few wise men now-a-days. Such wisdom is a kind of gallantry, that few are brought up to, and most think folly. Fine clothes, great feathers, civility towards men that will not swallow injuries, and injury towards them that will, is the present gallantry. But when the Parliament afterwards, having gotten the power into their hands, levied money for their own use; what said the people to that?

A. What else, but that it was legal and to be paid, as being imposed by consent of Parliament?

B. I have heard often that they ought to pay what

was imposed by consent of Parliament to the use of the King, but to their own use never before. I see by this, it is easier to gull the multitude, than any one man amongst them. For what one man, that has not his natural judgment depraved by accident, could be so easily cozened in a matter that concerns his purse, had he not been passionately carried away by the rest to change of government, or rather to a liberty of every one to govern himself?

A. Judge then, what kind of men such a multitude of ignorant people were like to elect for their burgesses and knights of shires.

B. I can make no other judgment, but that they who were then elected, were just such as had been elected for former Parliaments, and as likely to be elected for Parliaments to come. For people always have been, and always will be, ignorant of their duty to the public, as never meditating anything but their particular interest; in other things following their immediate leaders; which are either the preachers, or the most potent of the gentlemen that dwell amongst them: as common soldiers for the most part follow their immediate captains, if they like them. If you think the late miseries have made them wiser, that will quickly be forgot, and then we shall be no wiser than we were.

A. Why may not men be taught their duty, that is, the science of *just* and *unjust*, as divers other sciences have been taught, from true principles and evident demonstration; and much more easily than any of those preachers and democratical gentlemen could teach rebellion and treason?

B. But who can teach what none have learned? Or, if any man have been so singular, as to have studied the science of justice and equity; how can he teach it safely, when it is against the interest of those that are in possession of the power to hurt him?

A. The rules of *just* and *unjust* sufficiently demonstrated, and from principles evident to the meanest capacity, have not been wanting; and notwithstanding the obscurity of their author, have shined, not only in this, but also in foreign countries, to men of good education. But they are few, in respect of the rest of the men, whereof many cannot read: many, though they can, have no leisure; and of them that have leisure, the greatest part have their minds wholly employed and taken up by their private businesses or pleasures. So that it is impossible that the multitude should ever learn their duty, but from the pulpit and upon holidays; but then, and from thence, it is, that they learned their disobedience. And, therefore, the light of that doctrine has been hitherto covered and kept under here by a cloud of adversaries, which no private man's reputation can break through, without the authority of the *Universities*. But out of the *Universities*, came all those preachers that taught the contrary. The *Universities* have been to this nation, as the wooden horse was to the Trojans.[40]

---

40 *B*. Can you tell me why and when the Universities here, and in other places, first began?

A. It seems (for the time) they began in the reign of the

B. What was the Pope's design in setting up the Universities?[41]

A. What other design was he like to have, but (what you heard before) the advancement of his own authority in the countries where the Universities were erected? There they learned to dispute for him, and with unintelligible distinctions to blind men's eyes, whilst they encroached upon the rights of kings. And it was an evident argument of that design, that they fell in hand with the work so quickly. For the first Rector of the University of Paris (as I have read somewhere) was Peter Lombard, who first brought in them the learning called School-divinity; and was seconded by John Scot of Duns, who lived in, or near the same time; whom any ingenious reader, not knowing it was the design, would judge to have been two of the most egregious blockheads in the world, so ob-

---

Emperor Charles the Great. Before which time, I doubt not, but that there were many grammar schools for the Latin tongue, which was the natural language of the Roman Church; but for Universities, that is to say, schools for the sciences in general, and especially for divinity, it is manifest that the institution of them was recommended by the Pope's letter to the Emperor Charles the Great, and recommended further by a Council held in his time, I think, at Chalons-sur-Saone; and not long after was elected an University at Paris, and the college called University College at Oxford. And so by degrees several bishops, noblemen, and rich men, and some Kings and Queeens, contributing thereunto, the Universities obtained at last their present splendour.

This question and answer, exhibited by formed edd. have been eraded in MS. by the amanuensis as a repetition from p. [26].

41 But what was the Pope's design in it? Edd.

scure and senseless are their writings. And from these the schoolmen that succeeded, learnt the trick of imposing what they list upon their readers, and declining the force of true reason by verbal forks; I mean, distinctions that signify nothing, but serve only to astonish the multitude of ignorant men. As for the understanding readers, they were so few, that these new sublime doctors cared not what they thought. These schoolmen were to make good all the articles of faith, which the Popes from time to time should command to be believed: amongst which, there were very many inconsistent with the rights of kings, and other civil sovereigns, asserting to the Pope all authority whatsoever they should declare to be necessary in *ordine ad spiritualia*, that is to say, in order to religion.

From the Universities also it was, that all preachers proceeded, and were poured out into city and country, to terrify the people into an absolute obedience to the Pope's canons and commands, which, for fear of weakening kings and princes too much, they durst not yet call laws.

From the Universities it was, that the philosophy of Aristotle was made an ingredient in religion, as serving for a salve to a great many absurd articles, concerning the nature of Christ's body, and the estate of angels and saints in heaven; which articles they thought fit to have believed, because they brought some of them profit, and others reverence to the clergy, even to the meanest of them. For when they shall have made the people believe that the meanest of them can make the body of Christ; who is there that will not both show them reverence, and be liberal to them or to the Church, especially in the time of their sickness, when they think they make and bring unto them their Saviour?

B. But, what advantage to them, in these impostures, was the doctrine of Aristotle?

A. They have made more use of his obscurity than of his doctrine. For none of the ancient philosophers' writings are comparable to those of Aristotle, for their aptness to puzzle and entangle men with words, and to breed disputation, which must at last be ended in the determination of the Church of Rome. And yet in the doctrine of Aristotle, they made use of many points; as, first, the doctrine of *Separated Essences*.

B. What are *Separated Essences*?

A. Separated beings.

B. Separated from what?

A. From every thing that is.

B. I cannot understand the being of any thing, which I understand not to be. But what can they make of that?

A. Very much, in questions concerning the nature of God, and concerning the estate of man's soul after death, in heaven, hell, and purgatory; by which you and every man know, how great obedience, and how much money they gain from the common people.—Whereas Aristotle holdeth the soul of man to be the *first giver of motion* to the body, and consequently to itself; they make use of that in the doctrine of free will. What, and how they gain by that, I will not say.—He holdeth further, that there be many things that come to pass in this world from no *necessity* of causes, but mere *contingency*, *casuality*, and *fortune*.

B. Methinks, in this they make God stand idle, and to be a mere spectator of the games of Fortune. For what God is the cause of, must needs come to pass, and (in my opinion) nothing else. But, because there must be some ground for the justice of the eternal torment of the damned; perhaps it is this, that men's wills and propensions are not (they think) in the hands of God, but of themselves; and in this also I see somewhat conducing to the authority of the Church.

A. This is not much; nor was Aristotle of such credit with them, but that when his opinion was against theirs, they could slight him. Whatsoever he says is impossible in nature, they can prove well enough to be possible, from the Almighty power of God, who can make many bodies to be in one and the self-same place, and one body to be in many places at the same time, if the doctrine of transubstantiation require it, though Aristotle deny it. I like not the design of drawing religion into an art, whereas it ought to be a law; and though not the same in all countries, yet in every country indisputable; nor that they teach it not, as arts ought to be taught, by showing first the meaning of their terms, and then deriving from them the truth they would have us believe: nor that their terms are for the most part unintelligible; though, to make it seem rather want of learning in the reader, than want of fair dealing in themselves, they are, for the most part, Latin and Greek words, wryed a little at the point, towards the native language of the several countries where they are used. But that which is most intolerable is, that all clerks are forced to make as if they believed them, if they mean to have any Church preferment, the keys whereof are in the Pope's hands; and the common people, whatsoever they believe of those subtile doctrines, are never esteemed better sons of the Church for their learning. There is but one way there to salvation; that is, extraordinary devotion and liberality to the Church, and readiness for the Church's sake, if it be required, to fight against their natural and lawful sovereigns.

B. I see what use they make of Aristotle's logic, physics, and metaphysics; but I see not yet how his politics can serve their turn.

A. Nor I. It has, I think, done them no good, though it has done us here much hurt by accident. For men, grown weary at last of the insolence of the priests, and examining the truth of those doctrines that were put upon them, began to search the sense of the Scriptures, as they are in the learned languages; and consequently (studying Greek and Latin) became acquainted with the democratical principles of Aristotle and Cicero, and from the love of their eloquence fell in love with their politics, and that more and more, till it grew into the rebellion we now talk of, without any other advantage to the Roman Church but that it was a weakening to us, whom, since we broke out of their net in the time of Henry VIII., they have continually endeavoured to recover.

B. What have they gotten by the teaching of Aristotle's ethics?

A. It is some advantage to them, that neither the morals of Aristotle, nor of any other, have done them any harm, nor us any good. Their doctrines have caused a great deal of dispute concerning virtue and vice, but no knowledge of what they are, nor any method of attaining virtue nor of avoiding vice.—The end of moral philosophy is, to teach men of all sorts their duty, both to the public and to one another. They estimate virtue, partly by a mediocrity of the passions of men, and partly by that that they are praised. Whereas, it is not the Much or Little that makes an action virtuous, but the cause; nor Much or Little that makes an action vicious, but its being un-conformable to the laws in such men as are subject to the law, or its being unconformable to equity or charity in all men whatsoever.

B. It seems you make a difference between the ethics of subjects and the ethics of sovereigns.

A. So I do. The virtue of a subject is comprehended wholly in obedience to the laws of the commonwealth. To obey the laws, is justice and equity, which is the law of nature, and, consequently, is civil law in all nations of the world; and nothing is injustice or iniquity, otherwise, than it is against the law. Likewise, to obey the laws, is the prudence of a subject; for without such obedience the commonwealth (which is every subject's safety and protection) cannot subsist. And though it be prudence also in private men, justly and moderately to enrich themselves, yet craftily to withhold from the public or defraud it of such part of their wealth, as is by law required, is no sign of prudence, but of want of knowledge of what is necessary for their own defence.

The virtues of sovereigns are such as tend to the maintenance of peace at home, and to the resistance of foreign enemies. Fortitude is a royal virtue; and though it be necessary in such private men as shall be soldiers, yet, for other men, the less they dare, the better it is both for the commonwealth and for themselves. Frugality (though perhaps you will think it strange) is also a royal virtue: for it increases the public stock, which cannot be too great for the public use, nor any man too sparing of what he has in trust for the good of others. Liberality also is a royal virtue: for the commonwealth cannot be well served without extraordinary diligence and service of ministers, and great fidelity to their Sovereign; who ought therefore to be encouraged, and especially those that do him service in the wars. In sum, all actions and habits are to be esteemed good or evil by their causes and usefulness in reference to the commonwealth, and not by their mediocrity, nor by their being commended.

For several men praise several customs, and that which is virtue with one, is blamed by others; and, contrarily, what one calls vice, another calls virtue, as their present affections lead them.

B. Methinks you should have placed among the virtues that, which, in my opinion, is the greatest of all virtues, religion.

A. So I have; though, it seems, you did not observe it. But whither do we digress from the way we were in?

B. I think you have not digressed at all; for I suppose, your purpose was, to acquaint me with the history, not so much of those actions that passed in the time of the late troubles, as of their causes, and of the councils and artifice by which they were brought to pass. There be divers men that have written the history, out of whom I might have learned what they did, and somewhat also of the contrivance; but I find little in them of what I would ask. Therefore, since you were pleased to enter into this discourse at my request, be pleased also to inform me after my own method; and for the danger of confusion that may arise from that, I will take care to bring you back to the place from whence I drew you; for I well remember where it was.

A. Well then, to your question concerning religion, inasmuch as I told you, that all virtue is comprehended in obedience to the laws of the commonwealth, whereof religion is one, I have placed religion amongst the virtues.

B. Is religion then the law of a commonwealth?

A. There is no nation in the world, whose religion is not established, and receives not its authority from the laws of that nation. It is true, that the law of God receives no evidence from the laws of men. But because men can never by their own wisdom come to the knowledge of what God hath spoken and commanded to be observed, nor be obliged to obey the laws whose author they know not, they are to acquiesce in some human authority or other. So that the question will be, whether a man ought in matter of religion, that is to say, when there is question of his duty to God and the King, to rely upon the preaching of his fellow-subjects or of a stranger, or upon the voice of the law?

B. There is no great difficulty in that point. For there are none that preach here or anywhere else, or at least ought to preach, but such as have authority so to do from him or them that have the sovereign power. So that if the King give us leave, you or I may as lawfully preach as any of them; and I believe we should perform that office a great deal better, than they that preached us into the rebellion.

A. The Church morals are in many points very different from these, that I have here set down, for the doctrine of virtue and vice; and yet without any conformity with that of Aristotle. For in the Church of Rome, the principal virtues are, to obey their doctrine, though it be treason, and that is to be religious; to be beneficial to the clergy, that is their piety and liberality; and to believe upon their word that which a man knows in his conscience to be false, which is the faith they require. I could name a great many more such points of their morals, but that I know you know them already, being so well versed in the cases of conscience written by their schoolmen, who measure the goodness and wickedness of all actions, by their congruity with the doctrine of the Roman clergy.

B. But what is the moral philosophy of the Protestant clergy in England?

A. So much as they show of it in their life and conversation, is for the most part very good, and of very good example; much better than their writings.

B. It happens many times that men live honestly for fear, who, if they had power, would live according to their own opinions; that is, if their opinions be not right, unrighteously.

A. Do the clergy in England pretend, as the Pope does, or as the Presbyterians do, to have a right from God immediately, to govern the King and his subjects in all points of religion and manners? If they do, you cannot doubt but that if they had number and strength, which they are never like to have, they would attempt to obtain that power, as the others have done.

B. I would be glad to see a system of the present morals, written by some divine of good reputation and learning, of the late King's party.

A. I think I can recommend unto you the best that is extant, and such a one as (except a few passages that I mislike) is very well worth your reading. The title of it is, *The whole Duty of Man laid down in a plain and familiar way.*[42] And, yet, I dare say, that if the Presbyterian ministers, even those of them which were the most diligent preachers of the late sedition, were to be tried by it, they would go near to be found *not guilty*. He has divided the duty of man into three great branches; which are, his duty to God, to himself, and to his neighbour. In his duty to God, he puts the acknowledgment of him in his essence and his attributes, and in the believing of his word. His attributes are omnipotence, omniscience, infiniteness, justice, truth, mercy, and all the rest that are found in Scripture. Which of these did not those seditious preachers acknowledge equally with the best of Christians? The word of God are the books of Holy Scripture, received for canonical in England.

B. They receive the word of God; but according to their own interpretation.

A. According to whose interpretation was it received by the bishops and the rest of the loyal party, but their own? He puts for another duty, obedience and submission to God's will. Did any of them, nay, did any man living, do any thing, at any time, against God's will?

B. By God's will, I suppose, he means there his revealed will, that is to say, his commandments,

42 Published anonymously in 1658, it is currently thought that this English High Church Protestant devotional book was written by Richard Allestree (1621/2 – 1681), a Royalist churchman, although authorship is well concealed. —Ed.

which I am sure they did most horribly break, both by their preaching and otherwise.

A. As for their own actions, there is no doubt but all men are guilty enough, if God deal severely with them, to be damned. And for their preaching, they will say, they thought it agreeable to God's revealed will in the Scriptures. If they thought it so, it was not disobedience, but error. And how can any man prove they thought otherwise?

B. Hypocrisy hath *indeed* this great prerogative above other sins, that it cannot be accused.

A. Another duty he sets down is, to honour him in his house (that is, the Church), in his possessions, in his day, in his word and sacraments.

B. They perform this duty as well, I think, as any other ministers, I mean the loyal party; and the Presbyterians have always had an equal care to have God's house free from profanation; to have tithes duly paid, and offerings accepted; to have the sabbath day kept holy, the word preached, and the Lord's supper and baptism duly administered. But is not keeping of the feasts and fasts one of those duties that belong to the honour of God? If it be, the Presbyterians fail in that.

A. Why so? They kept some holidays, and they had fasts amongst themselves, though not upon the same days that the Church ordains, but when they thought fit; as when it pleased God to give the King any notable victory. And they governed themselves in this point by the Holy Scripture, as they pretend to believe. And who can prove they do not believe so?

B. Let us pass over all other duties, and come to that duty which we owe to the King, and consider whether the doctrine taught by those divines which adhered to the King, be such in that point, as may justify the Presbyterians, that incited the people to rebellion. For that is the thing you call in question.

A. Concerning our duty to our rulers, he hath these words: "*An obedience we must pay, either active or passive; the active, in the case of all lawful commands, that is, whenever the magistrate commands something which is not contrary to some command of God, we are then bound to act according to that command of the magistrate, to do the things he requires; but when he enjoins anything contrary to what God hath commanded, we are not then to pay him this active obedience; we may, nay we must, refuse thus to act (yet, here we must be very well assured, that the thing is so contrary, and not pretend conscience for a cloak of stubbornness); we are, in that case, to obey God rather than men; but even this is a season for the passive obedience; we must patiently suffer what he inflicts on us for such refusal, and not, to secure ourselves, rise up against him.*"

B. What is there in this, to give colour to the late rebellion?

A. They will say they did it in obedience to God, inasmuch as they did believe it was according to the Scripture; out of which they will bring examples, perhaps of David and his adherents, that resisted King Saul, and of the prophets afterward, that vehemently from time to time preached against the idolatrous Kings of Israel and Judah. Saul was their lawful King, and yet they paid him neither active nor passive obedience; for they did put themselves into a posture of defence against him, though David himself spared his person. And so did the Presbyterians put into their commissions to their general, that they should spare the King's person. Besides, you cannot doubt but that they, who in the pulpit did animate the people to take arms in the defence of the then Parliament, alleged Scripture, that is, the word of God, for it. If it be lawful then for subjects to resist the King, when he commands anything that is against the Scripture, that is, contrary to the command of God, and to be judge of the meaning of the Scripture, it is impossible that the life of any King, or the peace of any Christian kingdom, can be long secure. It is this doctrine that divides a kingdom within itself, whatsoever the men be, loyal or rebels, that write or preach it publicly. And thus you see that if those seditious ministers be tried by this doctrine, they will come off well enough.

B. I see it; and wonder at people that have never spoken with God Almighty, nor knowing one more than another what he hath said, when the laws and the preacher disagree, should so keenly follow the minister (for the most part an ignorant, though a ready-tongued, scholar), rather than the laws, that were made by the King with the consent of the Peers and Commons of the land.

A. Let us examine his words a little nearer. First, concerning passive obedience. When a thief hath broken the laws, and according to the law is therefore executed, can any man understand that this suffering of his is in obedience to the law? Every law is a command *to do*, or *to forbear*: neither of these is fulfilled by suffering. If any suffering can be called obedience, it must be such as is voluntary; for no involuntary action can be counted a submission to the law. He that means that his suffering should be taken for obedience, must not only not resist, but also not fly, nor hide himself to avoid his punishment. And who is there amongst them that discourse of *passive obedience*, when his life is in extreme danger, that will voluntarily present himself to the officers of justice? Do not we see that all men, when they are led to execution, are both bound and guarded, and would break loose if they could, and get away? Such is their *passive obedience*. Christ saith (Matthew xxiii. 2, 3): *The Scribes and Pharisees sit in Moses' chair; all, therefore, whatsoever they bid you observe, that observe and do*: which is a *doing* an active obedience. And yet the Scribes and Pharisees appear not by the Scripture to have been such godly men, as never to command anything against the revealed will of God.

B. Must tyrants also be obeyed in everything actively? Or is there nothing wherein a lawful King's command may be disobeyed? What if he should command me with my own hands to execute my father, in case he should be condemned to die by the law?

A. This is a case that need not be put. We never have read nor heard of any King or tyrant so inhuman as to command it. If any did, we are to consider whether that command were one of his laws. For by disobeying Kings, we mean the disobeying of his laws, those his laws that were made before they were applied to any particular person; for the King, though as a father of children, and a master of domestic servants *command many things which bind those children and servants* yet he commands the people in general never but by a precedent law, and as a politic, not a natural person. And if such a command as you speak of were contrived into a general law (which never was, nor never will be), you were bound to obey it, unless you depart the kingdom after the publication of the law, and before the condemnation of your father.

B. Your author says further, in refusing active obedience to the King, that commanded anything contrary to God's law, *we must be very well assured that the thing is so contrary.* I would fain know how it is possible to be *well* assured.

A. I think you do not believe that any of those refusers do, immediately from God's own mouth, receive any command contrary to the command of the King, who is God's lieutenant, nor any other way than you and I do, that is to say, than by the Scriptures. And because men do, for the most part, rather draw the Scripture to their own sense, than follow the true sense of the Scripture, there is no other way to know, certainly, and in all cases, what God commands, or forbids us to do, but by the sentence of him or them that are constituted by the King to determine the sense of the Scripture, upon hearing of the particular case of conscience which is in question. And they that are so constituted are easily known in all Christian commonwealths, whether they be bishops, or ministers, or assemblies, that govern the Church under him or them that have the sovereign power.

B. Some doubts may be raised from this that you now say. For if men be to learn their duty from the sentence which other men shall give concerning the meaning of the Scriptures, and not from their own interpretation, I understand not to what end they were translated into English, and every man not only permitted, but also exhorted, to read them. For what could that produce, but diversity of opinion, and consequently (as man's nature is) disputation, breach of charity, disobedience, and at last rebellion? Again, since the Scripture was allowed to be read in English, why are not the translations such as might make all that is read, understood even by mean capacities? Did not the Jews, such as could read, understand their law in the Jewish language, as well as we do our statute laws in English? And as for such places of the Scripture, as had nothing of the nature of a law, it was nothing to the duty of the Jews, whether they were understood or not, seeing nothing is punishable but the transgression of some law. The same question I may ask concerning the New Testament. For, I believe, that those men to whom the original language was natural, did understand sufficiently what commands and councils were given them by our Saviour and his apostles, and his immediate disciples. Again, how will you answer that question which was put by St. Peter and St. John (Acts iv. 19), when by Annas the high-priest, and others of the Council of Jerusalem, they were forbidden to teach any more in the name of Jesus: *Whether is it right in the sight of God, to hearken unto you more than unto God?*

A. The case is not the same. Peter and John had seen and daily conversed with our Saviour; and by the miracles he wrought, did know he was God, and consequently knew certainly that their disobedience to the high-priest's present command was just. Can any minister now say, that he hath immediately from God's own mouth received a command to disobey the King, or know otherwise than by the Scripture, that any command of the King, that hath the form and nature of a law, is against the law of God, which in divers places, directly and evidently, commandeth to obey him in all things? The text you cite does not tell us, that a minister's authority, rather than a Christian King's, shall decide the questions that arise from the different interpretations of the Scripture. And therefore, where the King is head of the Church, and by consequence (to omit that the Scripture itself was not received but by the authority of Kings and States) chief judge of the rectitude of all interpretations of the Scripture, to obey the King's laws and public edicts, is not to disobey, but to obey God. A minister ought not to think that his skill in the Latin, Greek, or Hebrew tongues, if he have any, gives him a privilege to impose upon all his fellow subjects his own sense, or what he pretends to be his sense, of every obscure place of Scripture: nor ought he, as oft as he *thinks he* hath found out some fine interpretation, not before thought on by others, to think he had it by inspiration: for he cannot be assured of that; no, nor that his interpretation, as fine as he thinks it, is not false: and then all this stubbornness and contumacy towards the King and his laws, is nothing but pride of heart and ambition, or else imposture. And whereas you think it needless, or perhaps hurtful, to have the Scriptures in English, I am of another mind. There are so many places of Scripture easy to be understood, that teach both true faith and good morality (and that as fully as is necessary to salvation), of which no seducer is able to dispossess the mind (of any ordinary readers), that the reading of them is so profitable as not to be forbidden without great damage to them and the commonwealth.

B. All that is required, both in faith and manners, for man's salvation is (I confess) set down in Scripture as plainly as can be. *Children obey your parents in all things: Servants obey your masters: Let all men be subject to the higher powers, whether it be the King or those that are sent by him: Love God with all your soul, and your neighbour as yourself*: are words of the Scripture, which are well enough understood; but neither children, nor the greatest part of men, do understand why it is their duty to do so. They see not that the safety of the commonwealth, and consequently their own, depends upon their doing it. Every man by nature (without discipline) does in all his actions look upon, as far as he can see, the benefit that shall redound to himself from his obedience. He reads that covetousness is the root of all evil; but he thinks, and sometimes finds, it is the root of his estate. And so in other cases, the Scripture says one thing, and they think another, weighing the commodities or incommodities of this present life only, which are in their sight, never putting into the scales the good and evil of the life to come, which they see not.

A. All this is no more than happens where the Scripture is sealed up in Greek and Latin, and the people taught the same things out of them by preachers. But they that are of a condition and age, fit to examine the sense of what they read, and that take a delight in searching out the grounds of their duty, certainly cannot choose but by their reading of the Scriptures come to such a sense of their duty, as not only to obey the laws themselves, but also to induce others to do the same. For commonly men of age and quality are followed by their inferior neighbours, that look more upon the example of those men whom they reverence, and whom they are unwilling to displease, than upon precepts and laws.

B. These men, of the condition and age you speak of, are, in my opinion, the unfittest of all others to be trusted with the reading of the Scriptures. I know you mean such as have studied the Greek or Latin, or both tongues, and that are withal such as love knowledge, and consequently take delight in finding out the meaning of the most hard texts, or in thinking they have found it, in case it be new and not found out by others. These are therefore they, that prætermitting the easy places which teach them their duty, fall to scanning only of the mysteries of religion. Such as are: how it may be made out with wit, *That there be three that bear rule in heaven, and those three but one? How the Deity could be made flesh? How that flesh could be really present in many places at once? Where is the place, and what the torments, of hell? And other metaphysical doctrines: Whether the will of man be free, or governed by the will of God? Whether sanctity comes by inspiration or education? By whom Christ now speaks to us, whether by the King, or by the clergy, or by the Bible, to every man that reads it and interprets it to himself, or by private spirit to every private man?* These and the like points are the study of the curious, and the cause of all our late mischief, and the cause that makes the plainer sort of men, whom the Scripture had taught belief in Christ, love towards God, obedience to the King, and sobriety of behaviour, forget it all, and place their religion in the disputable doctrines of these your wise men.

A. I do not think these men fit to interpret the Scripture to the rest, nor do I say that the rest ought to take their interpretation for the word of God. Whatsoever is necessary for them to know, is so easy, as not to need interpretation: whatsoever is more, does them no good. But in case any of those unnecessary doctrines shall be authorized by the laws of the King or other state, I say it is the duty of every subject not to speak against them: inasmuch as it is every man's duty to obey him or them that have the sovereign power, and the wisdom of all such powers to punish such as shall publish or teach their private interpretations, when they are contrary to the law, and likely to incline men to sedition or disputing against the law.

B. They must punish then the most of those that have had their breeding in the Universities. For such curious questions in divinity are first started in the Universities, and so are all those politic questions concerning the rights of civil and ecclesiastic government; and there they are furnished with arguments for liberty out of the works of Aristotle, Plato, Cicero, Seneca, and out of the histories of Rome and Greece, for their disputation against the necessary power of their sovereigns. Therefore I despair of any lasting peace amongst ourselves, till the Universities here shall bend and direct their studies to the settling of it, that is, to the teaching of absolute obedience to the laws of the King, and to his public edicts under the Great Seal of England. For I make no doubt, but that solid reason, backed with the authority of so many learned men, will more prevail for the keeping of us in peace within ourselves, than any victory can do over the rebels. But I am afraid that it is impossible to bring the Universities to such a compliance with the actions of state, as is necessary for the business.

A. Seeing the Universities have heretofore from time to time maintained the authority of the Pope, contrary to all laws divine, civil, and natural, against the right of our Kings, why can they not as well, when they have all manner of laws and equity on their side, maintain the rights of him that is both sovereign of the kingdom, and head of the Church?

B. Why then were they not in all points for the King's power, presently after that King Henry VIII. was in Parliament declared head of the Church, as much as they were before for the authority of the Pope?

A. Because the clergy in the Universities, by whom all things there are governed, and the clergy without the Universities, as well bishops as inferior clerks, did think that the pulling down of the Pope was the setting up of them (as to England) in his place, and made no question, the greatest part of them, but that their spiritual power did depend not upon the authority of the King, but of Christ himself, derived to them by a successive imposition of hands from bishop to bishop; notwithstanding they knew that this derivation passed through the hands of popes and bishops whose authority they had cast off. For though they were content that the divine right, which the Pope pretended to in England, should be denied him, yet they thought it not so fit to be taken from the Church of England, whom they now supposed themselves to represent. It seems they did not think it reasonable that a woman, or a child, or a man that could not construe the Hebrew, Greek, or Latin Bible, nor knew perhaps the declensions and conjugations of Greek or Latin nouns and verbs, should take upon him to govern so many learned doctors in matters of religion; meaning matters of divinity: for religion has been for a long time, and is now by most people, taken for the same thing with divinity, to the great advantage of the clergy.

B. And especially now amongst the Presbyterians. For I see few that are by them esteemed very good Christians, besides such as can repeat their sermons, and wrangle for them about the interpretation of the Scripture, and fight for them also with their bodies or purses, when they shall be required. To believe in Christ is nothing with them, unless you believe as they bid you. Charity is nothing with them, unless it be charity and liberality to them, and partaking with them in faction. How we can have peace while this is our religion, I cannot tell. *Hæret lateri lethalis arundo.* The seditious doctrine of the Presbyterians has been stuck so hard into the people's heads and memories (I cannot say into their hearts; for they understand nothing in it, but that they may lawfully rebel), that I fear the commonwealth will never be cured.

A. The two great virtues, that were severally in Henry VII. and Henry VIII., when they shall be jointly in one King, will easily cure it. That of Henry VII. was, without much noise of the people to fill his coffers; that of Henry VIII. was an early severity; but this without the former cannot be exercised.

B. This that you say looks (methinks) like an advice to the King, to let them alone till he have gotten ready money enough to levy and maintain a sufficient army, and then to fall upon them and destroy them.

A. God forbid that so horrible, unchristian, and inhuman a design should ever enter into the King's heart. I would have him to have money enough readily to raise an army to suppress any rebellion, and to take from his enemies all hope of success, that they may not dare to trouble him in the reformation of the Universities; but to put none to death without actual committing such crimes as are already made capital by the laws. The core of rebellion, as you have seen by this, and read of other rebellions, are the Universities; which nevertheless are not to be cast away, but to be better disciplined: that is to say, that the politics there taught be made to be (as true politics should be) such as are fit to make men know, that it is their duty to obey all laws whatsoever that shall by the authority of the King be enacted, till by the same authority they shall be repealed; such as are fit to make men understand, that the civil laws are God's laws, as they that make them are by God appointed to make them; and to make men know, that the people and the Church are one thing, and have but one head, the King; and that no man has title to govern under him, that has it not from him; that the King owes his crown to God only, and to no man, ecclesiastic or other; and that the religion they teach there, be a quiet waiting for the coming again of our blessed Saviour, and in the mean time a resolution to obey the King's laws (which also are God's laws); to injure no man, to be in charity with all men, to cherish the poor and sick, and to live soberly and free from scandal; without mingling our religion with points of natural philosophy, as freedom of will, incorporeal substance, everlasting nows, ubiquities, hypostases, which the people understand not, nor will ever care for. When the Universities shall be thus disciplined, there will come out of them, from time to time, well-principled preachers, and they that are now ill-principled, from time to time fall away.

B. I think it a very good course, and perhaps the only one that can make our peace amongst ourselves constant. For if men know not their duty, what is there that can force them to obey the laws? An army, you will say. But what shall force the army? Were not the trained bands an army? Were they not the janissaries, that not very long ago slew Osman in his own palace at Constantinople? I am therefore of your opinion, both that men may be brought to a love of obedience by preachers and gentlemen that imbibe good principles in their youth at the Universities, and also that we never shall have a lasting peace, till the Universities themselves be in such manner, as you have said, reformed; and the ministers know they have no authority but what the supreme civil power gives them; and the nobility and gentry know that the liberty of a state is not an exemption from the laws of their own country, whether made by an assembly or by a monarch, but an exemption from the constraint and insolence of their neighbours.

And now I am satisfied in this point, I will bring you back to the place from whence my curiosity drew you to this long digression. We were upon the point of ship-money; one of those grievances which the Parliament exclaimed against as tyranny and arbitrary government; thereby to single out (as you called it) the King from his subjects, and to make a party against him, when they should need it. And now you may proceed, if it please you, to such other artifices as they used to the same purpose.

A. I think it were better to give over here our discourse of this business, and refer it to some other day that you shall think fit.

B. Content. That day I believe is not far off.

Dialogue II

A. You are welcome; yet, if you had staid somewhat longer, my memory would have been so much the better provided for you.

B. Nay, I pray you give me now what you have about you; for the rest I am content you take what time you please.

A. After the Parliament had made the people believe that the exacting of ship-money was unlawful, and the people thereby inclined to think it tyrannical; in the next place, to increase their disaffection to his Majesty, they accused him of a purpose to introduce and authorize the Roman religion in this kingdom: than which nothing was more hateful to the people; not because it was erroneous (which they had neither learning nor judgment enough to examine), but because they had been used to hear it inveighed against in the sermons and discourses of the preachers whom they trusted to. And this was indeed the most effectual calumny, to alienate the people's affections from him, that could be possibly invented. The colour they had for this slander was, first, that there was one Rosetti, Resident (at and a little before that time) from the Pope, with the Queen;[1] and one Mr. George Con,[2] Secretary to the Cardinal Francisco Barberini,[3] nephew to Pope Urban VIII., sent over, under favour and protection of the Queen (as was conceived) to draw as many persons of quality about the court, as he should be able, to reconcile themselves to the Church of Rome: with what success I cannot tell; but it is likely he gained some, especially of the weaker sex;[4] if I may say, they were gained by him,

---

1 From 1639, Carlo Rosetti (1614 – 1681), a nobleman from Ferrara who had taken the habit of a prelate, was Pope Urban VIII's secret nuncio in London, his mission being clandestine on account of the conflict between England and the Church. As a result, while in London, he styled himself Count Charles Rosetti, using his title as a cover. The Queen, Henrietta Maria, who was a Roman Catholic, perceived his usefulness, and at one point had him petition the Pope for £100,000 to replenish the King's coffers. The Pope, of course, replied expressing readiness to supply the funds as soon as the King declared himself a Catholic. Rosetti also persuaded the Court to expel Catholic priests from England, rather than execute them, and even suggested to the King, when the latter faced accusations of Catholicism, that he may as well consider conversion. —Ed.

2 The Scottish Roman Catholic priest, George Conn (d. 1640), also a Franciscan, was Carlo Rosetti's predecessor. —Ed.

3 (1597 – 1679). —Ed.

4 One such success was Anne Blount, Lady Newport, the hitherto ardently Protestant wife of the 1st Earl, who converted to Catholicism in November 1637. Her younger sister, Olivia Porter, had herself previously converted and had also persuaded her father to do the same on his deathbed. Lady Newport strongly

when not his arguments, but hope of favour from the Queen, in all probability prevailed upon them.

B. In such a conjuncture as that was, it had perhaps been better they had not been sent.

A. There was exception taken also at a convent of friars-capucins in Somerset-House,[5] though allowed by the articles of marriage: and it was reported, that the Jesuits also were shortly after to be allowed a convent in Clerkenwell. And in the mean time, the principal secretary, Sir Francis Windebank,[6] was accused for having by his warrant set

---

opposed this and entered into a theological debate with the Capuchin priests at court. One by one her arguments were defeated, until she finally yielded, and took catechism lessons from Conn. The conversion generated a crisis. The Earl, according to Conn 'one of the chielf Puritans', accused Toby Matthew and Water Montague of conspiring with Conn to seduce his wife, and urged William Laud, Archbishop of Canterbury, to urge the Privy Council to banish the trio of seducers; he was distressed that his wife's actions would jeopardise his career at court. The increase of the Catholics was treated as a matter of national security. Charles then urged the Archbishop to strengthen the laws against conversion. However, Conn, in turn, urged the Queen, who was annoyed with Laud's intervention, to plead with Charles for leniency. Charles personally favoured Conn anyway, and the result was a proclamation so mild that the Queen would not object. —Ed.

5 During 17th century (except during the English Civil War, the Interregnum, and after 1692) this was used as residence for the Queens consort. To the south-west of the Great Court, Inigo Jones (1573 – 1652) build a chapel, which was put under the care of Capuchin monks, for Henrietta Maria to practice her Roman Catholic faith. —Ed.

6 Sir Francis Windebank (1582 – 1646) was Charles I's Secretary of State between 1632 and 1640. When summoned to answer

at liberty some English Jesuits, that had been taken and imprisoned for returning into England after banishment, contrary to the statute which had made it capital. Also the resort of English Catholics to the Queen's Chapel, gave them colour to blame the Queen herself, not only for that, but also for all the favours that had been shown to the Catholics; in so much that some of them did not stick to say openly, that the King was governed by her.

B. Strange injustice! The Queen was a Catholic by profession, and therefore could not but endeavour to do the Catholics all the good she could: she had not else been truly that which she professed to be. But it seems they meant to force her to hypocrisy, being hypocrites themselves. Can any man think it a crime in a devout lady, of what sect soever, to seek the favour and benediction of that Church whereof she is a member?

A. To give the Parliament another colour for their accusation on foot, of the King as to introducing of Popery, there was a great controversy between the Episcopal and Presbyterian clergy about free-will. The dispute began first in the Low Countries, between Gomar and Arminius,[7] in the time of King

the charge, Charles allowed him to escape to France. Windebank remained in Paris where he converted to Roman Catholicism shortly before he died. —Ed.

7 Francescus Gomarus (1563 – 1641) and Jacobus Arminius (1560 – 1609) were Dutch theologians who taught at the University of Leiden, Gomarus from 1594 and Arminius from 1603. When the latter joined the university, his doctrines roused Gomarus, a strict Calvinist, into active opposition; Go-

James, who foreseeing it might trouble the Church of England, did what he could to compose the difference. And an assembly of divines was thereupon got together at Dort,[8] to which also King James sent a divine or two, but it came to nothing; the question was left undecided, and became a subject to be disputed of in the universities here. All the Presbyterians were of the same mind with Gomar: but a very great many others not; and those were called here Arminians, who, because the doctrine of free-will had been exploded as a Papistical doctrine, and because the Presbyterians were far the greater number, and already in favour with the people, were generally hated. It was easy, therefore, for the Parliament to make that calumny pass currently with the people, when the Archbishop of Canterbury, Dr. Laud, was for Arminius, and had a little before, by his power ecclesiastical, forbidden

marus deemed Arminius' teachings pelagian and he opposed the latter's efforts to form of a new school of theology within the university. Arminius caused a split with Calvinism and his doctrines formed the basis for Arminianism and the Dutch Remonstrant movement (his followers after his death). —Ed.

8 Dort was the contemporary English name for Dordrecht, where the Synod of Dort referred to here was held by the Dutch Reformed Church between 13 November 1618 and 9 May 1619 to settle the controversy caused by the rise of Arminianism. The Synod ended with a rejection of the latter and the order for the Remonstrants to cease all ministerial activity. The Remonstrants agreed to do so within the government appointed churches, but thought it their duty to continue preaching their doctrines wherever people may assemble to hear them. They were then asked to sign an Act of Cessation, but they refused and were consequently expelled from the Dutch Republic. —Ed.

all ministers to preach to the people of predestination; and when all ministers that were gracious with him, and hoped for any Church preferment, fell to preaching and writing for free-will, to the uttermost of their power, as a proof of their ability and merit. Besides, they gave out, some of them, that the Archbishop was in heart a Papist; and in case he could effect a toleration here of the Roman religion, was to have a cardinal's hat: which was not only false, but also without any ground at all for a suspicion.

B. It is a strange thing, that scholars, obscure men, and such as could[9] receive no clarity but from the flame of the state, should be suffered to bring their unnecessary disputes, and together with them their quarrels, out of the universities into the commonwealth; and more strange, that the state should engage in their parties, and not rather put them both to silence.

A. A state can constrain obedience, but convince no error, nor alter the minds of them that believe they have the better reason. Suppression of doctrine does but unite and exasperate, that is, increase both the malice and power of them that have already believed them.

B. But what are the points they disagree in? Is there any controversy between Bishop and Presbyterian concerning the divinity or humanity of Christ? Do either of them deny the Trinity, or any article of the creed? Does either party preach open-

9 obscure men that could.

ly, or write directly, against justice, charity, sobriety, or any other duty necessary to salvation, except only the duty *we owe* to the King; and not that neither, but when they have a mind either to rule or destroy the King? Lord have mercy upon us! Can nobody be saved that understands not their disputations? Or is there more requisite, either of faith or honesty, for the salvation of one man than of another? What needs so much preaching of faith to us that are no heathens, and that believe already all that Christ and his apostles have told us is necessary to salvation, and more too? Why is there so little preaching of justice? I have indeed heard righteousness often recommended to the people, but I have seldom heard the word justice occur in their sermons; nay, though in the Latin and Greek Bible the word occur exceeding often, yet in the English, though it be a word that every man understands, the word righteousness (which few understand to signify the same, but take it rather for rightness of opinion, than of action or intention), is put in the place of it.

A. I confess I know very few controversies amongst Christians, of points necessary to salvation. They are the questions of authority and power over the Church, or of profit, or of honour to Churchmen, that for the most part raise all the controversies. For what man is he, that will trouble himself and fall out with his neighbours for the saving of my soul, or the soul of any other than himself? When the Presbyterian ministers and others did so seriously preach sedition, and animate men to rebellion in these late wars; who was there that had not a benefice, or having one feared not to lose it, or some other part of his maintenance, by the alteration of the Government, that did voluntarily, without any eye to reward, preach so earnestly against sedition, as the other party preached for it? I confess, that for aught I have observed in history, and other writings of the heathens, Greek and Latin, that those heathens were not at all behind us in point of virtue and moral duties, notwithstanding that we have had much preaching, and they none at all. I confess also, that considering what harm may proceed from a liberty that men have, upon every Sunday and oftener, to harangue all the people of a nation at one time, whilst the state is ignorant of what they will say; and that there is no such thing permitted in all the world out of Christendom, nor therefore any civil wars about religion; I have thought much preaching an inconvenience. Nevertheless, I cannot think that preaching to the people the points of their duty, both to God and man, can be too frequent; so it be done by grave, discreet, and ancient men, that are reverenced by the people; and not by light quibbling young men, whom no congregation is so simple as to look to be taught by (as being a thing contrary to nature), or to pay them any reverence, or to care what they say, except some few that may be delighted with their jingling. I wish with all my heart, there were enough of such discreet and ancient men, as might suffice for all the parishes of England, and that they would undertake it. But this is but a wish; I leave it to the wisdom of the State to do what it pleaseth.

B. What did they next?

A. Whereas the King had sent prisoners into places remote from London, three persons that had been condemned for publishing seditious doctrine, some in writing, some in public sermons; the Parliament (whether with his Majesty's consent or no, I have forgotten), caused them to be released and to return to London; meaning (I think) to try how the people would be pleased therewith, and, by consequence, how their endeavours to draw the people's affections from the King had already prospered. When these three came through London, it was a kind of triumph, the people flocking together to behold them, and receiving them with such acclamations, and almost adoration, as if they had been let down from heaven; insomuch as the Parliament was now sufficiently assured of a great and tumultuous party, whensoever they should have occasion to use it. On confidence whereof they proceeded to their next plot, which was to deprive the King of such ministers as by their wisdom, courage, and authority, they thought most able to prevent, or oppose their further designs against the King.—And first, the House of Commons resolved to impeach the Earl of Strafford, Lord Lieutenant of Ireland, of high-treason.

B. What was that Earl of Strafford before he

had that place? And how had he offended the Parliament or given them cause to think he would be their enemy? For I have heard that in former Parliaments he had been as parliamentary as any other.

A. His name was Sir Thomas Wentworth,[10] a gentleman both by birth and estate very considerable in his own county, which was Yorkshire; but more considerable for his judgment in the public affairs, not only of that county, but generally of the kingdom; and was therefore often chosen for the Parliament, either as a Burgess for some borough, or else Knight of the shire. For his principles of politics, they were the same that were generally proceeded upon by all men else that were thought fit to be chosen for the Parliament; which are commonly these: to take for the rule of justice and government the judgments and acts of former Parliaments, which are commonly called precedents; to endeavour to keep the people from being subject to extra-parliamentary taxes of money, and from being with parliamentary taxes too much oppressed; to preserve to the people their liberty of body from the arbitrary power of the King out of Parliament; to seek redress of grievances.

B. What grievances?

A. The grievances were commonly such as these: the King's too much liberality to some favourite; the too much power of some minister or officer of the commonwealth; the misdemeanour of judges, civil or spiritual; but especially all unparliamenta-

10 (1593 – 1641). —Ed.

ry raising of money upon the subjects. And commonly of late, till such grievances be redressed, they refuse, or at least make great difficulty, to furnish the King with money necessary for the most urgent occasions of the commonwealth.

B. How then can a King discharge his duty as he ought to do, or the subject know which of his masters he is to obey? For here are manifestly two powers, which, when they chance to differ, cannot both be obeyed.

A. It is true; but they have not often differed so much to the danger of the commonwealth, as they have done in this Parliament, 1640. In all the Parliaments of the late King Charles before the year 1640, my Lord of Strafford did appear in opposition to the King's demands as much as any man; and was for that cause very much esteemed and cried up by the people as a good patriot, and one that courageously stood up in defence of their liberties; and for the same cause was so much the more hated, when afterwards he endeavoured to maintain the royal and just authority of his Majesty.

B. How came he to change his mind so much as it seems he did?

A. After the dissolution of the Parliament holden in the years 1627 and 1628, the King, finding no money to be gotten from Parliaments which he was not to buy with the blood of such servants and ministers as he loved best, abstained a long time from calling any more, and had abstained longer if the rebellion of the Scots had not forced him to it.

During that Parliament the King made Sir Thomas Wentworth a baron, recommended to him for his great ability, which was generally taken notice of by the disservice he had done the King in former Parliaments, but which might be useful for him in the times that came on: and not long after he made him of the Council, and after that again Lieutenant of Ireland, which place he discharged with great satisfaction and benefit to his Majesty, and continued in that office, till, by the envy and violence of the Lords and Commons of that unlucky Parliament of 1640, he died. In which year he was made general of the King's forces against the Scots that then entered into England, and the year before, Earl of Strafford. The pacification being made, and the forces on both sides disbanded, and the Parliament at Westminster now sitting, it was not long before the House of Commons accused him to the House of Lords of High-Treason.

B. There was no great probability of his being a traitor to the King, from whose favour he had received his greatness, and from whose protection he was to expect his safety. What was the treason they laid to his charge?

A. Many articles were drawn up against him, but the sum of them was contained in these two: first, that he had traitorously endeavoured to subvert the fundamental laws and government of the realm; and in stead thereof to introduce an arbitrary and tyrannical government against law: secondly, that he had laboured to subvert the rights of

Parliaments, and the ancient course of Parliamentary proceedings.

B. Was this done by him without the knowledge of the King?

A. No.

B. Why then, if it were treason, did not the King himself call him in question by his attorney? What had the House of Commons to do, without his command, to accuse him to the Lords? They might have complained to the King, if he had not known it before. I understand not this law.

A. Nor I.

B. Had this been by any former statutes made treason?

A. Not that I ever heard of; nor do I understand how anything can be treason against the King, that the King, hearing and knowing, does not think treason. But it was a piece of that Parliament's artifice, to put the word traitorously to any article exhibited against any man whose life they meant to take away.

B. Was there no particular instance of action or words, out of which they argued that endeavour of his to subvert the fundamental laws of Parliament, whereof they accused him?

A. Yes; they said he gave the King counsel to reduce the Parliament to their duty by the Irish army, which not long before my Lord of Strafford himself had caused to be levied there for the King's service. But it was never proved against him, that he advised the King to use it against the Parliament.

B. What are those laws that are called fundamental? For I understand not how one law can be more fundamental than another, except only that law of nature that binds us all to obey him, whosoever he be, whom lawfully and for our own safety, we have promised to obey; nor any other fundamental law to a King, but *salus populi*, the safety and well-being of his people.

A. This Parliament, in the use of their words, when they accused any man, never regarded the signification of them, but the weight they had to aggravate their accusation to the ignorant multitude, which think all faults heinous that are expressed in heinous terms, if they hate the person accused, as they did this man, not only for being of the King's party, but also for deserting the Parliament's party as an apostate.

B. I pray you tell me also what they meant by arbitrary government, which they seemed so much to hate? Is there any governor of a people in the world that is forced to govern them, or forced to make this and that law, whether he will or no? I think not: or if any be, he that forces him does certainly make laws, and govern arbitrarily.

A. That is true; and the true meaning of the Parliament was, that not the King, but they themselves, should have the absolute government, not only of England, but of Ireland, and (as it appeared by the event) of Scotland also.

B. How the King came by the government of Scotland and Ireland by descent from his ancestors, everybody can tell; but if the King of England and his heirs should chance (which God forbid) to fail, I cannot imagine what title the Parliament of England can acquire thereby to either of those nations.

A. Yes; they will say they had been conquered anciently by the English subjects' money.

B. Like enough, and suitable to the rest of their impudence.

A. Impudence in democratical assemblies[11] does almost all that's done; 'tis the goddess of rhetoric, and carries proof with it. For what ordinary man will not, from so great boldness of affirmation, conclude there is great probability in the thing affirmed? Upon this accusation he was brought to his trial in Westminster Hall before the House of Lords, and found guilty, and presently after declared traitor by a bill of attainder, that is, by Act of Parliament.

B. It is a strange thing that the Lords should be induced, upon so light grounds, to give a sentence, or give their assent to a bill, so prejudicial to themselves and their posterity.

A. It was not well done, and yet, as it seems, not ignorantly; for there is a clause in the bill, that it should not be taken hereafter for an example, that is for a prejudice, in the like case hereafter.

B. That is worse than the bill itself, and is a plain confession that their sentence was unjust. For

---

11 *After* 'democratical assemblies', *there follows in the MS an illegible word and three further words:* 'and generally in all assemblies', *which have been crossed.*

what harm is there in the examples of just sentences? Besides, if hereafter the like case should happen, the sentence is not at all made weaker by such a provision.

A. Indeed I believe that the Lords, most of them, *following the principles of warlike and savage natures, envied his greatness, but yet* were not of themselves willing to condemn him of treason. They were awed to it by the clamour of common people that came to Westminster, crying out, "*Justice, Justice against the Earl of Strafford!*" The which were caused to flock thither by some of the House of Commons, that were well assured, after the triumphant welcome of Prynne, Burton, and Bastwick, to put the people into tumult upon any occasion they desired. They were awed unto it partly also by the House of Commons itself, which if it desired to undo a Lord, had no more to do but to vote him a *Delinquent*.

B. A delinquent; what is that? A sinner, is it not? Did they mean to undo all sinners?

A. By delinquent they meant only a man to whom they would do all the hurt they could. But the Lords did not yet, I think, suspect they meant to cashier their whole House.

B. It is a strange thing the whole House of Lords should not perceive that the ruin of the King's power, and the weakening of it, was the ruin or weakening of themselves. For they could not think it likely that the people ever meant to take the sovereignty from the King to give it to them, who were few in number, and less in power than so many Commoners, because less beloved by the people.

A. But it seems not so strange to me. For the Lords, for their personal abilities, as they were no less, so also they were no more skilful in the public affairs, than the knights and burgesses. For there is no reason to think, that if one that is to-day a knight of the shire in the lower House, be to-morrow made a Lord and a member of the higher House, he is therefore wiser than he was before. They are all, of both Houses, prudent and able men as any in the land, in the business of their private estates, which require nothing but diligence and natural wit to govern them. But for the government of a commonwealth, neither wit, nor prudence, nor diligence, is enough, without infallible rules and the true science of equity and justice.

B. If this be true, it is impossible that any commonwealth in the world, whether monarchy, aristocracy, or democracy, should continue long without change, or sedition tending to change, either of the government or of the governors.

A. It is true; nor have any the greatest commonwealths in the world been long free from sedition. The Greeks had for awhile their petty kings, and then by sedition came to be petty commonwealths; and then growing to be greater commonwealths, by sedition again became monarchies; and all for want of rules of justice for the common people to take notice of; which if the people had known in the beginning of every of these seditions, the ambitious persons could never have had the hope to disturb their government after it had been once settled. For ambition can do little without hands, and few hands it would have, if the common people were as diligently instructed in the true principles of their duty, as they are terrified and amazed by preachers, with fruitless and dangerous doctrines concerning the nature of man's will, and many other philosophical points that tend not at all to the salvation of their souls in the world to come, nor to their ease in this life, but only to the direction towards the clergy of that duty which they ought to perform to the King.

B. For aught I see, all the states of Christendom will be subject to these fits of rebellion, as long as the world lasteth.

A. Like enough; and yet the fault (as I have said) may be easily mended, by mending the Universities.

B. How long had the Parliament now sitten?

A. It began November the 3rd, 1640. My Lord of Strafford was impeached of treason before the Lords, November the 12th, sent to the Tower November the 22nd, his trial began March the 22nd, and ended April the 13th. After his trial he was voted guilty of high-treason in the House of Commons, and after that in the Lords' House, May the 6th; and on the 12th of May beheaded.

B. Great expedition; but could not the King, for all that, have saved him by a pardon?

A. The King had heard all that passed at his trial, and had declared himself unsatisfied concerning the justice of their sentence. And, I think, notwithstanding the danger of his own person from the fury of the people, and that he was counselled to give way to his execution, not only by such as he most relied on, but also by the Earl of Strafford himself, he would have pardoned him, if that could have preserved him against the tumult raised and countenanced by the Parliament itself, for the terrifying of those they thought might favour him. And yet the King himself did not stick to confess afterwards, that he had done amiss, in that he did not rescue him.

B. It was an argument of good disposition in the King. But I never read that Augustus Cæsar acknowledged that he had done a fault, in abandoning Cicero to the fury of his enemy Antonius: perhaps because Cicero, having been of the contrary faction to his father, had done Augustus no service at all out of favour to him, but only out of enmity to Antonius, and out of love to the senate, that is indeed out of love to himself that swayed the senate; as it is very likely the Earl of Strafford came over to the King's party for his own ends, having been so much against the King in former Parliaments.

A. We cannot safely judge of men's intentions. But, I have observed often, that such as seek preferment, by their stubbornness have missed of their aim; and on the other side, that those princes that with preferment are forced to buy the obedience of their subjects, are already, or must be soon after, in a very weak condition. For in a market where honour and power is to be bought with stubbornness, there will be a great many as able to buy as my Lord Strafford was.

B. You have read, that when Hercules fighting with the Hydra, had cut off any one of his many heads, there still arose two other heads in its place; and yet at last he cut them off all.

A. The story is told false. For Hercules at first did not cut off those heads, but bought them off; and afterwards, when he saw it did him no good, then he cut them off, and got the victory.

B. What did they next?

A. After the first impeachment of the Earl of Strafford, the House of Commons, upon December the 18th, accused the Archbishop of Canterbury also of high-treason, that is, of design to introduce arbitrary government, &c.; for which he was, February the 28th, sent to the Tower; but his trial and execution were deferred a long time, till January the 10th, 1643, for the entertainment of the Scots, that were come into England to aid the Parliament.

B. Why did the Scots think there was so much danger in the Archbishop of Canterbury? He was not a man of war, nor a man able to bring an army into the field; but he was perhaps a very great politician.

A. That did not appear by any remarkable event of his counsels. I never heard but he was a very honest man for his morals, and a very zealous promoter of the Church-government by bishops, and that desired to have the service of God performed, and the house of God adorned, as suitable as was possible to the honour we ought to do to the Divine Majesty. But to bring, as he did, into the State his former controversies, I mean his squabblings in the University about free-will, and his standing upon punctilios concerning the service-book and its rubrics, was not, in my opinion, an argument of his sufficiency in affairs of State.—About the same time they passed an act (which the King consented to) for a triennial Parliament; wherein was enacted, that after this present Parliament there should be a Parliament called by the King within the space of three years, and so from three years to three years, to meet at Westminster upon a certain day named in the act.

B. But what if the King did not call it, finding it perhaps inconvenient, or hurtful to the safety or peace of his people, which God hath put into his charge? For I do not well comprehend how any sovereign can well keep a people in order when his hands are tied, or when he hath any other obligation upon him than the benefit of those he governs; and at this time, for anything you have told me, they acknowledged the King for their sovereign.

A. I know not; but such was the act. And it was further enacted, that if the King did it not by his own command, then the Lord Chancellor or the Lord Keeper for the time being, should send out the writs of summons; and if the Chancellor refused, then the Sheriffs of the several counties should of themselves, in their next county-courts before the day set down for the Parliament's meeting, proceed to the election of the members for the said Parliament.

B. But what if the sheriffs refused?

A. I think they were to be sworn to it: but for that, and other particulars, I refer you to the act.

B. To whom should they be sworn, when there is no Parliament?

A. No doubt but to the King, whether there be a Parliament sitting or no.

B. Then the King may release them of their oath.[12] Besides, if the King, upon the refusal, should fall upon them in his anger; who shall (the Parliament not sitting) protect either the Chancellor or the sheriffs in their disobedience?

A. I pray you do not ask me any reason of such things as I understand no better than you. I tell you only an act passed to that purpose, and was signed by the King in the middle of February, a little before the Archbishop was sent to the Tower. Besides this bill, the two Houses of Parliament agreed upon another, wherein it was enacted, that the present Parliament should continue till both the Houses did consent to the dissolution of it; which bill also the King signed the same day he signed the warrant for the execution of the Earl of Strafford.

12 *The words of A:* "Besides . . . Courts", *have been transposed to a wrong place, after* "release them of their oath", *in the former edd.*

B. What a great progress made the Parliament *towards their ends, or at least* towards the ends of the most seditious Members of both Houses in so little time! They sat down in November, and now it was May; in this space of time, which is but half a year, they won from the King the adherence which was due to him from his people; they drove his faithfullest servants from him; beheaded the Earl of Strafford; imprisoned the Archbishop of Canterbury; obtained a triennial Parliament after their own dissolution, and a continuance of their own sitting as long as they listed: which last amounted to a total extinction of the King's right, in case that such a grant were valid; which I think it is not, unless the Sovereignty itself be in plain terms renounced, which it was not.

A. Besides, they obtained of the King the putting down the Star-chamber and High-Commission Courts.

B. But what money, by way of subsidy or otherwise, did they grant the King, in recompense of all these his large concessions?

A. None at all; but often promised they would make him the most glorious King that ever was in England; which were words that passed well enough for well meaning with the common people.

B. But the Parliament was contented now? For I cannot imagine what they could desire more from the King, than he had now granted them.

A. Yes; they desired the whole and absolute sovereignty, and to change the monarchical government into an oligarchy; that is to say, to make the Parliament, consisting of a few Lords and about four hundred Commoners, absolute in the sovereignty, for the present, and shortly after to lay the House of Lords aside. For this was the design of the Presbyterian ministers, who taking themselves to be, by divine right, the only lawful governors of the Church, endeavoured to bring the same form of Government into the civil state. And as the spiritual laws were to be made by their synods, so the civil laws should be made by the House of Commons; who, as they thought, would no less be ruled by them afterwards, than they formerly had been: wherein they were deceived, and found themselves outgone by their own disciples, though not in malice, yet in wit.

B. What followed after this?

A. In August following, the King supposing he had now sufficiently obliged the Parliament to proceed no further against him, took a journey into Scotland, to satisfy his subjects there, as he had done here; intending, perhaps, so to gain their good wills, that in case the Parliament here should levy arms against him, they should not be aided by the Scots: wherein he also was deceived. For though they seemed satisfied with what he did, whereof one thing was his giving way to the abolition of episcopacy; yet afterwards they made a league with the Parliament, and for money, when the King began to have the better of the Parliament, invaded England in the Parliament's quarrel. But this was a year or two after.

B. Before you go any further, I desire to know the ground and original of that right, which either the House of Lords, or House of Commons, or both together, now pretend to.

A. It is a question of things so long past, that they are now forgotten. Nor have we anything to conjecture by, but the records of our own nation, and some small and obscure fragments of Roman histories: and for the records, seeing they are of things done only, sometimes justly, sometimes unjustly, you can never by them know what right they had, but only what right they pretended.

B. Howsoever, let me know what light we have in this matter from the Roman histories.

A. It would be too long, and an useless digression, to cite all the ancient authors that speak of the forms of those commonwealths, which were amongst our first ancestors the Saxons and other Germans, and of other nations, from whom we derive the titles of honour now in use in England; nor will it be possible to derive from them any argument of right, but only examples of fact, which, by the ambition of potent subjects, have been oftener unjust than otherwise. And for those Saxons or Angles, that in ancient times by several invasions made themselves masters of this nation, they were not in themselves one body of a commonwealth, but only a league of divers petty German lords and states, such as was the Grecian army in the Trojan war, without other obligation than that which proceeded from their own fear and weakness. Nor were those lords, for the most part, the sovereigns at home in their own country, but chosen by the people for captains of the forces they brought with them. And therefore it was not without equity, when they had conquered any part of the land, and made some one of them king thereof, that the rest should have greater privileges than the common people and soldiers: amongst which privileges, a man may easily conjecture this to be one; that they should be made acquainted, and be of council, with him that hath the sovereignty in matter of government, and have the greatest and most honourable offices both in peace and war. But because there can be no government where there is more than one sovereign, it cannot be inferred that they had a right to oppose the King's resolutions by force, nor to enjoy those honours and places longer than they should continue good subjects. And we find that the Kings of England did, upon every great occasion, call them together by the name of discreet and wise men of the kingdom, and hear their counsel, and make them judges of all causes, that during their sitting were brought before them. But as he summoned them at his own pleasure, so had he also ever the power at his pleasure to dissolve them. The Normans also, that descended from the Germans, as we did, had the same customs in this particular; and by this means, this privilege of the lords to be of the King's great council, and when they were assembled, to be the highest of the

King's courts of justice, continued still after the Conquest to this day. But though there be amongst the lords divers names or titles of honour, yet they have their privilege only by the name of baron, a name received from the ancient Gauls; amongst whom, that name signified the King's man, or rather one of his great men: by which it seems to me, that though they gave him counsel when he required it, yet they had no right to make war upon him if he did not follow it.

B. When began first the House of Commons to be part of the King's great council?

A. I do not doubt but that before the Conquest some discreet men, and known to be so by the King, were called by special writ to be of the same council, though they were not lords; but that is nothing to the House of Commons. The knights of shires and burgesses were never called to Parliament, for aught that I know, till the beginning of the reign of Edward I.,[13] or the latter end of the reign of Henry III.,[14] immediately after the misbehaviour of the barons; and, for aught any man knows, were called on purpose to weaken that power of the lords, which they had so freshly abused. Before the time of Henry III., the lords were descended, most of them, from such as in the invasions and conquests of the Germans were peers and fellow-kings, till one was made king of them all; and their ten-

13 Edward I (1239 – 1307) reigned from 1272 until his death. —Ed.

14 Edward I's father, Henry III (1207 – 1272) reigned from 1216 until his death. —Ed.

ants were their subjects, as it is this day with the lords of France. But after the time of Henry III., the kings began to make lords in the place of them whose issue failed, titulary only, without the lands belonging to their title; and by that means, their tenants being no longer bound to serve them in the wars, they grew every day less and less able to make a party against the King, though they continued still to be his great council. And as their power decreased, so the power of the House of Commons increased; but I do not find they were part of the King's council at all, nor judges over other men; though it cannot be denied, but a King may ask their advice, as well as the advice of any other. But I do not find that the end of their summoning was to give advice, but only, in case they had any petitions for redress of grievances, to be ready there with them whilst the King had his great council about him. But neither they nor the lords could present to the King, as a grievance, that the King took upon him to make the laws; to choose his own privy-counsellors; to raise money and soldiers; to defend the peace and honour of the kingdom; to make captains in his army, and governors of his castles, whom he pleased. For this had been to tell the King, that it was one of their grievances that he was King.

B. What did the Parliament do, whilst the King was in Scotland?

A. The King went in August; after which, the Parliament, September the 8th, adjourned till the

20th of October; and the King returned in the beginning of December following. In which time the most seditious of both Houses, and which had designed the change of government and to cast off monarchy (but yet had not wit enough to set up any other government in its place, and consequently left it to the chance of war), made a cabal amongst themselves; in which they projected how, by seconding one another, to govern the House of Commons, and invented how to put the kingdom, by the power of that House, into a rebellion, which they then called a posture of defence against such dangers from abroad, as they themselves should feign and publish. Besides, whilst the King was in Scotland, the Irish Papists got together a great party, with an intention to massacre the Protestants there, and had laid a design for the seizing of Dublin Castle, on October 23, where the King's officers of the government of that country made their residence; and had effected it, had it not been discovered the night before. The manner of the discovery, and the murders they committed in the country afterwards, I need not tell you, since the whole story of it is extant.

B. I wonder they did not expect and provide for a rebellion in Ireland, as soon as they began to quarrel with the King in England. For was there any body so ignorant, as not to know that the Irish Papists did long for a change of religion there, as well as the Presbyterians in England? Or, that in general, the Irish nation did hate the name of subjection to England, nor would longer be quiet, than they feared an army out of England to chastise them? What better time then could they take for their rebellion than this, wherein they were encouraged, not only by our weakness caused by this division between the King and his Parliament, but also by the example of the Presbyterians, both of the Scotch and English nation? But what did the Parliament do upon this occasion, in the King's absence?

A. Nothing; but consider what use they might make of it to their own ends; partly, by imputing it to the King's evil counsellors, and partly, by occasion thereof to demand of the King the power of pressing and ordering soldiers; which power whosoever has, has also, without doubt, the whole sovereignty.

B. When came the King back?

A. He came back the 25th of November; and was welcomed with the acclamations of the common people, as much as if he had been the most beloved of all the Kings that were before him; but found not a reception by the Parliament, answerable to it. They presently began to pick new quarrels against him, out of everything he said to them. December the 2nd, the King called together both Houses of Parliament, and then did only recommend unto them the raising of succours for Ireland.

B. What quarrel could they pick out of that?

A. None: but in order thereto, as they may pretend, they had a bill in agitation to assert the power of levying and pressing soldiers to the two Houses of the Lords and Commons; which was as much as to take from the King the power of the *militia*, which is in effect the whole sovereign power. For he that hath the power of levying and commanding the soldiers, has all other rights of sovereignty which he shall please to claim. The King, hearing of it, called the Houses of Parliament together again, on December the 14th, and then pressed again the business of Ireland (as there was need; for all this while the Irish were murdering the English in Ireland, and strengthening themselves against the forces they expected to come out of England): and withal, told them he took notice of the bill in agitation for pressing of soldiers, and that he was contented it should pass with a *salvo jure* both for him and them, because the present time was unseasonable to dispute it in.

B. What was there unreasonable in this?

A. Nothing: what is unreasonable is one question, what they quarrelled at is another. They quarrelled at this: that his Majesty took notice of that bill, while it was in debate in the House of Lords, before it was presented to him in the course of Parliament; and also that he showed himself displeased with those that propounded the said bill; both which they declared to be against the privileges of Parliament, and petitioned the King to give them reparation against those by whose evil counsel he was induced to it, that they might receive condign punishment.

B. This was a cruel proceeding. Do not the Kings of England use to sit in the Lords' House when they please? And was not this bill in debate then in the House of Lords? It is a strange thing that a man should be lawfully in the company of men, where he must needs hear and see what they say and do, and yet must not take notice of it so much as to the same company; for though the King was not at the debate itself, yet it was lawful for any of the Lords to make him acquainted with it. Any one of the House of Commons, though not present at a proposition or debate in the House, nevertheless hearing of it from some of his fellow-members, may certainly not only take notice of it, but also speak to it in the House of Commons: but to make the King give up his friends and counsellors to them, to be put to death, banishment, or imprisonment, for their good-will to him, was such a tyranny over a king, no king ever exercised over any subject but in cases of treason or murder, and seldom then.

A. Presently hereupon began a kind of war between the pens of the Parliament and those of the secretaries, and other able men that were with the King. For upon the 15th of December they sent to the King a paper called *A Remonstrance of the State of the Kingdom*,[15] and with it a petition; both which they caused to be published. In the remomstrance they complained of certain mischievous de-

15 First proposed by John Pym (1584 – 1643), leader of the Long Parliament and chief critic of Charles I. —Ed.

signs of a malignant party, then, before the beginning of the Parliament, grown ripe; and did set forth what means had been used for the preventing of it by the wisdom of the Parliament; what rubs they had found therein; what course was fit to be taken for restoring and establishing the ancient honour, greatness, and safety, of the Crown and nation.

And of these designs the promoters and actors were (they said) 1. Jesuited Papists:

2. The bishops, and that part of the clergy that cherish formality as a support of their own ecclesiastical tyranny and usurpation:

3. Counsellors and courtiers, that for private ends (they said) had engaged themselves to further the interests of some foreign princes.

B. It may very well be, that some of the bishops, and also some of the court, may have, in pursuit of their private interest, done something indiscreetly, and perhaps wickedly. Therefore I pray you tell me in particular what their crimes were: for methinks the King should not have connived at anything against his own supreme authority.

A. The Parliament were not very keen against those that were for the King,[16] they made no doubt but all they did was by the King's command; but accused thereof the bishops, counsellors, and courtiers, as being a more mannerly way of accusing the King himself, and defaming him to his subjects.

---

16 "keen against them that were against the King" *edd., which has been corrected as above, by the author's own hand, in the MS.*

For the truth is, the charge they brought against them was so general as not to be called an accusation, but railing. As first (they said) they nourished questions of prerogative and liberty between the King and his people, to the end that, seeming much addicted to his Majesty's service, they might get themselves into places of greatest trust and power in the kingdom.

B. How could this be called an accusation, in which there is no fact, for any accusers to apply their proofs to, or their witnesses. For granting that these questions of prerogative had been moved by them, who can prove that their end was to gain to themselves and friends the places of trust and power in the kingdom?

A. A second accusation was, that they endeavoured to suppress the purity and power of religion.

B. That is canting. 'Tis not in man's power to suppress the power of religion.

A. They meant that they would suppress the doctrine of the Presbyterians; that is to say, the very foundation of the then Parliament's treacherous pretensions.

A third, that they cherished Arminians, Papists, and libertines (by which they meant the common Protestants, which meddle not with disputes), to the end they might compose a body fit to act according to their counsels and resolutions.

A fourth, that they endeavoured to put the King upon other courses of raising money, than by the ordinary way of Parliaments.

Judge whether these may be properly called accusations, or not rather spiteful reproaches of the King's government.

B. Methinks this last was a very great fault. For what good could there be in putting the King upon any odd course of getting money, when the Parliament was willing to supply him, as far as to the security of the kingdom, or to the honour of the King, should be necessary?

A. But I told you before, they would give him none, but with a condition he should cut off the heads of whom they pleased, how faithfully soever they had served him. And if he would have sacrificed all his friends to their ambition, yet they would have found other excuses for denying him subsidies; for they were resolved to take from him the sovereign power to themselves; which they could never do without taking great care that he should have no money at all. In the next place, they put into the remonstrance, as faults of them whose counsel the King followed, all those things which since the beginning of the King's reign were by them misliked, whether faults or not, and whereof they were not able to judge for want of knowledge of the causes and motives that induced the King to do them, and were known only to the King himself, and such of his privy-council as he revealed them to.

B. But what were those particular pretended faults?

A. 1. The dissolution of his first Parliament at Oxford. 2. The dissolution of his second Parliament, being in the second year of his reign. 3. The dissolution of his Parliament in the fourth year of his reign. 4. The fruitless expedition against Calais. 5. The peace made with Spain, whereby the Palatine's cause was deserted, and left to chargeable and hopeless treaties. 6. The sending of commissions to raise money by way of loan. 7. Raising of ship-money. 8. Enlargement of forests, contrary to Magna Charta. 9. The design of engrossing all the gunpowder into one hand, and keeping it in the Tower of London. 10. A design to bring in the use of brass money. 11. The fines, imprisonments, stigmatizings, mutilations, whippings, pillories, gags, confinements, and banishments, by sentence in the Court of Star-Chamber. 12. The displacing of judges. 13. Illegal acts of the Council-table. 14. The arbitrary and illegal power of the Earl Marshal's Court. 15. The abuses in Chancery, Exchequer-chamber, and Court of Wards. 16. The selling of titles of honour, of judges, and serjeants' places, and other offices. 17. The insolence of bishops and other clerks, in suspensions, excommunications, deprivations, and degradations of divers painful, learned and pious ministers.

B. Was there any such ministers degraded, deprived, or excommunicated?

A. I cannot tell. But I remember I have heard threatened divers painful, unlearned and seditious ministers.

18. The excess of severity of the High Commission-Court. 19. The preaching before the King

against the property of the subject, and for the prerogative of the King above the law. And divers other petty quarrels they had to the government; which though they were laid upon this faction, yet they knew they would fall upon the King himself in the judgment of the people, to whom, by printing, they were communicated.

Again, after the dissolution of the Parliament May the 5th, 1640, they find other faults: as the dissolution itself, the imprisoning some members of both Houses, a forced loan of money attempted in London, the continuance of the Convocation, when the Parliament was ended; and the favour showed to Papists by Secretary Windebank and others.

B. All this will go current with common people for misgovernment, and for faults of the King, though some of them were misfortunes; and both the misfortunes and the misgovernment (if any were) were the faults of the Parliament; who, by denying to give him money, did both frustrate his attempts abroad, and put him upon those extraordinary ways (which they call illegal) of raising money at home.

A. You see what a heap of evils they have raised to make a show of ill-government to the people, which they second with an enumeration of the many services they have done the King in overcoming a great many of them, though not all, and in divers other things; and say, that though they had contracted a debt to the Scots of 220,000*l*. and had granted six subsidies, and a bill of poll-money worth six subsidies more, yet that God had so blessed the endeavours of this Parliament, that the kingdom was a gainer by it: and then follows the catalogue of those good things they had done for the King and kingdom. For the kingdom they had done (they said) these things: they had abolished ship-money *which cost the kingdom 200 thousand pounds a year*; they had taken away coat and conduct money, and other military charges, which, they said, amounted to little less than the ship-money; that they suppressed all monopolies, which they reckoned above a million yearly saved by the subject; that they had quelled living grievances, meaning evil counsellors and actors, by the death of my Lord of Strafford, by the flight of Chancellor Finch,[17] and of Secretary Windebank, by the imprisonment of the Archbishop of Canterbury, and of Judge Bartlet, and the impeachment of other bishops and judges; that they had passed a bill for a triennial Parliament, and another for the continuance of the present Parliament, till they should think fit to dissolve themselves.

B. That is to say, for ever, if they be suffered. But the sum of all these things, which they had done for the kingdom, is: that they had left it without government, without strength, without money, without law, and without good counsel.

A. They reckoned, also, putting down of the

17 John Finch, 1st Baron Finch (1584 – 1660), Lord Keeper of the Great Seal. —Ed.

High-Commission, and the abating of the power of the Council-table, and of the bishops and their courts; the taking away of unnecessary ceremonies in religion; removing of ministers from their livings, that were not of their faction, and putting in *their places* such as were.

B. All this was but their own, and not the kingdom's business.

A. The good they had done the King, was first (they said) the giving of 25,000*l*. a month for the relief of the northern counties.

B. What need of relief had the northern, more than the rest of the counties of England?

A. Yes, in the northern counties were quartered the Scotch army which the Parliament called in to oppose the King, and consequently their quarter was to be discharged.

B. True; but by the Parliament that called them in.

A. But they say no; and that this money was given to the King, because he was bound to protect his subjects.

B. He is no further bound to that, than they give him money wherewithal to do it. This is very great impudence; to raise an army against the King, and with that army to oppress their fellow-subjects, and then require that the King should relieve them, that is to say, be at the charge of paying the army that was raised to fight against him.

A. Nay, further; they put to the King's account the 300,000*l*. given to the Scots, without which they would not have invaded England; besides many other things, that I now remember not.

B. I did not think there had been so great impudence and villainy in mankind.

A. You have not observed the world long enough to see all that's ill. Such was their remonstrance, as I have told you. With it they sent a petition, containing three points: 1. That his Majesty would deprive the bishops of their votes in Parliament, and remove such oppressions in religion, church-government, and discipline, as they had brought in; 2. That he would remove from his council all such as should promote the people's grievances, and employ in his great and public affairs, such *persons* as the Parliament should confide in; 3. That he would not give away the lands escheated to the Crown by the rebellion in Ireland.

B. This last point, methinks, was not wisely put in at this time: it should have been reserved till they had subdued the rebels, against whom there were yet no forces sent over. 'Tis like selling the lion's skin before they had killed him. But what answer was made to the other two propositions?

A. What answer should be made, but a denial? About the same time the King himself exhibited articles against six persons of the Parliament, five whereof were of the House of Commons and one of the House of Lords, accusing them of high-treason; and upon the 4th of January, went himself to the House of Commons to demand those five of them. But private notice having been given by some treacherous person about the King, they had absented themselves; and by that means frustrated his Majesty's intention. And after he was gone, the House making a heinous matter of it, and a high breach of their privileges, adjourned themselves into London, there to sit as a general committee, pretending they were not safe at Westminster: for the King, when he went to the House to demand those persons, had somewhat more attendance with him (but not otherwise armed than his servants used to be) than he ordinarily had. And would not be pacified, though the King did afterwards waive the prosecution of those persons, unless he would also discover to them those that gave him counsel to go in that manner to the Parliament House, to the end they might receive *condign punishment*; which was the word they used instead of *cruelty*.

B. This was a harsh demand. Was it not enough that the King should forbear his enemies, but that he must also betray his friends? If they thus tyrannize over the King before they have gotten the sovereign power into their hands, how will they tyrannize over their fellow-subjects when they have gotten it?

A. So as they did.

B. How long stayed that committee in London?

A. Not above two or three days; and then were brought from London to the Parliament House by water in great triumph, guarded with a tumultuous number of armed men, there to sit in security in despite of the King, and make traitorous acts against him, such and as many as they listed; and under favour of these tumults, to frighten away from the House of Peers all such as were not of their faction. For at this time the rabble *of people* were so insolent, that scarce any of the bishops durst go to the House for fear of violence upon their persons; in so much as twelve of them excused themselves of coming thither, and by way of petition to the King, remonstrated that they were not permitted to go quietly to the performance of that duty, and protesting against all determinations, as of none effect, that should pass in the House of Lords during their forced absence. Which the House of Commons taking hold of, sent to the Peers one of their members, to accuse them of high-treason. Whereupon ten of them were sent to the Tower; after which time there were no more words of their high-treason; but there passed a bill, by which they were deprived of their votes in Parliament; and to this bill they got the King's assent. And, in the beginning of September after, they voted that the bishops should have no more to do in the government of the Church; but to this they had not the King's assent, the war being now begun.

B. What made the Parliament so averse to episcopacy; and especially the House of Lords, whereof the bishops were members? For I see no reason why they should do it to gratify a number of poor parish priests that were Presbyterians, and that were never likely any way to serve the Lords; but, on the contrary, to do their best to pull down their power, and subject them to their synods and classes.

A. For the Lords, very few of them did perceive the intentions of the Presbyterians; and, besides that, they durst not (I believe) oppose the Lower House.

B. But why were the Lower House so earnest against them?

A. Because they meant to make use of their tenets, and with pretended sanctity to make the King and his party odious to the people, by whose help they were to set up democracy, and depose the King, or to let him have the title only so long as he should act for their purposes. But not only the Parliament, but in a manner all the people of England, were their enemies, upon the account of their behaviour, as being (they said) too imperious. *[For indeed the most of them so carried themselves, as if they owed their greatness not to the King's favour and to his letters patent, which gives them their authority, but to the merit of their (own?) conceived (wit and?) learning (and had?) no less care of the praises of each other, than they showed irritability to defend the dignity of their jurisdiction and of their office, being ever highly offended with those that dissented from their spirit or their ideas; (and consequently?) . . . they were reputed a little too diligent in making the best of themselves.]* This was all that was colourably laid to their charge. The main cause of pulling them down, was the envy of the Presbyterians, that incensed the people against them, and against episcopacy itself.

B. How would the Presbyterians have the Church to be governed?

A. By national and provincial synods.

B. Is not this to make the national assembly an archbishop, and the provincial assemblies so many bishops?

A. Yes; but every minister shall have the delight of sharing in the government, and consequently of being able to be revenged on those that do not admire their learning and help to fill their purses, and win to their service those that do.

B. It is a hard case, that there should be two factions to trouble the commonwealth, without any interest in it of their own, other than every particular man may have; and that their quarrel should be only about opinions, that is, about who has the most learning; as if their learning ought to be the rule of governing all the world. What is it they are learned in? Is it politics and rules of state? I know, it is called divinity; but I hear almost nothing preached but matter of philosophy. For religion in itself admits no controversy. It is a law of the kingdom, and ought not to be disputed. I do not think they pretend to speak with God and know his will by any other way than reading the Scriptures, which we also do.

A. Yes, some of them do, and give themselves out for prophets by extraordinary inspiration. But the rest pretend only (for their advancement to benefices and charge of souls) a greater skill in the Scriptures than other men have, by reason of their breeding in the Universities, and knowledge there gotten of the Latin tongue, and some also of the Greek and Hebrew tongues, wherein the Scripture was written; besides their knowledge of natural philosophy, which is there publicly taught.

B. As for the Latin, Greek, and Hebrew tongues, it was once (to the detection of Roman fraud, and to the ejection of the Romish power) very profitable, or rather necessary; but now that is done, and we have the Scripture in English, and preaching in English, I see no great need of Greek, Latin, and Hebrew. I should think myself better qualified by understanding well the languages of our neighbours, French, Dutch, and Spanish.—I think it was never seen in the world, before the power of popes was set up, that philosophy was much conducing to power in a commonwealth.

B. But philosophy, together with divinity, have very much conduced to the advancement of the professors thereof to places of greatest authority, next to the authority of kings themselves, in most of the ancient kingdoms of the world; as is manifestly to be seen in the history of those times.

B. I pray you cite me some of the authors and places.

A. First, what were the Druids of old time in Britanny and France? What authority these had you may see in Cæsar, Strabo, and others, and especially in Diodorus Siculus,[18] the greatest antiquary perhaps that ever was; who speaking of the Druids (whom he calls Sarovides) in France, says thus:—"*There be also amongst them certain philosophers and theologians, that are exceedingly honoured, whom they also use as prophets. These men, by their skill in augury and inspection into the bowels of beasts sacrificed, foretell what is to come, and have the multitude obedient to them.*" And a little after—"*It is a custom amongst them, that no man may sacrifice without a philosopher; because (say they) men ought not to present their thanks to the Gods, but by them that know the divine nature, and are as it were of the same language with them; and that all good things ought by such as these to be prayed for.*"

B. I can hardly believe that those Druids were very skilful, either in natural philosophy, or moral.

A. Nor I; for they held and taught the transmigration of souls from one body to another, as did Pythagoras; which opinion whether they took from him, or he from them, I cannot tell.

What were the Magi in Persia, but philosophers and astrologers? You know how they came to find our Saviour by the conduct of a star, either from Persia itself, or from some country more eastward than Judea. Were not these in great authority in

18 Greek historian from the 1st century BCE, who wrote a monumental universal history, *the Bibliotheca historica*, in forty books over a period of thirty years, from the mythic past up until 60 BCE. —Ed.

their country? And are they not in most parts of Christendom thought to have been Kings?

Egypt hath been by many thought the most ancient kingdom, and nation of the world; and their priests had the greatest power in civil affairs, that any subjects ever had in any nation. And what were they but philosophers and divines? Concerning whom, the same Diodorus Siculus says thus: "*The whole country (of Egypt) being divided into three parts, the body of the priests have one as being of most credit with the people, both for their devotion towards the Gods, and also for their understanding gotten by education*"; and presently after, "*For generally these men, in the greatest affairs of all, are the King's counsellors, partly executing, and partly informing and advising him; foretelling him also (by their skill in astrology and art in the inspection of sacrifices) the things that are to come, and reading to him out of their holy books such of the actions there recorded, as are profitable for him to know. It is not there as in Greece, one man or one woman that has the priesthood; but they are many that attend the honours and sacrifices of the Gods, and leave the same employment to their posterity, which, next to the King, have the greatest power and authority.*"

Concerning the judicature amongst the Egyptians, he saith thus: "*From out of the most eminent cities, Hieropolis, Thebes, and Memphis, they choose judges, which are a council not inferior to that of Areopagus in Athens, or that of the senate in Lacedæmon. When they are met, being in number thirty, they choose one from amongst themselves to be chief-justice, and the city whereof he is, sendeth another in his place. This chief-justice wore about his neck, hung in a gold chain, a jewel of precious stones, the name of which jewel was* truth; *which, when the chief-justice had put on, then began the pleading, &c.; and when the judges had agreed on the sentence, then did the chief-justice put this jewel of truth to one of the pleas.*" You see now what power was acquired in civil matters by the conjuncture of philosophy and divinity.[19]

Let us come now to the commonwealth of the Jews. Was not the priesthood in a family (namely, the Levites) as well as the priesthood of Egypt? Did not the high-priest give judgment by the breastplate of Urim and Thummim? Look upon the kingdom of Assyria, and the philosophers called Chaldeans. Had they not lands and cities belonging to their family, even in Abraham's time, who dwelt (you know) in Ur of the Chaldeans? Of these the same author says thus: "*The Chaldeans are a sect in politics, like to that of the Egyptian priests; for being ordained for the service of the Gods, they spend the whole time of their life in philosophy; being of exceeding great reputation in astrology,*

19 *B.* Was this kind of government and judicature in Egypt used in the time that [Jews] Moses lived there?
A. [Yes.] I know not. *This question and answer have been erased in the MS. by H.'s own hand.*

and pretending much also to prophecy, foretelling things to come by purifications and sacrifices, and to find out by certain incantations the preventing of harm, and the bringing to pass of good. They have also skill in augury, and in the interpretation of dreams and wonders, nor are they unskilful in the art of foretelling by the inwards of beasts sacrificed; and have their learning not as the Greeks; for the philosophy of the Chaldeans goes to their family by tradition, and the son receives it from his father."

From Assyria let us pass into India, and see what esteem the philosophers had there. "*The whole multitude*" (says Diodorus) "*of the Indians, is divided into seven parts; whereof the first, is the body of philosophers; for number the least, for eminence the first; for they are free from taxes, and as they are not masters of others, so are no others masters of them. By private men they are called to the sacrifices and to the care of burials of the dead, as being thought most beloved of the Gods and skilful in the doctrine concerning hell; and for this employment receive gifts and honours very considerable. They are also of great use to the people of India; for being taken at the beginning of the year into the great assembly, they foretell them of great drouths, great rains, also of winds, and of sickness, and of whatsoever is profitable for them to know beforehand.*"

The same author, concerning the laws of the Æthiopians, saith thus: "*The laws of the Æthio-*

pians seem very different from those of other nations, and especially about the election of their Kings. For the priests propound some of the chief men amongst them, named in a catalogue, and whom the God (which, according to a certain custom, is carried about to feastings) does accept of; him the multitude elect for their King, and presently adore and honour him as a God, put into the government by divine providence. The King being chosen, he has the manner of his life limited to him by the laws, and does all other things according to the custom of the country, neither rewarding nor punishing any man otherwise than from the beginning is established amongst them by law. Nor use they to put any man to death, though he be condemned to it, but to send some officer to him with a token of death; who seeing the token, goes presently to his house, and kills himself." And presently after: *"But the strangest thing of all is, that which they do concerning the death of their Kings. For the priests that live in Meroe, and spend their time about the worship and honour of their Gods, and are in greatest authority; when they have a mind to it, send a messenger to the King to bid him die, for that the Gods have given such order, and that the commandments of the immortals are not by any means to be neglected by those that are, by nature, mortal; using also other speeches to him, which men of simple judgment, and that have not reason enough to dispute against those unnecessary commands, as being educated in an old and indelible custom, are content to admit of. Therefore in former times the Kings did obey the priests, not as mastered by force and arms, but as having their reason mastered by superstition. But in the time of Ptolemy II., Ergamenes, King of the Æthiopians, having had his breeding in philosophy after the manner of the Greeks, being the first that durst despise their power, took heart as befitted a King; came with soldiers to a place called Abaton, where was then the golden temple of the Æthiopians; killed all the priests, abolished the custom, and rectified the kingdom according to his will."*

B. Though they that were killed were damnable impostors, yet the act was cruel.

A. It was so. But were not the priests cruel, to cause their Kings, whom a little before they adored as Gods, to make away themselves? The King killed them, for the safety of his person; they him, out of ambition, or love of change. The King's act may be coloured with the good of his people; the priests had no pretence against their kings, who were certainly very godly, or else would never have obeyed the command of the priests by a messenger unarmed, to kill themselves. Our late King, the best King perhaps that ever was, you know, was murdered, having been first persecuted by war, at the incitement of Presbyterian ministers; who are therefore guilty of the death of all that fell in that war; which were, I believe, in England, Scotland, and Ireland, near 100,000 persons. Had it not been much better that those seditious ministers, which were not perhaps 1000, had been all killed before they had preached? It had been (I confess) a great massacre; but the killing of 100,000 is a greater.

B. I am glad the bishops were out at this business. As ambitious as some say they are, it did not appear in that business, for they were enemies to them that were in it. *[Though they pretended a divine right (not depending upon the King's leave) to the government of the Church, yet being but few in number, and not much in favour with the people, how could they choose but be (on the King's side?)]*

A. I intend not by these quotations to commend either the divinity or the philosophy of those heathen people; but to show only what the reputation of those sciences can effect among the people. For their divinity was nothing but idolatry; and their philosophy (excepting the knowledge which the Egyptian priests, and from them the Chaldeans, had gotten by long observation and study in astronomy, geometry, and arithmetic), very little; and that in great part abused in astrology and fortune-telling. Whereas the divinity of the clergy in this nation, considered apart from the mixture (that has been introduced by the Church of Rome, and in part retained here) of the babbling philosophy of Aristotle and other Greeks, that has no affinity with religion, and serves only to breed disaffection, dissension, and finally sedition and civil war (as we have lately found by dear experience in the differences between the Presbyterians and Episcopals), is the true religion. But for these differences both parties, as they came into power, not only suppressed the tenets of one another, but also whatsoever doctrine looked with an ill aspect upon their interest; and consequently all true philosophy, especially civil and moral, which can never appear propitious to ambition, or to an exemption from their obedience due to the sovereign power. *[That reputation they have in the sciences, hath not proceeded from anything they have effected by those sciences, but from the infirmity of the people that understand nothing in them, and admire nothing but what they understand not. There was lately erected a company of gentlemen for the promoting of natural philosophy and mathematics. What they will produce, I know not yet, but this I am sure of, that the authority of licensing the books that are to be written of that subject, is not in them, but in some divines, who have little knowledge in physics, and none at all in mathematics.]*

After the King had accused the Lord Kimbolton,[20] a member of the Lords' house; and Hollis, Haslerigg, Hampden, Pym, and Stroud,[21] five

---

20 Edward Montagu, 2nd Earl of Manchester (1602 -1671). He was raised to the peerage in May 1626 and inherited the Barony of Kimbolton from his father; he was styled Viscount Mandeville as a courtesy title (also a title from his father), since his father had been created Earl of Manchester only three months earlier. He inherited the Earldom in 1642. —Ed.

21 Denzil Holles, 1st Baron Holles (1599 – 1680); Sir Arthur

members of the Lower House, of high-treason; and after the Parliament had voted out the bishops from the House of Peers; they pursued especially two things in their petitions to his Majesty: the one was, that the King would declare who were the persons that advised him to go, as he did, to the Parliament-house to apprehend them, and that he would leave them to the Parliament to receive condign punishment. And this they did, to stick upon his Majesty the dishonour of deserting his friends, and betraying them to his enemies. The other was, that he would allow them a guard out of the city of London, to be commanded by the Earl of Essex; for which they pretended, they could not else sit in safety; which pretence was nothing but an upbraiding of his Majesty for coming to Parliament better accompanied than ordinary, to seize the five seditious members.

B. I see no reason *why* in petitioning for a guard, they should determine it to the city of London in particular, and the command by name to the Earl of Essex, unless they meant the King should understand it for a guard against himself.

A. Their meaning was, that the King should understand it so, and (as I verily believe) they meant he should take it for an affront; and the King himself understanding it so, denied to grant it, though

---

Haselrig, 2nd Baronet (1601 – 1661), MP for Leicestershire; John Hampden (ca. 1595 – 1643), MP for Grampound, Cornwall; John Pym (1584 – 1643), MP for Calne, Wiltshire; and William Strode (1598 – 1645), MP for Bere Alston, Devon. —Ed.

he were willing, if they could not otherwise be satisfied, to command such a guard to wait upon them as he would be responsible for to God Almighty. Besides this, the city of London petitioned the King (put upon it, no doubt, by some members of the Lower House) to put the Tower of London into the hands of persons of trust, meaning such as the Parliament should approve of, and to appoint a guard for the safety of his Majesty and the Parliament. This method of bringing petitions in tumultuary manner, by great multitudes of clamorous people, was ordinary with the House of Commons, whose ambition could never have been served by way of prayer and request, without extraordinary terror.

After the King had waived the prosecution of the five members, but denied to make known who had advised him to come in person to the House of Commons, they questioned the Attorney-General,[22] who by the King's command had exhibited the articles against them, and voted him a breaker of the privilege of Parliament; and no doubt had made him feel their cruelty, if he had not speedily fled the land.

About the end of January, they made an order of both Houses of Parliament, to prevent the going over of popish commanders into Ireland; not so much fearing that, as that by this occasion the King himself choosing his commanders for that service,

22 Sir Edward Herbert (1591 – 1658), Attorney General from 1641 until 1645. —Ed.

might aid himself out of Ireland against the Parliament. But this was no great matter, in respect of a petition they sent his Majesty about the same time, that is to say, about the 27th or 28th of January, 1641, wherein they desired in effect the absolute sovereignty of England; though by the name of sovereignty they challenged it not whilst the King was living. For to the end that the fears and dangers in this kingdom might be removed, and the mischievous designs of those who are enemies to the peace of it might be prevented, they pray: that his Majesty would be pleased to put forthwith, first, the Tower of London, secondly, all other forts, thirdly, the whole *militia* of the kingdom, into the hands of such persons as should be recommended to him by both the Houses of Parliament. And this they style a necessary petition.

B. Were there really any such fears and dangers generally conceived here, or did there appear any enemies at that time with such designs as are mentioned in the petition?

A. Yes. But no other fear of danger, than such as any discreet and honest man might justly have of the designs of the Parliament itself, who were the greatest enemies to the peace of the kingdom that could possibly be. It is also worth observing, that this petition began with these words, "Most gracious Sovereign": so stupid they were as not to know, that he that is master of the *militia*, is master of the kingdom, and consequently is in possession of a most absolute sovereignty. The King was now at Windsor, to avoid the tumults of the common people before the gates of Whitehall, together with their clamours and affronts there. The 9th of February after, he came to Hampton Court, and thence he went to Dover with the Queen, and the Princess of Orange, his daughter; where the Queen with the Princess of Orange embarked for Holland, but the King returned to Greenwich, whence he sent for the Prince of Wales and the Duke of York, and so went with them towards York.

B. Did the Lords join with the Commons in this petition for the *militia*?

A. It appears so by the title; but I believe they durst not but do it. The House of Commons took them but for a cypher; men of title only, without real power. Perhaps also the most of them thought, that the taking of the *militia* from the King would be an addition to their own power; but they were very much mistaken, for the House of Commons never intended them sharers in it.

B. What answer made the King to this petition?

A. "*That when he shall know the extent of power which is intended to be established in those persons, whom they desire to be the commanders of the militia in the several counties; and likewise to what time it shall be limited, that no power shall be executed by his Majesty alone without the advice of Parliament; then he will declare, that (for the securing them from all dangers or jealousies) his Majesty will be content to put into all the places, both of forts and militia in the several coun-*

ties, such persons as both the Houses of Parliament shall either approve, or recommend unto him; so that they declare before unto his Majesty the names of the persons whom they approve or recommend, unless such persons shall be named, against whom he shall have just and unquestionable exceptions."

B. What power, for what time, and to whom, did the Parliament require,[23] concerning the *militia*?

A. The same power which the King had placed before[24] in his lieutenants and deputy-lieutenants, in the several counties, and without other limitation of time but their own pleasure.

B. Who were the men that should have this power?[25]

A. There is a catalogue of them printed. They are very many, and most of them lords; nor is it necessary to have them named; for to name them is (in my opinion) to brand them with the mark of disloyalty or of folly. When they had made a catalogue of them, they sent it to the King, with a new petition for the *militia*. Also presently after, they sent a message to his Majesty, praying him to leave the Prince at Hampton Court; but the King granted neither.

B. Howsoever, it was wisely done[26] of them to get hostages (if they could) of the King, before he went from them.

---

23 did the Parliament grant.

24 which the King had before planted.

25 the men that had this power?

26 it waswell done.

A. In the meantime, to raise money for the reducing of Ireland, the Parliament invited men to bring in money by way of adventure, according to these propositions. 1. That two millions and five hundred thousand acres of land in Ireland, should be assigned to the adventurers, in this proportion:

For an adventure of 200*l*. 1,000 acres in Ulster.
For an adventure of 300*l*. 1,000 acres in Connaught.
For an adventure of 450*l*. 1,000 acres in Munster.
For an adventure of 600*l*. 1,000 acres in Leinster.

All according to English measure, and consisting of meadow, arable, and profitable pasture; bogs, woods, and barren mountains being cast in over and above. 2. A revenue was reserved to the Crown, from one penny to three-pence on every acre. 3. That commissions should be sent by the Parliament, to erect manors, settle wastes and commons, maintain preaching ministers, to create corporations, and to regulate plantations. The rest of the propositions concern only the times and manner of payment of the sums subscribed by the adventurers. And to these propositions his Majesty assented; but to the petition of the *militia*, his Majesty denied his assent.

B. If he had not, I should have thought it a great wonder. What did the Parliament after this?

A. They sent him another petition, which was presented to him when he was at Theobald's, in his way to York; wherein they tell him plainly, *that unless he be pleased to assure them by those messengers then sent, that he would speedily apply his royal assent to the satisfaction of their former desires, they shall be enforced, for the safety of his Majesty and his kingdoms, to dispose of the militia by the authority of both Houses, &c.* They petition his Majesty also to let the Prince stay at St. James's, or some other of his Majesty's houses near London. They tell him also, that the power of raising, ordering, and disposing of the *militia*, cannot be granted to any corporation, without the authority and consent of the Parliament; and that those parts of the kingdom, which have put themselves into a posture of defence, have done nothing therein but by direction of both Houses, and what is justifiable by the laws of this kingdom.

B. What answer made the King to this?

**A.* He gave them a flat denial, not only of the *militia*, but also of the Prince's residence about London. After which they presently fell to voting as followeth: first, That this his Majesty's answer was a denial of the *militia*. 2. That those that advised his Majesty to it were enemies to the State. 3. That such parts of this kingdom, as had put themselves into a posture of defence, had done nothing but what was justifiable.

B. What is it which they called a posture of defence?*

A. It was a putting of themselves into arms, and under officers such as the Parliament should approve of. 4. They vote that his Majesty should be again desired that the Prince might continue about London. Lastly, they vote a declaration to be sent to his Majesty by both the Houses; wherein they accuse his Majesty of a design of altering religion, though not directly him, but them that counselled him; whom they also accused of being the inviters and fomenters of the Scotch war, and framers of the rebellion in Ireland; and upbraid the King again for accusing the Lord Kimbolton and the five members, and of being privy to the purpose of bringing up his army, which was raised against the Scots, to be employed against the Parliament. To which his Majesty sent his answer from Newmarket. Whereupon it was resolved by both Houses, that in this case of extreme danger and of his Majesty's refusal, the ordinance agreed upon by both Houses for the *militia* doth oblige the people by the fundamental laws of this kingdom; and also, that whosoever shall execute any power over the *militia*, by colour of any commission of lieutenancy, without consent of both Houses of Parliament, shall be accounted a disturber of the peace of the kingdom. Whereupon his Majesty sent a message to both Houses from Huntingdon, requiring obedience to the laws established, and prohibiting all subjects, upon pretence of their ordinance, to execute anything concerning the *militia* which is not by those laws warranted. Upon this, the Parliament vote a standing to their former votes; as also, that when the Lords and Commons in Parliament, which is the supreme court of judicature in the kingdom, shall declare what the law of the land is, to have this not only questioned, but contradicted, is a high breach of the privilege of Parliament.

B. I thought that he that makes the law, ought to declare what the law is. For what is it else to make a law, but to declare what it is? So that they have taken from the King, not only the *militia*, but also the legislative power.

A. They have so; but I make account that the legislative power (and indeed all power possible) is contained in the power of the *militia*. After this, they seize such money as was due to his Majesty upon the bill of tonnage and poundage, and upon the bill of subsidies, that they might disable him every way they possibly could. They sent him also many other contumelious messages and petitions after his coming to York; amongst which one was: "That whereas the Lord Admiral, by indisposition of body, could not command the fleet in person, he would be pleased to give authority to the Earl of Warwick[27] to supply his place;" when they knew the King had put Sir John Pennington[28] into *that employment* before.[29]

B. To what end did the King entertain so many petitions, messages, declarations and remonstrances, and vouchsafe his answers to them, when he could not choose but clearly see they were resolved to take from him his royal power, and consequently his life? For it could not stand with their safety to let either him or his issue live, after they

---

27 Robert Rich, 2nd Earl of Warwick (1587 – 1658). —Ed.

28 (probably 1584 – 1646). —Ed.

29 Pennington in it before.

had done him so great injuries.

A. Besides this, the Parliament had at the same time a committee residing in York *both* to spy what his Majesty did, and to inform the Parliament thereof, and also to hinder the King from gaining the people of that county to his party: so that when his Majesty was courting the gentlemen there, the committee was instigating of the yeomanry against him. To which also the ministers did very much contribute; so that the King lost his opportunity at York.

B. Why did not the King seize the committee into his hands, or drive them out of the town?

A. I know not; but I believe he knew the Parliament had a greater party than he, not only in Yorkshire but also in York. Towards the end of April, the King, upon petition of the people of Yorkshire to have the magazine of Hull to remain still there, for the greater security of the northern parts, thought fit to take it into his own hands. He had a little before appointed governor of that town the Earl of Newcastle;[30] but the townsmen, having been already corrupted by the Parliament, refused to receive him, but refused not to receive Sir John Hotham,[31] appointed to be governor *there* by the Parliament. The King therefore coming before the town, guarded only by his own servants, and a few gentlemen of the country thereabouts, was

30 William Cavendish, Earl (1628), Marquis (1643), and Duke of Newcastle (1665) (1592 – 1676). —Ed.

31 (1589 – 1645). —Ed.

denied entrance by Sir John Hotham, that stood upon the wall; for which act he presently caused Sir John Hotham to be proclaimed traitor, and sent a message to the Parliament, requiring justice to be done upon the said Hotham, and that the town and magazine might be delivered into his hands. To which the Parliament made no answer, but instead thereof published another declaration, in which they omitted nothing of their former slanders against his Majesty's government, but inserted certain propositions declarative of their own pretended right: viz. 1. That whatsoever they declare to be law, ought not to be questioned by the King: 2. That no precedents can be limits to bound their proceedings: 3. That a Parliament, for the public good, may dispose of anything wherein the King or subject hath a right; and that they, without the King, are this Parliament, and the judge of this public good, and that the King's consent is not necessary: 4. That no member of either House ought to be troubled for treason, felony, or any other crime, unless the cause be first brought before the Parliament, that they may judge of the fact and give leave to proceed, if they see cause: 5. That the sovereign power resides in both Houses, and that the King ought to have no negative voice: 6. That the levying of forces against the personal commands of the King (though accompanied with his presence) is not levying war against the King, but the levying of war against *his politic person,* viz., his laws, &c., though not *accompanied with* his person, is levying war against the King: 7. That treason cannot be committed against his person, otherwise than as he is entrusted with the kingdom and discharges that trust; and that they have a power to judge whether he *have* discharged this trust or not: 8. That they may dispose of the King when they will.

B. This is plain dealing and without hypocrisy. Could the city of London swallow this?

A. Yes; and more too, if need be. London, you know, has a great belly, but no palate nor taste of right and wrong. In the Parliament-roll of Henry IV., amongst the articles of the oath the King at his coronation took, there is one runs thus: *Concedes justas leges et consuetudines esse tenendas; et promittis per te eas esse protegendas, et ad honorem Dei corroborandas, quas vulgus elegerit*. Which the Parliament urged for their legislative authority, and therefore interpret *quas vulgus elegerit, which the people shall choose*; as if the King should swear to protect and corroborate laws before they were made, whether they be good or bad; whereas the word signifies no more, but that he shall protect and corroborate such laws as they have chosen, that is to say, the Acts of Parliament then in being. And in the records of the Exchequer it is thus: "*Will you grant to hold and keep the laws and rightful customs which the commonalty of this your kingdom have, and will you defend and uphold them? &c.*" And this was the answer his Majesty made to that point.

B. And I think this answer very full and clear. But if the words were to be interpreted in the other sense, yet I see no reason why the King should be bound to swear to them. For Henry IV. came to the Crown by the votes of a Parliament not much inferior in wickedness to this Long Parliament, that deposed and murdered their lawful King; saving that it was not the Parliament itself, but the usurper that murdered King Richard II.[32]

A. About a week after, in the beginning of May, the Parliament sent the King another paper, which

32 Richard II (1367 – 1400) became King of England at the age of 10, and during the early years of his reign, England was ruled through a series of councils, which most of the aristocracy preferred to a regency led by the king's uncle, John of Gaunt. In 1386, a group of nobles, called the Lords Appellant, sought to restrain what they felt was Richard's tyrannical and capricious rule. Joining them later were Henry Bolingbroke (the future Henry IV), who was John of Gaunt's son, and Thomas de Mowbray. They established a Commission to govern England for a year and then, the year following, launched a successful armed rebellion, which left Richard as a figurehead. John of Gaunt, however, returned from Spain in 1389 and from that point Richard was able to rebuild his power. By 1397 he was ready to exact vengeance on the Lords Appellant, which he did, albeit without punishing Henry. The following year, Henry overheard a remark by Thomas de Mowbray that he deemed treasonous and accordingly reported to the King. Richard called for a duel of honour, but, rather than allow it to happen, he exiled the two, Henry with his father's approval. When John of Gaunt died, however, Richard disinherited Henry without explanation and extended the exile to life. Consequently, Henry sailed for England, along with Thomas Arundel, one of the exiled Lords Appellant, while Richard was away in Ireland, ostensibly to reclaim his patrimony, but in reality coveting the crown. He faced little opposition and was able

they styled the humble petition and advice of both Houses, containing nineteen propositions; which, when you shall hear, you will be able to judge what power they meant to leave to the King, more than to any one of his subjects. The first of them is this:

1. That the Lords and others of his Majesty's privy-council, and all great officers *and ministers* of state, both at home and abroad, be put from their employments and from his council, save only such as should be approved of by both Houses of Parliament; and none put into their places but by approbation of the said Houses. And that all privy-councillors take an oath for the due execution of their places, in such form as shall be agreed upon by the said Houses.

2. That the great affairs of the kingdom be debated, resolved, and transacted only in Parliament; and such as shall presume to do anything to the contrary, be reserved to the censure of the Parliament; and such other matters of state, as are proper for his Majesty's privy-council, shall be de-

---

to amass sufficient power and support to challenge the King. When the latter arrived in Wales in August 1399, he was taken prisoner and transported to London, where he was locked up in the Tower. The Bishop of St Asaph then read thirty-three articles of deposition in Parliament, both houses of which unanimously approved it. Richard was formally deposed on 1 October 1399 and then left, allegedly, to starve to death in a cell at Pontefract Castle. The official record, read by Thomas Arundel at the House of Lords, had Richard ratifying to the deposition, citing his own inability and unworthiness. The anonymous *Chronicque de la traïson et mort de Richart Deux roy d'Engleterre*, on the other hand, states otherwise. —Ed.

bated and concluded, by such as shall from time to time be chosen for that place by both Houses of Parliament; and that no public act concerning the affairs of the kingdom, which are proper for his privy-council, be esteemed valid, as proceeding from the royal authority, unless it be done by the advice and consent of the major part of the council, attested under their hands; and that the council be not more than twenty-five, nor less than fifteen; and that when a councillor's place falls void in the interval of Parliament, it shall not be supplied without the assent of the major part of the council; and that such choice also shall be void, if the next Parliament after confirm it not.

3. That the Lord High Steward of England, Lord High Constable, Lord Chancellor, or Lord Keeper of the Great Seal, Lord Treasurer, Lord Privy-Seal, Earl Marshal, Lord Admiral, Warden of the Cinque Ports, Chief Governor of Ireland, Chancellor of the Exchequer, Master of the Wards, Secretaries of State, two Chief Justices and Chief Baron, be always chosen with approbation of both Houses of Parliament; and in the intervals of Parliaments by the major part of the privy-council.

4. That the governors of the King's children shall be such as both Houses shall approve of; and in the intervals of Parliament, such as the privy-council shall approve of; that the servants then about them, against whom the Houses have just exception, shall be removed.

5. That no marriage be concluded or treated of

for any of the King's children, without consent of Parliament.

6. That the laws in force against Jesuits, priests, and popish recusants, be strictly put in execution.

7. That the votes of Popish lords in the House of Peers be taken away, and that a bill be passed for the education of the children of Papists in the Protestant religion.

8. That the King will be pleased to reform the Church-government and liturgy in such manner as both Houses of Parliament shall advise.

9. That he would be pleased to rest satisfied with that course that the Lords and Commons have appointed for ordering the *militia*; and recall his declarations and proclamations against it.

10. That such members as have been put out of any place or office since this Parliament began, may be restored, or have satisfaction.

11. That all privy-councillors and judges take an oath (the form whereof shall be agreed on and settled by act of Parliament), for the maintaining of the Petition of Right, and of certain statutes made by this Parliament.

12. That all the judges and officers placed by approbation of both Houses of Parliament, may hold their places *quam diu bene se gesserint*.[33]

13. That the justice of Parliament may pass upon all delinquents, whether they be within the kingdom or fled out of it; and that all persons cited by either House of Parliament, may appear and abide

33 Latin: as long as he shall behave himself well. —Ed.

the censure of Parliament.

14. That the general pardon offered by his Majesty, be granted with such exceptions as shall be advised by both Houses of Parliament.

B. What a spiteful article was this! All the rest proceeded from ambition, which many times well-natured men are subject to; but this proceeded from an inhuman and devilish cruelty.

A. 15. That the forts and castles be put under the command of such persons as, with the approbation of the Parliament, the King shall appoint.

16. That the extraordinary guards about the King be discharged; and for the future none raised but according to the law, in case of actual rebellion or invasion.

B. Methinks these very propositions sent to the King are an actual rebellion.

A. 17. That his Majesty *be pleased to* enter into a more strict alliance with the United Provinces, and other neighbour Protestant Princes and States.

18. That his Majesty be pleased, by act of Parliament, to clear the Lord Kimbolton and the five members of the House of Commons, in such manner as that future Parliaments may be secured from the consequence of that evil precedent.

19. That his Majesty be pleased to pass a bill for restraining peers made hereafter, from sitting or voting in Parliament, unless they be admitted with the consent of both Houses of Parliament.

These propositions granted, they promise to apply themselves to regulate his Majesty's revenue to his best advantage, and to settle it to the support of his royal dignity in honour and plenty; and also to put the town of Hull into such hands as his Majesty shall appoint with consent of Parliament.

B. Is not that to put it into such hands as his Majesty shall appoint by the consent of the petitioners, which is no more than to keep it in their hands as it is? Did they want, or think the King wanted, common sense, so as not to perceive that their promise herein was worth nothing?

A. After the sending of these propositions to the King, and his Majesty's refusal to grant them, they began, on both sides, to prepare for war. The King raising a guard for his person in Yorkshire; and the Parliament, thereupon having voted that the King intended to make war upon his Parliament, gave order for the mustering and exercising the people in arms, and published propositions to invite and encourage them to bring in either ready money or plate, or to promise under their hands to furnish and maintain certain numbers of horse, horsemen, and arms, for the defence of the King and Parliament (meaning by King, as they had formerly declared, not his person, but his laws); promising to repay their money with interest of 8*l.* in the 100*l.* and the value of their plate with twelve-pence the ounce for the fashion. On the other side, the King came to Nottingham, and there did set up his standard royal, and sent out commissions of array to call those to him, which by the ancient laws of England were bound to serve him in the wars. Upon this occasion there passed divers declarations between the King and Parliament concerning the legality of this array, which are too long to tell you at this time.

B. Nor do I desire to hear any mooting about this question. For I think that general law of *salus populi*, and the right of defending himself against those that had taken from him the sovereign power, are sufficient to make legal whatsoever he should do in order to the recovery of his kingdom, or to the punishing of the rebels.

A. In the meantime the Parliament raised an army, and made the Earl of Essex general thereof; by which act they declared what they meant formerly, when they petitioned the King for a guard to be commanded by the said Earl of Essex. And now the King sends out his proclamations, forbidding obedience to the orders of the Parliament concerning the *militia*; and the Parliament send out orders against the execution of the commissions of array. Hitherto, though it were a war before, yet there was no blood shed; they shot at one another nothing but paper.

B. I understand now, how the Parliament destroyed the peace of the kingdom; and how easily, by the help of seditious Presbyterian ministers, and of ambitious ignorant orators, they reduced this government into anarchy. But I believe it will be a harder task for them to bring in peace again, and settle the government, either in themselves, or in any other governor, or form of government. For, granting that they obtained the victory in this war, they must be beholding for it to the valour, good conduct, or felicity of those to whom they give the command of their armies; especially to the general, whose good success will, without doubt, draw with it the love and admiration of the soldiers; so that it will be in his power, either to take the government upon himself, or to place it where he himself thinks good. In which case, if he take it not to himself, he will be thought a fool; and if he do, he shall be sure to have the envy of his subordinate commanders, who *will* look for a share either in the present government, or in the succession to it. For they will say: "Has he obtained this power by his own, without our danger, valour, and counsel? and must we be his slaves, whom we have thus raised? Or, is not there as much justice on our side against him, as was on his side against the King?"

A. They will, and did; insomuch, that it was the reason why Cromwell, after he had gotten into his own hands the absolute power of England, Scotland, and Ireland, by the name of Protector, did never dare to take upon him the title of King, nor was ever able to settle it upon his children. His officers would not suffer it, as pretending after his death to succeed him; nor would the army consent to it, because he had ever declared to them against the government of a single person.

B. But to return to the King. What means had he to pay, what provision had he to arm, nay, means to levy, an army able to resist the army of the Parliament, maintained by the great purse of the city of London, and contributions of almost all the towns corporate in England, and furnished with arms, as fully as they could require?

A. 'Tis true, the King had great disadvantages, and yet by little and little he got a considerable army, with which he so prospered, as to grow stronger every day, and the Parliament weaker; till they had gotten the Scots, with an army of 21,000 men, to come into England to their assistance. But to enter into the particular narration of what was done in the war, I have not now time.

B. Well then; we will talk of that at next meeting.

Dialogue III

B. We left at the preparations on both sides for war; which, when I considered by myself, I was mightily puzzled to find out what possibility there was for the King to equal the Parliament in such a course, and what hopes he had of money, men, arms, fortified places, shipping, counsel, and military officers, sufficient for such an enterprise against the Parliament, that had men and money as much at command, as the city of London, and other corporation towns, were able to furnish, which was more than they needed. And for the men they should set forth for soldiers, they were almost all of them spitefully bent against the King and his whole party, whom they took to be either papists, or flatterers of the King, or that had designed to raise their fortunes by the plunder of the city and other corporation towns. And though I believe not that they were more valiant than other men, nor that they had so much experience in the war, as to be accounted good soldiers; yet they had that in them, which in time of battle is more conducing to victory than valour and experience both together; and that was spite.

And for arms, they had in their hands the chief magazines, the Tower of London, and the town of Kingston-upon-Hull; besides most of the powder and shot that lay in several towns for the use of the trained bands.

Fortified places, there were not many then in England, and most of them in the hands of the Parliament.

The King's fleet was wholly in their command, under the Earl of Warwick.

Counsellors, they needed no more than such as were of their own body; so that the King was every way inferior to them, except it were, perhaps, in officers.

A. I cannot compare their chief officers. For the Parliament, the Earl of Essex (after the Parliament had voted the war) was made general of all their forces both in England and Ireland, from whom all other commanders were to receive their commissions.

B. What moved them to make general the Earl of Essex? And for what cause was the Earl of Essex so displeased with the King, as to accept that office?

A. I do not certainly know what to answer to either of those questions; but the Earl of Essex had been in the wars abroad, and wanted neither experience, judgment, nor courage, to perform such an undertaking. And besides that, you have heard, I believe, how great a darling of the people his father had been before him, and what honour he had gotten by the success of his enterprise upon Calais, and in some other military actions. To which I may add, that this Earl himself was not held by the people to be so great a favourite at court, as that they might not trust him with their army against the King. And by this, you may perhaps conjecture the cause for which the Parliament made choice of him for general.

B. But why did they think him discontented with the Court?

A. I know not that; nor indeed that he was so. He came to the court, as other noblemen did, when occasion was, to wait upon the King; but had no office (till a little before this time) to oblige him to be there continually. But I believe verily, that the unfortunateness of his marriages had so discountenanced his conversation with the ladies, that the court could not be his proper element, unless he had had some extraordinary favour there, to balance that calamity. But for particular discontent from the King, or intention of revenge for any supposed disgrace, I think he had none, nor that he was any ways addicted to Presbyterian doctrines, or other fanatic tenets in Church or State; saving only, that he was carried away with the stream (in a manner) of the whole nation, to think that England was not an absolute, but a mixed monarchy;

not considering that the supreme power must always be absolute, whether it be in the King or in the Parliament.

B. Who was general of the King's army?

A. None yet but himself; nor indeed had he yet any army. But there coming to him at that time[1] his two nephews, Prince Rupert and Maurice,[2] he put the command of his horse into the hands of Prince Rupert, a man than whom no man living has a better courage, nor was more active and diligent in prosecuting his commissions; and, though but a young man then, was not without experience in the conducting of soldiers, as having been an actor in part of his father's wars in Germany.

B. But how could the King find money to pay such an army as was necessary for him against the Parliament?

A. Neither the King nor Parliament had much money at that time in their own hands, but were fain to rely upon the benevolence of those that took their parts. Wherein (I confess) the Parliament had a mighty great advantage. Those that helped the King in that kind were only lords and gentlemen, which, not approving the proceedings of the Parliament, were willing to undertake the payment, every one, of a certain number of horse;

1 August 1642. —Ed.

2 Prince Rupert (1619 – 1662) was the son of Frederick V of the Palatinate (1596 – 1632) and his wife Elizabeth (1596 – 1662), eldest daughter of James I and at that time Queen of Bohemia. Maurice was Rupert's younger brother (1620 – 1652). —Ed.

which cannot be thought any great assistance, the persons that paid them being so few. For other moneys that the King then had, I have not heard of any, but what he borrowed upon jewels in the Low Countries. Whereas the Parliament had a very plentiful contribution, not only from London, but generally from their faction in all other places of England, upon certain propositions (published by the Lords and Commons in June 1642, at what time they had newly voted that the King intended to make war upon them), for bringing in of money or plate to maintain horse and horsemen, and to buy arms for the preservation of the public peace, and for the defence of the King and both Houses of Parliament; for the repayment of which money and plate, they were to have the public faith.

B. What public faith is there, when there is no public? What is it that can be called public, in a civil war, without the King?

A. The truth is, the security was nothing worth, but served well enough to gull those seditious blockheads, that were more fond of change than either of their peace or profit.

Having by this means gotten contributions from those that were the well-affected to their cause, they made use of it afterward to force the like contribution from others. For in November following, they made an ordinance for assessing also of those that had not contributed then, or had contributed, but not proportionably to their estates. And yet this was contrary to what the Parliament promised and declared in the propositions themselves. For they declared, in the first proposition, that no man's affection should be measured by the proportion of his offer, so that he expressed his good-will to the service in any proportion whatsoever.

Besides this, in the beginning of March following, they made an ordinance, to levy weekly a great sum of money upon every county, city, town, place, and person of any estate almost, in England; which weekly sum (as may appear by the ordinance itself, printed and published in March 1642, by order of both Houses) comes to almost 33,000*l.*, and consequently to above 1,700,000*l.* for the year. They had, besides all this, the profits of the King's lands and woods, and whatsoever was remaining unpaid of any subsidies formerly granted him, and the tonnage and poundage usually received by the King; besides the profit of the sequestrations of great persons, whom they pleased to vote delinquents, and the profits of the bishops' lands, which they took to themselves a year, or a little more, after.

B. Seeing then the Parliament had such advantage of the King in money and arms and multitude of men, and had in their hands the King's fleet, I cannot imagine what hope the King could have, either of victory or (unless he resigned into their hands the sovereignty) of subsisting. For I cannot well believe he had any advantage of them, either in counsellors, conductors, or in the resolutions of his soldiers.

A. On the contrary, I think he had some disadvantage also in that; for though he had as good officers at least as any that then served the Parliament, yet I doubt he had not so useful counsel as was necessary. And for his soldiers, though they were men as stout as theirs, yet, because their valour was not sharpened so with malice as theirs were of the other side, they fought not so keenly as their enemies did: amongst whom there were a great many London apprentices, who, for want of experience in the war, would have been fearful enough of death and wounds approaching visibly in glistering swords; but, for want of judgment, scarce thought of such death as comes invisibly in a bullet, and therefore were very hardly to be driven out of the field.

B. But what fault do you find in the King's counsellors, lords, and other persons of quality and experience?

A. Only that fault, which was generally in the whole nation, which was, that they thought the government of England was not an absolute, but a mixed monarchy; and that if the King should clearly subdue this Parliament, that his power would be what he pleased, and theirs as little as he pleased: which they counted tyranny. This opinion, though it did not lessen their endeavour to gain the victory for the King in a battle, when a battle could not be avoided, yet it weakened their endeavour to procure him an absolute victory in the war. And for this cause, notwithstanding that they saw that the Parliament was firmly resolved to take all kingly power whatsoever out of his hands, yet their counsel to the King was upon all occasions, to offer propositions to them of treaty and accommodation, and to make and publish declarations; which any man might easily have foreseen would be fruitless; and not only so, but also of great disadvantage to those actions by which the King was to recover his crown and preserve his life. For it took away the courage of the best and forwardest of his soldiers, that looked for great benefit by their service out of the estates of the rebels, in case they could subdue them; but none at all, if the business should be ended by a treaty.

B. And they had reason: for a civil war never ends by treaty, without the sacrifice of those who were on both sides the sharpest. You know well enough how things passed at the reconciliation of Augustus and Antonius in Rome. But I thought, that after they once began to levy soldiers one against another, that they would not any more have returned of either side to declarations, or other paper war, which, if it could have done any good, had done it long before this.

A. But seeing the Parliament continued writing, and set forth their declarations to the people against the lawfulness of the King's commission of array, and sent petitions to the King as fierce and rebellious as ever they had done before, demanding of him, that he would disband his soldiers, and come up to the Parliament, and leave those whom the Parliament called delinquents (which were none but the King's best subjects) to their mercy, and pass such bills as they should advise him; would you not have the King set forth declarations and proclamations against the illegality of their ordinances, by which they levied soldiers against him, and answer those insolent petitions of theirs?

B. No; it had done him no good before, and therefore was not likely to do him any afterwards. For the common people, whose hands were to decide the controversy, understood not the reasons of either party; and for those that by ambition were once set upon the enterprise of changing the government, they cared not much what was reason and justice in the cause, but what strength they might procure by seducing the multitude with remonstrances from the Parliament House, or by sermons in the churches. And to their petitions, I would not have had any answer made at all, more than this: that if they would disband their army, and put themselves upon his mercy, they should find him more gracious than they expected.

A. That had been a gallant answer indeed, if it had proceeded from him after some extraordinary great victory in battle, or some extraordinary assurance of a victory at last in the whole war.

B. Why, what could have happened to him worse, than at length he suffered, notwithstanding his gentle answers, and all his reasonable declarations?

A. Nothing; but who knew that?

B. Any man might see that he was never like to

be restored to his right without victory: and such his stoutness being known to the people, would have brought to his assistance many more hands than all the arguments of law, or force of eloquence, couched in declarations and other writings, could have done, by far. And I wonder what kind of men they were, that hindered the King from taking this resolution?

A. You may know by the declarations themselves, which are very long and full of quotations of records and of cases formerly reported, that the penners of them were either lawyers (by profession), or such gentlemen as had the ambition to be thought so. Besides, I told you before, that those which were then likeliest to have their counsel asked in this business, were averse to absolute monarchy, as also to absolute democracy or aristocracy, all which governments they esteemed tyranny; and were in love with mixarchy[3] which they used to praise by the name of mixed monarchy, though it were indeed nothing else but pure anarchy. And those men, whose pens the King most used in these controversies of law and politics, were such (if I have not been misinformed) as having been members of this Parliament, had declaimed against ship-money and other extra-parliamentary taxes, as much as any; but when they saw the Parliament grow higher in their demands than they thought they would have done, went

3 "In love with monarchy" all the edd. except the one of 1815, which has, "with a sort of monarchy", evidently by conjecture.

over to the King's party.

B. Who were those?

A. It is not necessary to name any man, seeing I have undertaken only a short narration of the follies and other faults of men during this trouble; but not (by naming the persons) to give you, or any man else, occasion to esteem them the less, now that the faults on all sides have been forgiven.

B. When the business was *now* brought to this height, by levying of soldiers and seizing of the navy and arms and other provisions on both sides, that no man was so blind as not to see they were in an estate of war one against another; why did not the King (by proclamation or message), according to his undoubted right, dissolve the Parliament, and thereby diminish, in some part, the authority of their levies, and of other their unjust ordinances?

A. You have forgotten that I told you, that the King himself, by a bill which he passed at the same time when he passed the bill for the execution of the Earl of Strafford, had given them authority to hold the Parliament till they should by consent of both Houses dissolve themselves. If therefore he had, by any proclamation or message to the Houses, dissolved them, they would, to their former defamations of his Majesty's actions, have added also this, that he was a breaker of his word: and not only in contempt of him have continued their session, but also have made advantage of it to the increase and strengthening of their own party.

B. Would not the King's raising of an army against them be interpreted as a purpose to dissolve them by force? And was it not as great a breach of promise to scatter them by force, as to dissolve them by proclamation? Besides, I cannot conceive that the passing of that act was otherwise intended than conditionally; so long as they should not ordain anything contrary to the sovereign right of the King; which condition they had already by many of their ordinances broken. And I think that even by the law of equity, which is the unalterable law of nature, a man that has the sovereign power, cannot, if he would, give away the right of anything which is necessary for him to retain for the good government of his subjects, unless he do it in express words, saying, that he will have the sovereign power no longer. For the giving away that, which by consequence only, draws the sovereignty along with it, is not (I think) a giving away of the sovereignty; but an error, such as works nothing but an invalidity in the grant itself. And such was the King's passing of this bill for the continuing of the Parliament as long as the two Houses pleased. But now that the war was resolved on, on both sides, what needed any more dispute in writing?

A. I know not what need they had. But on both sides they thought it needful to hinder one another, as much as they could, from levying of soldiers; and, therefore, the King did set forth declarations in print, to make the people know that they ought not to obey the officers of the new *militia* set up by ordinance of Parliament, and also to let them see the legality of his own commissions of array. And the Parliament on their part did the like, to justify to the people the said ordinance, and to make the commission of array appear unlawful.

B. When the Parliament were levying of soldiers, was it not lawful for the King to levy soldiers to defend himself and his right, though there had been no other title for it but his own preservation, and that the name of commission of array had never before been heard of?

A. For my part, I think there cannot be a better title for war, than the defence of a man's own right. But the people, at that time, thought nothing lawful for the King to do, for which there was not some statute made by Parliament. For the lawyers, I mean the judges of the courts at Westminster, and some few others, though but advocates, yet of great reputation for their skill in the common-laws and statutes of England, had infected most of the gentry of England with their maxims and cases prejudged, which they call precedents; and made them think so well of their own knowledge in the law, that they were very glad of this occasion to show it against the King, and thereby to gain a reputation with the Parliament of being good patriots and wise statesmen.

B. What was this commission of array?

A. King William the Conqueror had gotten into his hands by victory all the land in England, of which he disposed, some part as forests and chases for his recreation, and some part to lords and gentlemen that had assisted him or were to assist him in the wars. Upon which he laid a charge of service in his wars, some with more men and some with less, according to the lands he had given them: whereby, when the King sent men unto them with commission to make use of their service, they were obliged to appear with arms, and accompany the King to the wars for a certain time at their own charges: and such were the commissions by which this King did then make his levies.

B. Why then was it not legal?

A. No doubt but it was legal. But what did that amount to, with men that were already resolved to acknowledge for law nothing that was against their design of abolishing monarchy, and placing a sovereign and absolute arbitrary power in the House of Commons?

B. To destroy monarchy, and set up the House of Commons, are two businesses.

A. They found it so at last, but did not think it so then.

B. Let us come now to the military part.

A. I intended only the story of their injustice, impudence, and hypocrisy; therefore, for the proceeding of the war, I refer you to the history thereof written at large in English. I shall only make use of such a thread as is necessary for the filling up of such knavery, and folly also, as I shall observe in their several actions.

From York the King went to Hull, where was his

magazine of arms for the northern parts of England, to try if they would admit him. The Parliament had made Sir John Hotham governor of the town, who caused the gates to be shut, and presenting himself upon the walls flatly denied him entrance: for which the King caused him to be proclaimed traitor, and sent a message to the Parliament to know if they owned the action; *and they owned it*.

B. Upon what grounds?

A. Their pretence was this: that neither this nor any other town in England was otherwise the King's, than in trust for the people of England.

B. But what was that to the Parliament? *Is the town therefore theirs?*

A. Yes, say they; for we are the Representative of the people of England.

B. I cannot see the force of this argument: we represent the people, ergo, all that the people has is ours. The mayor of Hull did represent the King. Is therefore all that the King had in Hull, the mayor's? The people of England may be represented with limitations, as to deliver a petition or the like. Does it follow that they, who deliver the petition, have right to all the towns in England? When began this Parliament to be a Representative of England? Was it not November 3, 1640? Who was it the day before, that is, November 2, that had the right to keep the King out of Hull, and possess it for themselves? For there was then no Parliament. Whose was Hull then?

A. I think it was the King's, not only because it was called the King's town upon Hull, but because the King himself did then and ever represent the person of the people of England. If he did not, who then did, the Parliament having no being?

B. They might perhaps say, the people had then no Representative.

A. Then there was no commonwealth; and consequently, all the towns of England being the people's, you, and I, and any man else, might have put in for his share. You may see by this, what weak people they were, that were carried into the rebellion by such reasoning as the Parliament used, and how impudent they were that did put such fallacies upon them.

B. Surely they were such as were esteemed the wisest men in England, being upon that account chosen to be of the Parliament.

A. And were they also esteemed the wisest men of England, that chose them?

B. I cannot tell that. For I know it is usual with the freeholders in the counties, and with tradesmen in the cities and boroughs, to choose, as near as they can, such as are most repugnant to the giving of subsidies.

A. The King in the beginning of August, after he had summoned Hull, and tried some of the counties thereabout what they would do for him, sets up his standard at Nottingham; but there came not in thither men enough to make an army sufficient to give battle to the Earl of Essex. From thence he went to Shrewsbury, where he was quickly furnished; and appointing the Earl of Lindsey[4] to be general, he resolved to march towards London.—The Earl of Essex was now at Worcester with the Parliament's army, making no offer to stop him in his passage; but as soon as he was gone by, marched close after him.

The King, therefore, to avoid being enclosed between the army of the Earl of Essex and the city of London, turned upon him and gave him battle at Edgehill; where, though he got not an entire victory, yet he had the better, if either had the better; and had certainly the fruit of a victory, which was to march on, in his intended way towards London: in which the next morning he took Banbury-castle, and from thence went to Oxford, and thence to Brentford, where he gave a great defeat to three regiments of the Parliament's forces, and so returned to Oxford.

B. Why did not the King go on from Brentford?

A. The Parliament, upon the first notice of the King's marching from Shrewsbury, caused all the trained-bands and the auxiliaries of the city of London (which was so frightened as to shut up all their shops) to be drawn forth; so that there was a most complete and numerous army ready for the Earl of Essex, that was crept into London just at the time to head it. And this was it that made the King retire to Oxford.—In the beginning of February after, Prince Rupert took Cirencester from the Par-

4 Robert Bertie, 1st Earl of Lindsey (1582 – 1642). —Ed.

liament, with many prisoners and many arms: for it was newly made a magazine. And thus stood the business between the King's and the Parliament's greatest forces. The Parliament in the meantime caused a line of communication to be made about London and the suburbs, of twelve miles in compass; and constituted a committee for the association, and the putting into a posture of defence, of the counties of Essex, Cambridge, Suffolk, and some others; and one of these commissioners was Oliver Cromwell, from which employment he came to his following greatness.

B. What was done during this time in other parts of the country?

A. In the west, the Earl of Stamford[5] had the employment of putting in execution the ordinance of Parliament for the *militia*; and Sir Ralph Hopton[6] for the King executed the commission of array. Between these two was fought a battle at Liskeard in Cornwall, wherein Sir Ralph Hopton had the victory, and presently took a town called Saltash, with many arms and much ordnance and many prisoners. Sir William Waller[7] in the meantime seized Winchester and Chichester for the Parliament.—In the north, for the commission of array was my Lord of Newcastle, and for the *militia* of the Parliament was my Lord Fairfax.[8] My Lord of Newcas-

5 Henry Grey, 1st Earl of Stamford (c. 1599 – 1673). —Ed.

6 Ralph Hopton, 1st Baron Hopton DL (1596 – 1652). —Ed.

7 Sir William Waller (c. 1597 – 1668). —Ed.

8 Ferdinando Fairfax, 2nd Lord Fairfax of Cameron MP (1584

tle took from the Parliament Tadcaster, in which were a great part of the Parliament's forces for that country, and had made himself, in a manner, master of all the north. About this time, that is to say in February, the Queen landed at Burlington, and was conducted by my Lord of Newcastle and the Marquis of Montrose[9] to York, and thence not long after to the King. Divers other little advantages, besides these, the King's party had of the Parliament's in the north.

There happened also between the *militia* of the Parliament, and the Commission of Array[10] in Staffordshire, under my Lord Brook[11] for the Parliament, and my Lord of Northampton[12] for the King, great contention, wherein both these commanders were slain. For my Lord Brook, besieging Litchfield-Close, was killed with a shot; notwithstanding which they gave not over the siege, till they were masters of the Close. But presently after, my Lord of Northampton besieged it again for the

---

– 1648). —Ed.

9 James Graham, Earl (1628) Marquis (1644) of Montrose (1612 – 1650). —Ed.

10 A commission given by English sovereigns to officers or gentry in a given territory to muster and array the inhabitants and to see them in a condition for war, or to put soldiers of a country in a condition for military service. Long obsolete by the 17th century, Charles I revived it at the onset of the Civil War in order to counter the Militia Ordinance enacted by Parliament. —Ed.

11 Robert Greville, 2nd Baron Brooke (1607 – 1643). —Ed.

12 Spencer Compton, 2nd Earl of Northampton (1601 – 1643). —Ed.

King; which to relieve, Sir William Brereton[13] and Sir John Gell[14] advanced towards Litchfield, and were met at Hopton Heath by the Earl of Northampton, and routed. The Earl himself was slain; but his forces with victory returned to the siege again; and shortly after, seconded by Prince Rupert, who was then abroad in that country, carried the place. These were the chief actions of this year, 1642;[15] wherein the King's party had not much the worse.

B. But the Parliament had now a better army; insomuch that if the Earl of Essex had immediately followed the King to Oxford (not yet well fortified) he might in all likelihood have taken it. For he could not want either men or ammunition, whereof the city of London (which was wholly at the Parliament's devotion) had store enough.

A. I cannot judge of that. But this is manifest, considering the estate the King was in at his first marching from York, when he had neither money, nor men, nor arms enough to put him in hope of victory, that this year (take it altogether) was very prosperous.

B. But what great folly or wickedness do you observe in the Parliament's actions for this first year?

A. All that can be said against them in that point

---

13 William Brereton, 2nd Baron Brereton (1611 – 1664). —Ed.

14 Sir John Gell, 1st Baronet (1593 – 1671). —Ed.

15 Hobbes' chronology is a bit off, as the Battle of Hopton Heath where Spencer Compton, Earl of Northumberland was slain took place on 19 March 1643. —Ed.

will be excused with the pretext of war, and come under one name of rebellion; saving, that when they summoned any town, it was always in the name of the King and Parliament, the King being in the contrary army, and many times beating them from the siege; I do not see how the right of war can justify such impudence as that. But they pretended that the King was always virtually in the two Houses of Parliament; making a distinction between his person natural and politic; which made the impudence greater, besides the folly of it. For this was but an university quibble, such as boys make use of in maintaining (in the schools) such tenets as they cannot otherwise defend.

In the end of this year they solicited also the Scots to enter England with an army, to suppress the power of the Earl of Newcastle in the north; which was a plain confession, that the Parliament's forces were, at this time, inferior to the King's. And most men thought, that if the Earl of Newcastle had then marched southward, and joined his forces with the King's, that most of the members of Parliament would have fled out of England.

In the beginning of 1643, the Parliament, seeing the Earl of Newcastle's power in the North grown so formidable, sent to the Scots to hire them to an invasion of England, and (to compliment them in the meantime) made a covenant amongst themselves, such as the Scots had before taken against episcopacy, and demolished crosses and church windows (such as had in them any images of saints) throughout all England. Also in the middle of the year, they made a solemn league with the nation, which was called the Solemn League and Covenant.[16]

B. Are not the Scots as properly to be called foreigners as the Irish? Seeing then they persecuted the Earl of Strafford even to death, for advising the King to make use of Irish forces against the Parliament, with what face could they call in a Scotch army against the King?

A. The King's party might easily here have discerned their design, to make themselves absolute masters of the kingdom and to dethrone the King. Another great impudence, or rather a bestial incivility, it was of theirs, that they voted the Queen a traitor, for helping the King with some ammunition and English officers[17] from Holland.

B. Was it possible that all this could be done, and men not see that papers and declarations must be useless; and that nothing could satisfy them but the deposing of the King, and setting up of themselves in his place?

A. Yes; very possible. For who was there of them though knowing that the King had the sovereign power, that knew the essential rights of sovereignty? They dreamt of a mixed power, of the King and the two Houses. That it was a divided power, in which there could be no peace, was above their un-

16 It was accepted by the Church of Scotland on 17 August 1643 and by Parliament on 25 September 1643. —Ed.

17 Forces from Holland.

derstanding. Therefore they were always urging the King to declarations and treaties (for fear of subjecting themselves to the King in an absolute obedience); which increased the hope and courage of the rebels, but did the King little good. For the people either understand not, or will not trouble themselves with controversies in writing, but rather, by his compliance and messages, go away with an opinion that the Parliament was likely to have the victory in the war. Besides, seeing the penners and contrivers of these papers were formerly members of the Parliament, and of another mind, and now revolted from the Parliament, because they could not bear that sway in the House which they expected, men were apt to think they believed not what they writ.

As for military actions (to begin at the head-quarters) Prince Rupert took Birmingham, a garrison of the Parliament's. In July after, the King's forces had a great victory over the Parliament's, near Devizes on Roundway-Down, where they took 2,000 prisoners, four brass pieces of ordnance, twenty-eight colours, and all their baggage; and shortly after, Bristol was surrendered to Prince Rupert for the King; and the King himself marching into the west, took from the Parliament many other considerable places.

But this good fortune was not a little allayed by his besieging of Gloucester,[18] which, after it was

18 The siege took place from 10 August until 15 September 1643. —Ed.

reduced to the last gasp, was relieved by the Earl of Essex; whose army was before greatly wasted, but now suddenly recruited with the trained bands and apprentices of London.

B. It seems, not only by this, but also by many examples in history, that there can hardly arise a long or dangerous rebellion, that has not some such overgrown city, with an army or two in its belly to foment it.

A. Nay more; those great capital cities, when rebellion is upon pretence of grievances, must needs be of the rebel party: because the grievances are but taxes, to which citizens, that is, merchants, whose profession is their private gain, are naturally mortal enemies; their only glory being to grow excessively rich by the wisdom of buying and selling.

B. But they are said to be of all callings the most beneficial to the commonwealth, by setting the poorer sort of people on work.

A. That is to say, by making poor people sell their labour to them at their own prices; so that poor people, for the most part, might get a better living by working in Bridewell, than by spinning, weaving, and other such labour as they can do; saving that by working slightly they may help themselves a little, to the disgrace of our manufacture. And as most commonly they are the first encouragers of rebellion, presuming of their own strength; so also are they, for the most part, the first to repent, deceived by them that command their strength.

But to return to the war; though the King withdrew from Gloucester, yet it was not to fly from, but to fight with the Earl of Essex, which presently after he did at Newbury, where the battle was bloody, and the King had not the worst, unless Cirencester be put into the scale, which the Earl of Essex had in his way a few days before surprised.

But in the north and the west, the King had much the better of the Parliament. For in the north, at the very beginning of the year, March 29th, the Earls of Newcastle and Cumberland[19] defeated the Lord Fairfax (who commanded in those parts for the Parliament) at Bramham Moor; which made the Parliament to hasten the assistance of the Scots.

In June following the Earl of Newcastle routed Sir Thomas Fairfax (son to the Lord Fairfax) upon Adderton Heath; and, in pursuit of them to Bradford, took and killed 2,000 men; and the next day took the town and 2,000 prisoners more (Sir Thomas himself hardly escaping), with all their arms and ammunition; and besides this, made the Lord Fairfax quit Halifax and Beverley. Lastly, Prince Rupert relieved Newark, besieged by Sir John Meldrun[20] (for the Parliament) with 7,000 men; whereof 1,000 were slain, the rest upon articles departed, leaving behind them their arms, bag and baggage.

To balance (in part) this success, the Earl of

19 Henry Clifford, 5th Earl of Cumberland (1591 – 1643). —Ed.

20 Sir John Meldrum (d. 1645) had, until 1642 and for 36 years, served the Stuart kings of Scotland and England. He switched sides when he found himself opposed to Charles I's policies. —Ed.

Manchester whose lieutenant-general was Oliver Cromwell, got a victory over the royalists near Horncastle, of whom he slew 400 took 800 prisoners and 1,000 arms; and presently after took and plundered the city of Lincoln.

In the West (May the 16th) Sir Raph Hopton at Stratton, in Devonshire, had a victory over the Parliamentarians, wherein he took 1,700 prisoners, thirteen pieces of brass ordnance, and all their ammunition, which was seventy barrels of powder, and the magazine of their other provisions in the town.

Again at Lansdown, between Sir Raph Hopton and the Parliamentarians under Sir William Waller, was fought a fierce battle, wherein the victory was not very clear on either side; saving that the Parliamentarians might seem to have the better, because presently after Sir William Waller followed Sir Raph Hopton to Devizes, in Wiltshire, though to his cost; for there he was overthrown, as I have already told you.

After this the King in person marched into the West, and took Exeter, Dorchester, Barnstable, and divers other places; and had he not at his return besieged Gloucester, and thereby given the Parliament time for new levies, it was thought by many he might have routed the House of Commons.—But the end of this year was more favourable to the Parliament. For in January the Scots entered England, and, March the 1st, crossed the Tyne; and whilst the Earl of Newcastle was marching to them, Sir Thomas Fairfax gathered together a considerable party in Yorkshire, and the Earl of Manchester from Lyn advanced towards York; so that the Earl of Newcastle having two armies of the rebels, *one* behind him, and another before him, was forced to retreat to York; where *(the Earl of Manchester joining)*[21] three armies presently besieged him. And these are all the considerable military actions of the year 1643.

In the same year the Parliament caused to be made a new Great Seal. The Lord Keeper had carried the former seal to Oxford. Hereupon the King sent a messenger to the judges at Westminster, to forbid them to make use of it. This messenger was taken, and condemned at a council of war, and hanged for a spy.

B. Is that the law of war?

A. I know not: but it seems, when a soldier comes into the enemies' quarters, without address or notice given to the chief commander, that it is presumed he comes as a spy. The same year, when certain gentlemen at London received a commission of array from the King to levy men for his service in that city, being discovered, they were condemned, and some of them executed. This case is not much unlike the former.

B. Was not the making of a new Great Seal a sufficient proof that the war was raised, not to remove evil counsellors from the King, but to remove the King himself from the government? What hope

21 Which those three armies joining presently besieged—*corr. H.*

then could there be had in messages and treaties?

A. The entrance of the Scots was a thing unexpected to the King, who was made to believe by continual letters from his commissioner in Scotland, Duke Hamilton, that the Scots never intended any invasion. The Duke being then at Oxford, the King (assured that the Scotch were now entered) sent him prisoner to Pendennis Castle in Cornwall.

In the beginning of the year 1644, the Earl of Newcastle being (as I told you) besieged *in York* by the joint forces of the Scots, the Earl of Manchester and Sir Thomas Fairfax, the King sent Prince Rupert to relieve the town, and as soon as he could to give the enemy battle. Prince Rupert passing through Lancashire, and by the way having stormed the seditious town of Bolton, and taken in Stopford and Liverpool, came to York July the 1st, and relieved it; the enemy being risen thence to a place called Marston Moor, about four miles off; and there was fought that unfortunate battle, which lost the King in a manner all the north. Prince Rupert returned the way he came, and the Earl of Newcastle to York, and thence with some of his officers over the sea to Hamburgh.

The honour of this victory was attributed chiefly to Oliver Cromwell (the Earl of Manchester's lieutenant-general). The Parliamentarians returned from the field to the siege of York, which not long after, upon honourable articles, was surrendered;

not for favour,[22] but because the Parliament employed not much time, nor many men in sieges.

B. This was a great and sudden abatement of the King's prosperity.

A. It was so; but amends were made him for it within five or six weeks after. For Sir William Waller (after the loss of his army at Roundway-Down) had another raised for him by the city of London; who for the payment thereof imposed a weekly tax of the value of one meal's meat upon every citizen. This army, with that of the Earl of Essex, intended to besiege Oxford; which the King understanding, sent the Queen into the west, and marched himself towards Worcester. This made them to divide again, and the Earl to go into the west, and Waller to pursue the King. By this means (as it fell out) both their armies were defeated. For the King turned upon Waller, routed him at Cropredy-bridge, took his train of artillery and many officers; and then presently followed the Earl of Essex into Cornwall, where he had him at such advantage, that the Earl himself was fain to escape in a small boat to Plymouth; his horse broke through the King's quarters by night; but the infantry were all forced to lay down their arms, and upon condition never more to bear arms against the King, were permitted to depart.

In October following was fought a second and sharp battle at Newbury. For this infantry, making no conscience of the conditions made with the

22 not that they were favoured—*corr. H.*

King, being now come towards London as far as Basingstoke, had arms put again into their hands; to whom some of the trained-bands *of London* being added, the Earl of Essex had suddenly so great an army, that he attempted the King again at Newbury; and certainly had the better of the day, but the night parting them, had not a complete victory. And it was observed here, that no part of the Earl's army fought so keenly as they who had laid down their arms in Cornwall.

These were the most important fights of the year 1644; and the King was yet (as both himself and others thought) in as good condition as the Parliament, which despaired of victory, by the commanders they then used. Therefore they voted a new modelling of the army, suspecting the Earl of Essex, though I think wrongfully, to be too much a royalist, for not having done so much as they looked for, in this second battle at Newbury. The Earls of Essex and Manchester, perceiving what they went about, voluntarily laid down their commissions; and the House of Commons made an ordinance, that no member of either House should enjoy any office or command, military or civil; with which oblique blow they shook off those that had hitherto served them too well. And yet out of this ordinance they excepted Oliver Cromwell, in whose conduct and valour they had very great confidence (which they would not have done, if they had known him as well then as they did afterwards), and made him lieutenant-general to Sir Thomas Fairfax, their new-made general. In the commission to the Earl of Essex, there was a clause for the preservation of his Majesty's person; which in this new commission was left out; though the Parliament (as well as the general) were as yet Presbyterian.

B. It seems the Presbyterians also (in order to their ends) would fain have had the King murdered.

A. For my part I doubt it not. For a rightful king living, an usurping power can never be sufficiently secured.

In this same year the Parliament put to death Sir John Hotham and his son, for having tampered[23] with the Earl of Newcastle about the rendition of Hull; and Sir Alexander Carew,[24] for endeavouring to deliver up Plymouth, where he was governor for the Parliament; and the Archbishop of Canterbury, for nothing but to please the Scots; for the general article of going about to subvert the fundamental laws of the land, was no accusation, but only foul words. They then also voted down the Book of Common-prayer, and ordered the use of a Directory, which had been newly composed by an Assembly of Presbyterian ministers. They were also then, with much ado, prevailed with for a treaty with the King at Uxbridge; where they remitted nothing of their former demands. The King had also at this time a Parliament at Oxford, consisting of such discontented members as had left the Houses at

23 for tampering—*corr. H.*

24 Sir Alexander Carew, 2nd Baronet (1609 – 1644). —Ed.

Westminster; but few of them had changed their old principles, and therefore that Parliament was not much worth. Nay rather, because they endeavoured nothing but messages and treaties, that is to say, defeating of the soldiers' hope of benefit by the war, they were thought by most men to do the King more hurt than good.[25]

The year 1645 was to the King very unfortunate; for by the loss of one great battle, he lost all he had formerly gotten, and at length his life.—The new modelled army, after consultation whether they should lay siege to Oxford, or march westward to the relief of Taunton (then besieged by the Lord Goring, and defended by Blake,[26] famous afterwards for his actions at sea), resolved for Taunton; leaving Cromwell to attend the motions of the King, though not strong enough to hinder him. The King upon this advantage drew out his forces and artillery out of Oxford. This made the Parliament to call back their general, Fairfax, and order him to besiege Oxford. The King in the meantime relieved Chester, which was besieged by Sir William Brereton, and coming back took Leicester by force; a place of great importance, well provided of artillery and provision.

Upon this success it was generally thought that

25 The proceedings of this body are largely unknown, as all records would be burnt before Oxford fell to Parliament's forces in May 1646. —Ed.

26 Robert Blake (1598 – 1657), who, at this time, held the rank of Colonel in the New Model Army. —Ed.

the King's party was the stronger. The King himself thought so; and the Parliament in a manner confessed the same, by commanding Fairfax to rise from the siege, and endeavour to give the King battle. For the successes of the King, and the divisions and treacheries growing now amongst themselves, had driven them to rely upon the fortune of one day; in which, at Naseby, the King's army was utterly overthrown, and no hope left him to raise another. Therefore after the battle, with a small party he went up and down, doing the Parliament here and there some shrewd turns, but never much increasing his number.

Fairfax in the meantime first recovered Leicester, and then marching into the west, subdued it all, except only a few places, forcing with much ado my Lord Hopton (upon honourable conditions) to disband his army, and with the Prince of Wales to pass over to Scilly; whence not long after they went to Paris.

In April, 1646, General Fairfax began to march back to Oxford. In the meantime Rainsborough,[27] who besieged Woodstock, had it surrendered. The King therefore, who was now also returned to Oxford, from whence Woodstock is but six miles, not doubting but that he should there by Fairfax be besieged, and having no army, to relieve him, resolved to get away disguised to the Scotch army about Newark; and thither he came the 4th of May; and the Scotch army, being upon remove home-

27 Thomas Rainsborough (1610 – 1648). —Ed.

wards, carried him with them to Newcastle, whither he came May 13th.

B. Why did the King trust himself with the Scots? They were the first that rebelled. They were Presbyterians, *id est*, cruel; besides, they were indigent, and consequently might be suspected would sell him to his enemies for money. And lastly, they were too weak to defend him, or keep him in their country.

A. What could he have done better? For he had in the winter before sent to the Parliament to get a pass for the Duke of Richmond and others, to bring them propositions of peace; it was denied. He sent again; it was denied again. Then he desired he might come to them in person; this also was denied. He sent again and again to the same purpose; but instead of granting it, they made an ordinance: that the commanders of the *militia* of London, in case the King should attempt to come within the lines of communication, should raise what force they thought fit to suppress tumults, to apprehend such as came with him, and to secure (*id est*, to imprison) his person from danger. If the King had adventured to come, and had been imprisoned, what could the Parliament have done with him? They had dethroned him by their votes, and therefore could have no security whilst he lived, though in prison. It may be they would not have put him to death by a high court of justice publicly, but secretly some other way.

B. He should have attempted to get beyond sea.

A. That had been (from Oxford) very difficult. Besides, it was generally believed that the Scotch army had promised him, that not only his Majesty, but also his friends that should come with him, should be in their army safe; not only for their persons, but also for their honours and consciences.

B. 'Tis a pretty trick, when the army and the particular soldiers of the army are different things, to make the soldiers promise what the army mean not to perform.

A. July the 11th the Parliament sent their propositions to the King at Newcastle; which propositions they pretended to be the only way to a settled and well grounded peace. They were brought by the Earl of Pembroke,[28] the Earl of Suffolk,[29] Sir Walter Earle,[30] Sir John Hippisley,[31] Mr. Goodwin,[32] and Mr. Robinson;[33] whom the King asked if they had power to treat; and (when they said no) why they might not as well have been sent by a trumpeter. The propositions were the same dethroning ones, which they used to send, and therefore the King would not assent to them. Nor did the Scots swallow them at first, but made some exceptions against them; only, it seems, to make the Parliament perceive they meant not to put the

28 Philip Herbert, 5th Earl of Pembroke (1621 – 1669). —Ed.

29 James Howard, 3rd Earl of Suffolk (1606/6 – 1688). —Ed.

30 (1586 – 1665). —Ed.

31 (1621 – 1653). —Ed.

32 Robert Goodwin (1601 – 1681). —Ed.

33 Luke Robinson (1610 – 1669). —Ed.

King into their hands gratis. And so at last the bargain was made between them; and upon the payment of 200,000*l.* the King was put into the hands of the commissioners, which the English Parliament sent down to receive him.

B. What a vile complexion has this action, compounded of feigned religion, and very covetousness, cowardice, perjury, and treachery!

A. Now the war, that seemed to justify many unseemly things, is ended, you will see almost nothing else in these rebels but baseness and falseness besides their folly.

By this time the Parliament had taken in all the rest of the King's garrisons; whereof the last was Pendennis Castle, whither Duke Hamilton had been sent prisoner by the King.[34]

B. What was done during this time in Ireland and Scotland?

A. In Ireland there had been a peace made by order from his Majesty for a time, which by divisions amongst the Irish was ill kept. The Popish party (the Pope's nuncio being then there) took this to be the time for delivering themselves from their subjection to the English. Besides, the time of the peace was now expired.

B. How were they subject to the English, more than the English to the Irish? They were subject to the King of England; but so also were the English

34 James Hamilton was imprisoned in Pendennis Castle in January 1644; from 1645 he was held at St Michael's Mount, a tidal island in Mount's Bay, Cornwall. —Ed.

to the King of Ireland.

A. This distinction is somewhat too subtile for common understandings.—In Scotland the Marquis of Montrose for the King, with a very few men and miraculous victories, had overrun all Scotland, where many of his forces (out of too much security) were permitted to be absent for awhile; of which the enemy having intelligence, suddenly came upon them, and forced them to fly back into the Highlands to recruit; where he began to recover strength, when he was commanded by the King (then in the hands of the Scots at Newcastle) to disband; and *so* he departed from Scotland by sea.

In the end of the same year, 1646, the Parliament caused the King's Great Seal to be broken; also the King was brought to Holmeby, and there kept by the Parliament's commissioners. And here was an end of that war as to England and Scotland, but not to Ireland. About this time also died the Earl of Essex, whom the Parliament had *formerly* discarded.

B. Now that there was peace in England, and the King in prison, in whom was the sovereign power?

A. The right was certainly in the King, but the exercise was yet in nobody; but contended for, as in a game at cards, without fighting, all the years 1647 and 1648, between the Parliament and Oliver Cromwell, lieutenant-general to Sir Thomas Fairfax.

**B*. What cards could Cromwell have for it?

A.* You must know: that when King Henry VIII.

abolished the pope's authority here, and took upon him to be the head of this Church, the bishops, as they could not resist him, so neither were they discontented with it. For whereas before the pope allowed not the bishops to claim jurisdiction in their dioceses *jure divino*, that is of right immediately from God, but by the gift and authority of the pope, now that the pope was ousted, they made no doubt but the divine right was in themselves. After this, the city of Geneva, and divers other places beyond sea, having revolted from the papacy, set up presbyteries for the government of their several churches. And divers English scholars, that went beyond sea during the persecution in the time of Queen Mary, were much taken with this government, and at their return in the time of Queen Elizabeth, and ever since, have endeavoured, to the great trouble of the Church and nation, to set up that government here, wherein they might domineer and applaud their own wit and learning. And these took upon them not only a Divine right, but also a Divine inspiration. And having been connived at, and countenanced sometimes in their frequent preaching, they introduced many strange and many pernicious doctrines, out-doing the Reformation (as they pretended) both of Luther and Calvin; receding from the former divinity (or church philosophy, for religion is another thing) as much as Luther and Calvin had receded from the pope; and distracted their auditors into a great number of sects, as Brownists, Anabaptists, Independents, Fifth-monarchy-men, Quakers, and divers others, all commonly called by the name of fanatics: insomuch as there was no so dangerous an enemy to the Presbyterians, as this brood of their own hatching.

These were Cromwell's best cards, whereof he had a very great number in the army, and some in the House, whereof he himself was thought one; though he were nothing certain, but applying himself always to the faction which was strongest, and was of a colour like it.

There were in the army a great number (if not the greatest part) that aimed only at rapine and sharing the lands and goods of their enemies; and these also, upon the opinion they had of Cromwell's valour and conduct, thought they could not any way better arrive at their ends than by adhering to him. Lastly, in the Parliament itself, though not the major part, yet a considerable number were fanatics, enough to put in doubts, and cause delay in the resolutions of the House, and sometimes also by advantage of a thin House to carry a vote in favour of Cromwell, as they did upon the 26th of July. For whereas on the 4th of May precedent the Parliament had voted that the *militia* of London should be in the hands of a committee of citizens, whereof the Lord Mayor for the time being should be one; shortly after, the Independents, chancing to be the major part, made an ordinance, by which it was put into hands more favourable to the army.

The best cards the Parliament had, were the city of London and the person of the King. The General, Sir Thomas Fairfax, was right Presbyterian, but in the hands of the army, and the army in the hands of Cromwell; but which party should prevail, depended on the playing of the game. Cromwell protested still obedience and fidelity to the Parliament; but meaning nothing less, bethought him and resolved on a way to excuse himself of all that he should do to the contrary, upon the army. Therefore he and his son-in-law, Commissary-General Ireton,[35] as good at contriving as himself, and at speaking and writing better, contrive how to mutiny the army against the Parliament. To this end they *secretly* spread a whisper through the army, that the Parliament, now they had the King, intended to disband them, to cheat them of their arrears, and to send them into Ireland to be destroyed by the Irish. The army being herewith enraged, were taught by Ireton to erect a council amongst themselves of two soldiers out of every troop and every company, to consult for the good of the army, and to assist at the council of war, and to advise for the peace and safety of the kingdom. These were called adjutators; so that whatsoever Cromwell would have to be done, he needed nothing to make them do it, but secretly to put it into the heads of these adjutators. The effect of their first consultation was to take the King from Holmeby, and to bring him to the army.

35 Henry Ireton (1611 – 1651). —Ed.

The general hereupon, by letter to the Parliament, excuses himself and Cromwell, and the body of the army, as ignorant of the fact; and that the King came away willingly with those soldiers that brought him: assuring them withal, that the whole army intended nothing but peace, nor opposed Presbytery, nor affected Independency, nor did hold any licentious freedom in religion.

B. 'Tis strange that Sir Thomas Fairfax could be so abused by Cromwell as to believe this which he himself here writes.

A. I cannot imagine that Cornet Joyce[36] could go out of the army with 1,000 soldiers to fetch the King, and neither the general, nor the lieutenant-general, nor the body of the army take notice of it. And that the King went *with them* willingly, appears to be false by a message sent on purpose from his Majesty to the Parliament.

B. Here is perfidy upon perfidy: first, the perfidy of the Parliament against the King, and then the perfidy of the army against the Parliament.

A. This was the first trick Cromwell played *them,* whereby he thought himself to have gotten so great an advantage, that he said openly, "that he had the Parliament in his pocket;" as indeed he had, and the city too. For upon the news of it they were, both the one and the other, in very great disorder; and the more, because there came with it a rumour that the army was marching up to London.

36 (b. 1618), an officer in the Parliamentary New Model Army. —Ed.

The King in the meantime, till his residence was settled at Hampton Court, was carried from place to place, not without some ostentation; but with much more liberty, and with more respect shown him by far, than when he was in the hands of the Parliament's commissioners; for his own chaplains were allowed him, and his children and some friends permitted to see him. Besides that, he was much complimented by Cromwell, who promised him, in a serious and seeming passionate manner, to restore him to his right against the Parliament.

B. How was he sure he could do that?

A. He was not sure; but he was resolved to march up to the city and Parliament, to set up the King again (and be the second man), unless in the attempt he found better hope, than yet he had, to make himself the first man, by dispossessing the King.

B. What assistance against the Parliament and the city could Cromwell expect from the King?

A. By declaring directly for him, he might have had all the King's party, which were many more now since his misfortune, than ever they were before. For in the Parliament itself, there were many that had discovered the hypocrisy, and private aims of their fellows: many were converted to their duty by their own natural reason; and their compassion for the King's sufferings had begot generally an indignation against the Parliament: so that if they had been, by the protection of the present army, brought together and embodied, Cromwell might have done what he had pleased, in the first place for the King, and in the second for himself. But it seems he meant first to try what he could do without the King; and if that proved enough, to rid his hands of him.

B. What did the Parliament and city do to oppose the army?

A. First, the Parliament sent to the general to re-deliver the King to their commissioners. Instead of an answer to this, the army sent articles to the Parliament, and with them a charge against eleven of their members, all of them active Presbyterians: of which articles these are some: 1. That the House may be purged of those, who, by the , ought not to be there; 2. That such as abused and endangered the kingdom, might be disabled to do the like hereafter; 3. That a day might be appointed to determine this Parliament; 4. That they would make an account to the kingdom of the vast sums of money they had received; 5. That the eleven members might presently be suspended sitting in the House. These were the articles that put them to their trumps; and they answered none of them, but that of the suspension of the eleven members, which they said they could not do by law till the particulars of the charge were produced: but this was soon answered with their own proceeding against the Archbishop of Canterbury and the Earl of Strafford.

The Parliament being thus somewhat awed, and the King made somewhat confident, Cromwell undertakes[37] the city, requiring the Parliament to put the *militia* of London into other hands.

B. What other hands? I do not well understand you.

A. I told you that the *militia* of London was, on the 4th of May, put into the hands of the lord-mayor and other citizens, and soon after put into the hands of other men more favourable to the army. And now I am to tell you, that on July the 26th, the violence of certain apprentices and disbanded soldiers forced the Parliament to re-settle it as it was, in the citizens; and hereupon the two speakers and divers of the members ran away to the army, where they were invited and contented to sit and vote in the council of war in nature of a Parliament. And out of the citizens' hands they would have the *militia* taken away, and put again into those hands out of which it was taken the 26th of July.

B. What said the city to this?

A. The Londoners manned their works, *viz*.: the line of communication; raised an army of valiant men within the line; chose good officers, all being desirous to go out and fight whensoever the city should give them order; and in that posture stood expecting the enemy.

The soldiers in the meantime enter into an engagement to live and die with Sir Thomas Fairfax, and the Parliament, and the army.

B. That is very fine. They imitate that which the Parliament did, when they first took up arms against the King, styling themselves the King and

37 he undertakes—*corr. H.*

Parliament, maintaining that the King was always virtually in his Parliament: so the army now, making war against the Parliament, called themselves the Parliament and the army: but they might, with more reason, say, that the Parliament, since it was in Cromwell's pocket, was virtually in the army.

A. Withal they send out a declaration of the grounds of their march towards London; wherein they take upon them to be judges of the Parliament, and of who are fit to be trusted with the business of the kingdom, giving them the name, not of the Parliament, but of the gentlemen at Westminster. For since the violence they were under July the 26th, the army denied them to be a lawful Parliament. At the same time they sent a letter to the mayor and aldermen of London, reproaching them with those late tumults; telling them they were enemies to the peace, treacherous to the Parliament, unable to defend either the Parliament or themselves; and demanded to have the city delivered into their hands, to which purpose, they said, they were now coming to them. The general also sent out his warrants to the counties adjacent, summoning their trained soldiers to join with them.

B. Were the trained soldiers part of the general's army?

A. No, nor at all in pay, nor could be without an order of Parliament. But what might an army not do, after it had mastered all the laws of the land? The army being come to Hounslow Heath, distant from London but ten miles, the Court of Aldermen was called to consider what to do. The captains and soldiers of the city were willing, and well provided, to go forth and give them battle. But a treacherous officer, that had charge of a work on Southwark side, had let in within the line a small party of the enemies, who marched as far as to the gate of London-bridge; and then the Court of Aldermen, their hearts failing them, submitted on these conditions: to relinquish their *militia*; to desert the eleven members; to deliver up the forts and line of communication, together with the Tower of London, and all magazines and arms therein, to the army; to disband their forces and turn out the reformadoes, *id est*, all Essex's old soldiers; to draw off the guards from the Parliament. All which was done, and the army marched triumphantly through the principal streets of the city.

B. It is strange that the mayor and aldermen, having such an army, should so quickly yield. Might they not have resisted the party of the enemy at the bridge, with a party of their own; and the rest of the enemies, with the rest of their own?

A. I cannot judge of that: but to me it would have been strange if they had done otherwise. For I consider the most part of rich subjects, that have made themselves so by craft and trade, as men that never look upon anything but their present profit; and who, to everything not lying in that way, are in a manner blind, being amazed at the very thought of plundering. If they had understood what virtue there is to preserve their wealth in obedience to their lawful sovereign, they would never have sided with the Parliament; and so we had had no need of arming. The mayor and aldermen therefore, being assured by this submission to save their goods, and not sure of the same by resisting, seem to me to have taken the wisest course. Nor was the Parliament less tame than the city. For presently, August the 6th, the general brought the fugitive speakers and members to the House, with a strong guard of soldiers, and replaced the speakers in their chairs. And for this they gave the general thanks, not only there in the House, but appointed also a day for a holy thanksgiving; and not long after made him Generalissimo of all the forces of England and Constable of the Tower. But in effect all this was the advancement of Cromwell; for he was the usufructuary, though the property were in Sir Thomas Fairfax. For the Independents immediately cast down the whole line of communication; divided the *militia* of London, Westminster and Southwark, which were before united; displaced such governors of towns and forts as were not for their turn, though placed there by ordinance of Parliament; instead of whom, they put in men of their own party. They also made the Parliament to declare null all that had passed in the Houses from July the 26th to August the 6th, and clapped in prison some of the lords, and some of the most eminent citizens, whereof the lord mayor was one.

B. Cromwell had power enough now to restore

the King. Why did he it not?

A. His main end was to set himself in his place. The restoring of the King was but a reserve against the Parliament, which being in his pocket, he had no more need of the King, who was now an impediment to him. To keep him in the army was a trouble; to let him fall into the hands of the Presbyterians had been a stop to his hopes; to murder him privately (besides the horror of the act) now whilst he was no more than lieutenant-general, would have made him odious without furthering his design. There was nothing better for his purpose than to let him escape from Hampton Court (where he was too near the Parliament) whither he pleased beyond sea. For though Cromwell had a great party in the Parliament House whilst they saw not his ambition to be their master, yet they would have been his enemies as soon as that had appeared.—To make the King attempt an escape, some of those that had him in custody, by Cromwell's direction told him that the adjutators meant to murder him; and withal caused a rumour of the same to be generally spread, to the end it might that way also come to the King's ear, as it did.

The King, therefore, in a dark and rainy night, his guards being retired, as it was thought, on purpose, left Hampton Court and went to the sea-side about Southampton, where a vessel had been bespoken to transport him, but failed; so that the King was forced to trust himself with Colonel Hammond,[38] then governor of the Isle of Wight; expecting perhaps some kindness from him, for Dr. Hammond's sake, brother to the colonel and his Majesty's much favoured chaplain. But it proved otherwise; for the colonel sent to his masters of the Parliament, to receive their orders concerning him. This going into the Isle of Wight was not likely to be any part of Cromwell's design, who neither knew whither nor which way he would go; nor had Hammond known any more than other men, if the ship had come to the appointed place in due time.

B. If the King had escaped into France, might not the French have assisted him with forces to recover his kingdom, and so frustrated the designs both of Cromwell and all the King's other enemies?

A. Yes, much; just as they assisted his son, our present most gracious Sovereign, who two years before fled thither out of Cornwall.

B. It is methinks no great polity in neighbouring princes to favour, so often as they do, one another's rebels, especially when they rebel against monarchy itself. They should rather, first, make a league against rebellion and afterwards, (if there be no remedy) fight one against another. Nor will that serve the turn amongst Christian sovereigns, till preaching be better looked to, whereby the interpretation of a verse in the Hebrew, Greek, or Latin Bible, is oftentimes the cause of civil war and the deposing and assassinating of God's anointed. And yet, converse with those divinity-disputers as long

38 Robert Hammond (1621 – 1654). —Ed.

as you will, you will hardly find one in a hundred discreet enough to be employed in any great affair, either of war or peace. It is not the right of the sovereign, though granted to him by every man's express consent, that can enable him to do his office; it is the obedience of the subject, which must do that. For what good is it to promise allegiance, and then by and by to cry out (as some ministers did in the pulpit) *To your tents, O Israel!*? Common people know nothing of right or wrong by their own meditation; they must therefore be taught the grounds of their duty, and the reasons why calamities ever follow disobedience to their lawful sovereigns. But to the contrary, our rebels were publicly taught rebellion in the pulpits; and that there was no sin, but the doing of what the preachers forbade, or the omission of what they advised.—But now the King was the Parliament's prisoner, why did not the Presbyterians advance their own interest by restoring him?

A. The Parliament, in which there were more Presbyterians yet than Independents, might have gotten what they would of the King during his life, if they had not by an unconscionable and sottish ambition obstructed the way to their ends. They sent him four propositions, to be signed and passed by him as Acts of Parliament; telling him, when these were granted, they would send commissioners to treat with him of any other articles.

The propositions were these: First, that the Parliament should have the *militia*, and the power of levying money to maintain it, for twenty years; and after that term, the exercise thereof to return to the King, in case the Parliament think the safety of the kingdom concerned in it.

B. The first article takes from the King the *militia*, and consequently the whole sovereignty for ever.

A. The second was, that the King should justify the proceedings of the Parliament against himself; and declare void all declarations[39] made by him against the Parliament.

B. This was to make him guilty of the war, and of all the blood spilt therein.

A. The third was, to take away all titles of honour conferred by the King since the Great Seal was carried to him in May, 1642.

The fourth was, that the Parliament should adjourn themselves, when, and to what place, and for what time they pleased.

These propositions the King refused to grant, as he had reason; but sent others of his own, not much less advantageous to the Parliament, and desired a personal treaty upon them with the Parliament, for the settling of the peace of the kingdom. But the Parliament denying them to be sufficient for that purpose, voted that there should be no more addresses made to him, nor messages received from him; but that they would settle the kingdom without him. And this they voted partly upon the speeches and menaces of the army-faction then present in the House of Commons, whereof one

39 all oaths and declarations—*the two words erased in the MS.*

advised these three points: 1. To secure the King in some inland castle with guards; 2. To draw up articles of impeachment against him; 3. To lay him by, and settle the kingdom without him.

Another said, that his denying of the four bills was the denying protection to his subjects; and that therefore they might deny him subjection; and added, that till the Parliament forsook the army, the army would never forsake the Parliament. This was threatening.

Last of all, Cromwell himself told them, it was now expected that the Parliament should govern and defend the kingdom, and not any longer let the people expect their safety from a man whose heart God had hardened; nor let those, that had so well defended the Parliament, be left hereafter to the rage of an irreconcilable enemy, lest they seek their safety some other way. This again was threatening; as also the laying his hand upon his sword when he spake it.

And hereupon the vote of non-addresses was made an ordinance; which the House would afterwards have recalled, but was forced by Cromwell to keep their word.

The Scots were displeased with it; partly because their brethren the Presbyterians had lost a great deal of their power in England, and partly also, because they had sold the King into their hands.

The King now published a passionate complaint to his people of this hard dealing with him; which made them pity him, but not yet rise in his behalf.

B. Was not this, think you, the true time for Cromwell to take possession?

A. By no means. There were yet many obstacles to be removed. He was not general of the army. The army was still for a Parliament. The city of London discontented about their *militia*. The Scots expected with an army to rescue the King. His adjutators were levellers, and against monarchy, who though they had helped him to bring under the Parliament, yet, like dogs that are easily taught to fetch, and not easily taught to render, would not make him king. So that Cromwell had these businesses following to overcome, before he could formally make himself a sovereign prince: 1. To be Generalissimo: 2. To remove the King: 3. To suppress all insurrections here: 4. To oppose the Scots: and lastly, to dissolve the present Parliament. Mighty businesses, which he could never promise himself to overcome. Therefore I cannot believe he then thought to be King; but only by well serving the strongest party, which was always his main polity, to proceed as far as that and fortune would carry him.

B. The Parliament were certainly no less foolish than wicked, in deserting thus the King, before they had the army at a better command than they had.

A. In the beginning of 1648 the Parliament gave commission to Philip Earl of Pembroke, then made Chancellor of Oxford, together with some of the doctors there as good divines as he, to purge the

University. By virtue whereof they turned out all such as were not of their faction, and all such as had approved the use of the Common-prayer-book; as also divers scandalous ministers and scholars (that is, such as customarily without need took the name of God into their mouths, or used to speak wantonly, or haunt the company of lewd women). And for this last I cannot but commend them.

B. So shall not I; for it is just such another piece of piety, as to turn men out of an hospital because they are lame. Where can a man probably learn godliness, and how to correct his vices, better than in the universities erected for that purpose?

A. It may be, the Parliament thought otherwise. For I have often heard the complaints of parents, that their children were debauched there to drunkenness, wantonness, gaming, and other vices consequent to these. Nor is it a wonder amongst so many youths, if they did corrupt one another in despite of their tutors, who oftentimes were little elder than themselves. And therefore I think the Parliament did not much reverence that institution of universities, as to the bringing up of young men to virtue; though many of them learned there to preach, and became thereby capable of preferment and maintenance; and some others were sent thither by their parents, to save themselves the trouble of governing them at home, during that time wherein children are least governable. Nor do I think the Parliament cared more for the clergy than other men did. But certainly an university is an excellent servant to the clergy; and the clergy, if it be not carefully looked to (by their dissensions in doctrines and by the advantage to publish their dissensions), is an excellent means to divide a kingdom into factions.

B. But seeing there is no place in this part of the world, where philosophy and other humane sciences are not highly valued; where can they be learned better than in the Universities?

A. What other sciences? Do not divines comprehend all civil and moral philosophy within their divinity? And as for natural philosophy, is it not removed from Oxford and Cambridge to Gresham College in London, and to be learned out of their gazettes? But we are gone from our subject.

B. No; we are indeed gone from the greater businesses of the kingdom; to which, if you please, let us return.

A. The first insurrection, or rather tumult, was that of the apprentices, on the 9th of April. But this was not upon the King's account, but arose from a customary assembly of them for recreation in Moorfields, whence some zealous officers of the trained soldiers would needs drive them away by force; but were themselves routed with stones; and had their ensign taken away by the apprentices, which they carried about in the streets, and frighted the lord mayor into his house; where they took a gun called a drake; and then they set guards at some of the gates, and all the rest of the day childishly swaggered up and down: but the next day the general himself marching into the city, quickly dispersed them. This was but a small business, but enough to let them see that the Parliament was *but* ill-beloved of the people.

Next, the Welch took arms against them. There were three colonels in Wales, Langhorne,[40] Poyer,[41] and Powel,[42] who had formerly done the Parliament good service, but now were commanded to disband; which they refused to do; and the better to strengthen themselves, declared for the King; and were about 8,000.

About the same time, in Wales also, was another insurrection, headed by Sir Nicholas Keymish, and another under Sir John Owen;[43] so that now all Wales was in rebellion against the Parliament: and yet all these were overcome in a month's time by Cromwell and his officers; but not without store of bloodshed on both sides.

B. I do not much pity the loss of those men, that impute to the King that which they do upon their own quarrel.

A. Presently after this, some of the people of Surrey sent a petition to the Parliament for a personal treaty between the King and the Parliament; but their messengers were beaten home again by the soldiers that were quartered about Westminster and the mews. And then the Kentish men having

40 Rowland Laugharne (c. 1607 – 1675). —Ed.

41 John Poyer (d. 1649). —Ed.

42 Rice Powel. —Ed.

43 Sir John Owen of Clenennau (1600 – 1666). —Ed.

a like petition to deliver, and seeing how ill it was like to be received, threw it away and took up arms. They had many gallant officers, and for general the Earl of Norwich;[44] and increased daily by apprentices and old disbanded soldiers. Insomuch as the Parliament was glad to restore to the city their *militia*, and to keep guards on the Thames side: and then Fairfax marched towards the enemy.

B. And then the Londoners, I think, might easily and suddenly have mastered, first the Parliament, and next Fairfax his 8,000, and lastly Cromwell's army; or at least have given the Scotch army opportunity to march unfoughten to London.

A. It is true: but the city was never good at venturing; nor were they or the Scots principled to have a King over them, but under them. Fairfax marching with his 8,000 against the royalists, routed a part of them at Maidstone; another part were taking in of places in Kent further off; and the Earl of Norwich with the rest came to Blackheath, and thence sent to the city to get passage through it, to join with those which were risen in Essex under Sir Charles Lucas[45] and Sir George Lisle;[46] which being denied, the greatest part of his Kentish men deserted him. With the rest, not above 500, he crossed the Thames into the Isle of Dogs, and so to Bow, and thence to Colchester. Fairfax having notice of this, crossed the Thames at Gravesend;

44 George Goring, 1st Earl of Norwich (1585 – 1663). —Ed.

45 (1613 – 1648). —Ed.

46 (1610 – 1648). —Ed.

and overtaking them, besieged them in Colchester. The town had no defence but a breastwork, and yet held out, upon hope of the Scotch army to relieve them, the space of two months. Upon news of the defeat of the Scots they were forced to yield. The Earl of Norwich was sent prisoner to London. Sir Charles Lucas and Sir George Lisle, two loyal and gallant persons, were shot to death.[47] There was also another little insurrection, headed by the Earl of Holland,[48] about Kingston; but quickly suppressed, and he himself taken prisoner.

B. How came the Scots to be so soon dispatched?

A. Merely (as it is said) for want of conduct. Their army was led by Duke Hamilton, who was then set at liberty, when Pendennis Castle, where he was prisoner, was taken by the Parliamentarians. He entered England with horse and foot 15,000, to which came in above 3,000 English royalists. Against these Cromwell marched out of Wales with horse and foot 11,000, and near to Preston in Lancashire, in less than two hours, defeated them. And the cause of it is said to be, that the Scotch army was so ordered as they could not all come to the fight, nor relieve their fellows. After the defeat, they had no way to fly but further into England; so that in the pursuit they were almost all taken, and lost all that an army can lose; for the few that got home, did not all bring home their swords. Duke Hamilton was taken, and not long

47 On 28 August. —Ed.

48 Henry Rich, 1st Earl of Holland (baptised 1590 – 1649). —Ed.

after sent to London. But Cromwell marched on to Edinburgh, and there, by the help of the faction which was contrary to Hamilton's, he made sure not to be hindered in his designs; the first whereof was to take away the King's life by the hand of the Parliament.

Whilst these things passed in the north, the Parliament (Cromwell being away) came to itself, and recalling their vote of non-addresses, sent to the King new propositions, somewhat (but not much) easier than formerly. And upon the King's answer to them, they sent commissioners to treat with him at Newport in the Isle of Wight; where they so long dodged with him about trifles, that Cromwell was come to London before they had done, to the King's destruction. For the army was now wholly at the devotion of Cromwell, who set the adjutators on work again to make a remonstrance to the House of Commons, wherein they require: 1. That the King be brought to justice: 2. That the Prince and Duke of York be summoned to appear at a day appointed, and proceeded with, according as they should give satisfaction: 3. That the Parliament settle the peace and future government, and *then* set a reasonable period to their own sitting, and make certain future Parliaments, annual, or biennial: 4. That a competent number of the King's chief instruments be executed. And this to be done both by the House of Commons and by a general agreement of the people testified by their subscriptions. Nor did they stay for an answer, but presently set a guard of soldiers at the Parliament-house door, and other soldiers in Westminster Hall, suffering none to go into the House but such as would serve their turns. All others were frighted away, or made prisoners, and some upon divers quarrels suspended; above ninety of them, because they had refused to vote against the Scots; and others, because they had voted against the vote of non-addresses: and the rest were a House for Cromwell. The fanatics also in the city being countenanced by the army, pack a new common-council, whereof any forty was to be above the mayor; and their first work was to frame a petition for justice against the King, which Tichborne, the mayor (involving the city in the regicide) delivered to the Parliament.

At the same time, with the like violence, they took the King from Newport in the Isle of Wight, to Hurst Castle, till things were ready for his trial. The Parliament in the meantime (to avoid perjury) by an ordinance declared void the oaths of supremacy and allegiance, and presently after made another to bring the King to his trial.

B. This is a piece of law I understood not before, that when many swear singly, they may, when they are assembled, if they please, absolve themselves.

A. The ordinance being drawn up was brought into the House, where after three several readings it was voted, "that the Lords and Commons of England, assembled in Parliament, do declare, that by the fundamental laws of the realm, it is treason in the King of England to levy war against the Parliament." And this vote was sent up to the Lords; and they denying their consent, the Commons in anger made another vote: "That all members of committees should proceed and act in any ordinance, whether the Lords concurred or no; and that the people, under God, are the original of all just power; and that the House of Commons have the supreme power of the nation; and that whatsoever the House of Commons enacteth, is law." All this passed *nemine contradicente*.[49]

B. These propositions fight not only against the King of England, but against all the kings of the world. It were good they thought on it. But yet, I believe that under God the original of all laws was in the people.

A. But the people, for them and their heirs, by consent and oaths, have long ago put the supreme power of the nation into the hands of their kings, for them and their heirs; and consequently into the hands of this King, their known and lawful sovereign.[50]

B. But does not the Parliament represent the people?

A. Yes, to some purposes; as to put up petitions to the King, when they have leave, and are grieved; but not to make a grievance with the King's power. Besides, the Parliament never represents the people but when the King calls them; nor is it to be imagined that he calls a Parliament to depose him. Put the case, every county and borough should

49 Latin: with no one contradicting. —Ed.

50 lawful heir—*corr. H.*

have given this Parliament for a benevolence a sum of money; and that every county, meeting in their county-court or elsewhere, and every borough in their town-hall, should have chosen *certain* men to carry their several sums respectively to the Parliament. Had not these men represented the whole nation?

B. Yes, no doubt.

A. Do you think the Parliament would have thought it reasonable to be called to account by this representative?

B. No, sure; and yet I must confess the case is the same.

A. This ordinance contained, first, a summary of the charge against the King, in substance this: that not content with the encroachments of his predecessors upon the freedom of the people, he had designed to set up a tyrannical government; and to that end, had raised and maintained in the land a civil war against the Parliament, whereby the country hath been miserably wasted, the public treasure exhausted, thousands of people murdered, and infinite other mischiefs committed. Secondly, a constitution passed of a high court of justice, that is, of a certain number of commissioners, of whom any twenty had power to try the King, and to proceed to sentence according to the merit of the cause, and see it speedily executed.

The commissioners met on Saturday, January 20th, in Westminister Hall, and the King was brought before them; where, sitting in a chair, he heard the charge read, but denied to plead to it either guilty or not guilty, till he should know by what lawful authority he was brought thither. The president told him that the Parliament affirmed their own authority; and the King persevered in his refusal to plead. Though many words passed between him and the president, yet this was the substance of it all.

On Monday, January 22nd, the court met again; and then the solicitor moved that if the King persisted in denying the authority of the court, the charge might be taken *pro confesso*: but the King still denied their authority.

They met again January the 23rd, and then the solicitor moved the court for judgment; whereupon the King was required to give his final answer; which was again a denial of their authority.

Lastly, they met again January the 27th, where the King desired to be heard before the Lords and Commons in the Painted Chamber, and promising after that to abide the judgment of the court. The commissioners retired for half an hour to consider of it, and then returning caused the King to be brought again to the bar, and told him that what he proposed was but another denial of the court's jurisdiction; and that if he had no more to say, they would proceed. Then the King answering that he had no more to say, the president began a long speech in justification of the Parliament's proceedings, producing the examples of many kings killed or deposed by wicked Parliaments, ancient and modern, in England, Scotland, and other parts of the world. All which he endeavoured to justify from this only principle: that the people have the supreme power, and the Parliament is the people. This speech ended, the sentence of death was read; and the same upon Tuesday after, January 30th, executed at the gate of his own palace of Whitehall. He that can delight in reading how villainously he was used by the soldiers between the sentence and execution, may go to the chronicle itself; in which he shall see what courage, patience, wisdom, and goodness was in this prince, whom in their charge the members of that wicked Parliament styled tyrant, traitor, and murderer.

The King being dead, the same day they made an act of Parliament: that whereas several pretences might be made to the crown, &c., it is enacted by this present Parliament and by authority of the same, that no person presume to declare, proclaim, or publish, or any way promote Charles Stuart, son of Charles late King of England, commonly called Prince of Wales, or any other person, to be King of England or Ireland, &c.

B. Seeing the King was dead, and his successor barred; by what declared authority was the peace maintained?

A. They had, in their anger against the Lords, formerly declared the supreme power of the nation to be in the House of Commons; and now, on February the 5th, they vote the House of Lords to be useless and dangerous. And thus the kingdom is turned into a democracy, or rather an oligarchy; for presently they made an act: that none of those members, who were secluded for opposing the vote of non-addresses, should ever be re-admitted. And these were commonly called *the secluded members*; and the rest were by some styled a Parliament, and by others *the Rump*.

I think you need not now have a catalogue, either of the vices, or of the crimes, or of the follies of the greatest part of them that composed the Long Parliament; than which greater cannot be in the world. What greater vices than irreligion, hypocrisy, avarice and cruelty; which have appeared so eminently in the actions of Presbyterian members and Presbyterian ministers? What greater crimes than blaspheming and killing God's anointed? which was done by the hands of the Independents, but by the folly and first treason of the Presbyterians, who betrayed and sold him to his murderers? Nor was it a little folly in the Lords, not to see that by the taking away of the King's power they lost withal their own privileges; or to think themselves, either for number or judgment, any way a considerable assistance to the House of Commons. And for those men who had skill in the laws, it was no great sign of understanding not to perceive that the laws of the land were made by the King, to oblige his subjects to peace and justice, and not to oblige himself that made them. And lastly and generally, all men are fools which pull down anything which does them good, before they have set up something better in its place. He that would set up democracy with an army, should have an army to maintain it; but these men did it, when those men had the army that were resolved to pull it down. To these follies I might add the folly of those fine men, which out of their reading of Tully, Seneca, or other anti-monarchies, think themselves sufficient politics, and show their discontent when they are not called to the management of the state, and turn from one side to another upon every neglect they fancy from the King or his enemies.

Dialogue IV

A. You have seen the Rump in possession (as they believed) of the supreme power over the two nations England and Ireland, and the army their servant; though Cromwell thought otherwise, serving them diligently for the advancement of his own purposes. I am now therefore to show you their proceedings.

B. Tell me first, how this kind of government under the Rump or relic of a House of Commons is to be called?

A. It is doubtless an oligarchy. For the supreme authority must needs be in one man or in more. If in one, it is monarchy; the Rump therefore was no Monarch.[1] If the authority were in more than one, it was in all, or in fewer than all. When in all, it is democracy; for every man may enter into the assembly which makes the Sovereign Court; which

1 was no monarchy.

they could not do here. It is therefore manifest, that the authority was in a few, and consequently the state was an oligarchy.

B. Is it not impossible for a people to be well governed, that are to obey more masters than one?

A. Both the Rump and all other sovereign assemblies, if they have but one voice, though they be many men, yet are they but one person. For contrary commands cannot consist in one and the same voice, which is the voice of the greatest part; and therefore they might govern well enough, if they had honesty and wit enough.

The first act of the Rump, was the exclusion of those members of the House of Commons, which had been formerly kept out by violence for the procuring of an ordinance for the King's trial; for these men had appeared against the ordinance of non-addresses, and therefore to be excluded, because they might else be an impediment to their future designs.

B. Was it not rather, because in the authority of few they thought the fewer the better, both in respect of their shares and also of a nearer approach in every one of them to the dignity of a King?

A. Yes, certainly, that was their principal end.

B. When these were put out, why did not the counties and boroughs choose others in their places?

A. They could not do that without order from the House.

After this they constituted a council of forty persons, which they termed a Council of State,[2] whose office was to execute what the Rump should command.

B. When there was neither King nor House of Lords, they could not call themselves a Parliament; for a Parliament is a meeting of the King, Lords, and Commons, to confer together about the businesses of the commonwealth. With whom did the Rump confer?

A. Men may give to their assembly what name they please, what signification soever such name might formerly have had; and the Rump took the name of Parliament, as most suitable to their purpose, and such a name, as being venerable amongst the people, had for many hundred years countenanced and sweetened subsidies and other levies of money, otherwise very unpleasant to the

2 On 14 February 1649. The first Council met on 17 February and the first elected president, appointed on 12 March, was John Bradshaw, who had presided over the trial of Charles I and had been the first to sign his death warrant. The members of the first Council were: Basil Failding, 2nd Earl of Denbigh; Edmund Sheffield, 2nd Earl of Mulgrave; Philip Herbert, 5th Earl of Pembroke; William Cecil, 2nd Earl of Salisbury; Thomas Grey, Lord Grey of Groby; and Thomas Fairfax, 3rd Lord Fairfax of Cameron; John Lisle; Henry Rolle; Oliver St John; John Wilde; John Bradshaw; Oliver Cromwell; Philip Skippon; Sir Gilbert Pickering; Sir William Masham; Arthur Haselrig; Sir James Harington; Henry Vane the Younger; John Danvers; Sir William Armine; Henry Mildmay; William Constable; Pennington; Wilson; Bulstrode Whitelocke; Martin; Edmund Ludlow; Stapleton; William Heveningham; Robert Wallop; John Hutchinson; Denis Bond; Alexander Popham; Valentine Walton; Thomas Scot; William Purefoy; John Jones. —Ed.

subject. They took also afterwards another name, which was *Custodes Libertatis Angliæ*, which title they used only in their writs issuing out of the courts of justice.

B. I do not see how a subject that is tied to the laws, can have more liberty in one form of government than in another.

A. Howsoever, to the people that understand by liberty nothing but leave to do what they list, it was a title not ingrateful.

Their next work was to set forth a public declaration, that they were fully resolved to maintain the fundamental laws of the nation, as to the preservation of the lives, liberties, and proprieties of he people.

B. What did they mean by the fundamental laws of the nation?

A. Nothing but to abuse the people. For the only fundamental law in every commonwealth is to obey the laws from time to time, which he shall make to whom the people have given the supreme power. How likely then are they to uphold the fundamental laws, that had murdered him who was by themselves so often acknowledged for their lawful sovereign? Besides, at the same time that this declaration came forth, they were erecting that High Court of Justice which took away the lives of Duke Hamilton, the Earl of Holland, and the Lord Capel.[3] Whatsoever they meant by a fundamental law, the erecting of this court was a breach of it, as being

3 Arthur Capell, 1st Baron Capell (1608 – 1649). —Ed.

warranted by no former law or example in England.

At the same time also they levied taxes by soldiers, and to soldiers permitted free quarter, and did many other actions, which if the King had done, they would have said had been done against the liberty and propriety of the subject.

B. What silly things are the common sort of people, to be cozened as they were so grossly!

A. What sort of people, as to this matter, are not of the common sort? The craftiest knaves of all the Rump were no wiser than the rest whom they cozened. For the most of them did believe that the same things which they imposed upon the generality, were just and reasonable; and especially the great haranguers, and such as pretended to learning. For who can be a good subject to monarchy, whose principles are taken from the enemies of monarchy, such as were Cicero, Seneca, Cato, and other politicians of Rome, and Aristotle of Athens, who seldom speak of kings but as of wolves and other ravenous beasts? You may perhaps think a man has need of nothing else to know the duty he owes to his governor, and what right he has to order him, but a good natural wit; but it is otherwise. For it is a science, and built upon sure and clear principles, and to be learned by deep and careful study, or from masters that have deeply studied it. And who was there in the Parliament or in the nation, that could find out those evident principles, and derive from them the necessary rules of justice, and the necessary connexion of justice and peace? The people have one day in seven the leisure to hear instruction, and there are ministers appointed to teach them their duty. But how have those ministers performed their office? A great part of them, namely, the Presbyterian ministers, throughout the whole war, instigated the people against the King; so did also independent and other fanatic ministers. The rest, contented with their livings, preached in their parishes points of controversy, to religion impertinent, but to the breach of charity amongst themselves very effectual; or else elegant things,[4] which the people either understood not, or thought themselves not concerned in. But this sort of preachers, as they did little good, so they did little hurt. The mischief proceeded wholly from the Presbyterian preachers, who, by a long practised histrionic faculty, preached up the rebellion powerfully.

B. To what end?

A. To the end that the State becoming popular, the Church might be so too, and governed by an Assembly; and by consequence (as they thought) seeing politics are subservient to religion, they might govern, and thereby satisfy not only their covetous humour with riches, but also their malice with power to undo all men that admired not their wisdom. Your calling the people silly things, obliged me by this digression to show you, that it is not want of wit, but want of the science of justice, that brought them into these troubles. Persuade,

4 eloquent things.

if you can that man that has made his fortune, or made it greater, or an eloquent orator, or a ravishing poet, or a subtle lawyer, or but a good hunter or a cunning gamester, that he has not a good wit; and yet there were of all these a great many so silly, as to be deceived by the Rump and *yet were* members of the same Rump. They wanted not wit, but the knowledge of the causes and grounds upon which one person has a right to govern, and the rest an obligation to obey; which grounds are necessary to be taught the people, who without them cannot live long in peace amongst themselves.

B. Let us return, if you please, to the proceedings of the Rump.

A. In the rest of this year they voted a new stamp for the coin of this nation. They considered also of agents to be sent to foreign states; and having lately received applause from the army for their work done by the High Court of Justice, and encouragement to extend the same further, they created another High Court[5] of Justice, in which were tried Duke Hamilton, the Earl of Holland, Lord Capel, the Earl of Norwich, and Sir John Owen; whereof, as I mentioned before, the three first were beheaded. This affrighted divers of the King's party out of the land; for not only they, but all that had borne arms for the King, were at that time in very great danger of their lives. For it was put to the question by the army at a council of war, whether they should be all massacred or no; where the

5 they perfected the said High Court.

noes carried it but by two voices. Lastly, March the 24th, they put the Mayor of London out of his office, fined him 2,000*l.*, disfranchised him, and condemned him to two months' imprisonment in the Tower, for refusing to proclaim the act for abolishing the kingly power. And thus ended the year 1648 and the monthly fast; God having granted that which they fasted *and prayed* for, the death of the King and the possession of his inheritance. By these their proceedings they had already lost the hearts of the generality of the people, and had nothing to trust to but the army; which was not in their power, but in Cromwell's; who never failed, when there was occasion, to put them upon all exploits that might make them odious to the people, in order to his future dissolving them whensoever it should conduce to his ends.

In the beginning of 1649 the Scots, discontented with the proceedings of the Rump against the late King, began to levy soldiers in order to a new invasion of England. The Irish rebels, for want of timely resistance from England, were grown terrible; and the English army at home, infected by the adjutators, were casting how to share the land amongst the godly, meaning themselves and such others as they pleased, who were therefore called Levellers. Also the Rump for the present were not very well provided of money, and, therefore, the first thing they did, was the laying of a tax upon the people of 90,000*l.* a month for the maintenance of the army.

B. Was it not one of their quarrels with the King, that he had levied money without the consent of the people in Parliament?

A. You may see by this, what reason the Rump had to call itself a Parliament. For the taxes imposed by Parliament were always understood to be by the people's consent, and consequently legal.—To appease the Scots, they sent messengers with flattering letters to keep them from engaging for the present King; but in vain. For they would hear nothing from a *House of Commons* (as they called it) *at Westminster*, without a King and Lords. But they sent commissioners to the King, to let him know what they were doing for him: for they had resolved to raise an army of 17,000 foot and 6,000 horse (for themselves).

To relieve Ireland, the Rump had resolved to send eleven regiments thither out of the army in England. This happened well for Cromwell. For the levelling soldiers, which were in every regiment many, and in some the major part, finding that instead of dividing the land at home they were to venture their lives in Ireland, flatly denied to go; and one regiment, having cashiered their colonel, about Salisbury, was marching to join with three regiments more of the same resolution; but both the general and Cromwell falling upon them at Burford, utterly defeated them, and soon after reduced the whole army to their obedience. And thus another of the impediments to Cromwell's advancement was soon removed. This done, they came to Oxford, and thence to London. At Oxford, both the general and Cromwell were made doctors of the civil law; and at London, feasted and presented by the city.

B. Were they not first made masters, and then doctors?

A. They made themselves already masters, both of the laws and Parliament. The army now being obedient, the Rump sent over those eleven regiments into Ireland, under the command of Dr. Cromwell, intituled governor of that kingdom, the Lord Fairfax being still general of all the forces, both here and there.

The Marquis (now Duke) of Ormond[6] was the King's lieutenant of Ireland; and the rebels had made a confederacy amongst themselves; and these confederates had made a kind of league with the lieutenant, wherein they agreed, upon liberty given them in the exercise of their religion, to be faithful to and assist the King. To these also were joined some forces raised by the Earls of Castlehaven[7] and Clanricarde[8] and my Lord Inchiquin;[9] so that they were the greatest united strength in

6 James FitzThomas Butler, 1st Duke of Ormond, 1st Marquess of Ormond, 12th Earl of Ormond, 5th Earl of Ossory, 4th Viscount Thurles, 1st Baron Butler of Llanthony, 1st Earl of Brecknock, KG, PC (1610 – 1688). —Ed.

7 James Tuchet, 3rd Earl of Castlehaven (c. 1617 – 1684). —Ed.

8 Ulick MacRichard Burke, 1st Marquess of Clanricarde, 5th Earl of Clanricarde, 2nd Earl of St Albans (1604 – 1657). —Ed.

9 Murrough MacDermod O'Brien, 6th Baron Inchiquin, 1st Baron O'Brien of Burren, 1st Earl of Inchiquin (1614 – 1674). —Ed.

the island. But there were amongst them a great many other Papists, that would by no means subject themselves to Protestants; and these were called the Nuntio's party, as the others were called the confederate party. These parties not agreeing, and the confederate party having broken their articles, the lord-lieutenant seeing them ready to besiege him in Dublin, and not able to defend it, did, to preserve the place for the Protestants, surrender it to the Parliament of England; and came over to the King, at that time when he was carried from place to place by the army. From England he went over to the Prince (now King), residing then at Paris.

But the confederates, affrighted with the news that the Rump was sending over an army thither, desired the Prince by letters, to send back my Lord of Ormond, engaging themselves to submit absolutely to the King's authority, and to obey my Lord of Ormond as his lieutenant. And hereupon he was sent back. This was about a year before the going over of Cromwell.

In which time, by the dissension in Ireland between the confederate party and the Nuntio's party, and discontents about command, this otherwise sufficient power effected nothing; and was at last defeated, August the 2nd, by a sally out of Dublin, which they were besieging. Within a few days after arrived Cromwell, who with extraordinary diligence and horrid executions, in less than a twelvemonth that he stayed there, subdued in a manner the whole nation; having killed or exterminated a great part of them, and leaving his son-in-law Ireton to subdue the rest. But Ireton died there (before the business was quite done) of the plague. This was one step more towards Cromwell's exaltation to the throne.

B. What a miserable condition was Ireland reduced to by the learning of the Roman, as well as England was by the learning of the Presbyterian clergy!

A. In the latter end of the preceding year the King was come from Paris to the Hague; and shortly after came thither from the Rump their agent Dorislaus,[10] doctor of civil law, who had been employed in the drawing up of the charge against the late King. But the first night he came, as he was at supper, a company of cavaliers, near a dozen, entered his chamber, killed him, and got away. Not long after also their agent at Madrid, one Ascham,[11] one that had written in defence of his masters, was killed in the same manner. About this time came out two books, one written by Salmasius,[12] a Presbyterian, against the murder of the King; another written by Milton,[13] an English Independent, in answer to it.

B. I have seen them both. They are very good

10 Isaac Dorislaus (1595 – 1649). —Ed.

11 Anthony Ascham (c. 1614 – 1650). —Ed.

12 Claudius Salmasius, or, Claude Saumaise in French (1588 – 1653). —Ed.

13 John Milton (1608 – 1674). —Ed.

Latin both, and hardly to be judged which is better; and both very ill reasoning, hardly to be judged which is worse; like two declamations, pro and con, made for exercise only in a rhetoric school by one and the same man. So like is a Presbyterian to an Independent.

A. In this year the Rump did not much at home; save that in the beginning they made England a Free-State by an act which runs thus: "*Be it enacted and declared by this present Parliament, and by the authority thereof, that the people of England, and all the dominions and territories thereunto belonging, are, and shall be, and are hereby constituted, made, and declared a Commonwealth and Free-State, &c.*"

B. What did they mean by a Free-State and commonwealth? Were the people no longer to be subject to laws? They could not mean that: for the Parliament meant to govern them by their own laws, and punish such as broke them. Did they mean that England should not be subject to any foreign kingdom or commonwealth? That needed not be enacted, seeing there was no king nor people pretended to be their masters. What did they mean then?

A. They meant that neither this king, nor any king, nor any single person, but only that they themselves would be the people's masters, and would have set it down in those plain words, if the people could have been cozened with words intelligible, as easily as with words not intelligible.

After this they gave one another money and estates, out of the lands and goods of the loyal party. They enacted also an engagement to be taken by every man, in these words: *You shall promise to be true and faithful to the Commonwealth of England, as it is now established, without King or House of Lords.*

They banished also from within twenty miles of London all the royal party, forbidding also every one of them to depart more than five miles from his dwelling-house.

B. They meant perhaps to have them ready, if need were, for a massacre. But what did the Scots in this time?

A. They were considering the army which they were levying for the King, how they might exclude from command all such as had loyally served his father, and all Independents, and all such as had command in Duke Hamilton's army; and these were the main things that passed this year.

The Marquis of Montrose, that in the year 1645 had with a few men, and in little time, done things almost incredible against the late King's enemies in Scotland, landed now again, in the beginning of the year 1650, in the north of Scotland, with commission from the present King, hoping to do him as good service as he had formerly done his father. But the case was altered; for the Scotch forces were then in England in the service of the Parliament; whereas now they were in Scotland, and many more (for their intended invasion) newly raised. Besides, the soldiers which the Marquis brought over were few, and foreigners; nor did the Highlanders come in to him, as he expected; insomuch as he was soon defeated, and shortly after taken, and (with more spiteful usage than revenge required) executed by the Covenanters of Edinburgh, May the 2nd.

B. What good could the King expect from joining with these men, who during the treaty discovered so much malice to him in one of his best servants?

A. No doubt (their churchmen being then prevalent) they would have done as much to this King as the English Parliament had done to his father, if they could have gotten by it that which they foolishly aspired to, the government of the nation. Do not believe that the Independents were worse than the Presbyterians: both the one and the other were resolved to destroy whatsoever should stand in the way to their ambition. But necessity made the King pass over both this and many other indignities from them, rather than suffer the pursuit of his right in England to cool, and be little better than extinguished.

B. Indeed I believe, a kingdom, if suffered to become an old debt, will hardly ever be recovered. Besides, the King was sure, wheresoever the victory lighted, he could lose nothing in the war but enemies.

A. About the time of Montrose's death, which was in May, Cromwell was yet in Ireland, and his work unfinished. But finding, or by his friends advertised, that his presence in the expedition now preparing against the Scots would be necessary to his design, he sent to the Rump to know their pleasure concerning his return. But for all that, he knew, or thought it was not necessary to stay for their answer, but came away, and arrived at London the 6th of June following, and was welcomed by the Rump. Now General Fairfax, who was truly what he pretended to be, a Presbyterian, had been so catechised by the Presbyterian ministers here, that he refused to fight against the brethren in Scotland; nor did the Rump nor Cromwell go about to rectify his conscience in that point. And thus Fairfax laying down his commission, Cromwell was now made general of all the forces in England and Ireland; which was another step to the sovereign power. *And there appeared but one more, which was the mastering of Scotland. Towards which he began to march June the 12th, and came to Barwick July the 21st, his army being, horse and foot, 16,000.*

B. Where was the King?

A. In Scotland, newly come over. He landed in the north, and was honourably conducted to Edinburgh, though all things were not yet well agreed on between the Scots and him. For though he had yielded to as hard conditions as the late King had yielded to in the Isle of Wight, yet they had still somewhat to add, till the King, enduring no more, departed from them towards the north again. But they sent messengers after him to pray him to return, but they furnished these messengers with strength enough to bring him back, if he should have refused. In fine they agreed; but *they* would not suffer either the King, or any royalist, to have command in the army.

B. The sum of all is, the King was there a prisoner.

A. Cromwell from Barwick sends a declaration to the Scots, telling them he had no quarrel against the people of Scotland, but against a malignant party that had brought in the King, to the disturbance of the peace between the two nations; and that he was willing, either by conference to give and receive satisfaction, or to decide the justice of the cause by battle. To which the Scots answering, declare: that they will not prosecute the King's interest before and without his acknowledgment of the sins of his house, and his former ways, and satisfaction given to God's people in both kingdoms. Judge by this whether the present King were not in as bad a condition here, as his father was in the hands of the Presbyterians of England.

B. Presbyterians are everywhere the same: they would fain be absolute governors of all they converse with, having nothing to plead for it, but that where they reign, it is God that reigns, and nowhere else. But I observe one strange demand, that the King should acknowledge the sins of his house; for I thought it had been certainly held by all divines, that no man was bound to acknowledge any man's sins but his own.

A. The King having yielded to all that the Church

required, the Scots proceeded in their intended war. Cromwell marched on to Edinburgh, provoking them all he could to battle; which they declining, and provisions growing scarce in the English army, Cromwell retired to Dunbar, despairing of success; and intending by sea or land to get back into England. And such was the condition which this General (Cromwell), so much magnified for conduct, had brought his army to, that all his glories had ended in shame and punishment, if fortune and the faults of his enemies had not relieved him. For as he retired, the Scots followed him close all the way till within a mile of Dunbar. There is a ridge of hills, that from beyond Edinburgh goes winding to the sea, and crosses the highway between Dunbar and Berwick, at a village called Copperspeith, where the passage is so difficult, that had the Scots sent timely thither a very few men to guard it, the English could never have gotten home. For the Scots kept the hills, and needed not have fought but upon great advantage, and were almost two to one. Cromwell's army was at the foot of those hills, on the north side; and there was a great ditch or channel of a torrent between the hills and it; so that he could never have got home by land, nor without utter ruin of the army attempted to ship it; nor have stayed where he was, for want of provisions. Now Cromwell knowing the pass was free, and commanding a good party of horse and foot to possess it, it was necessary for the Scots to let them go, whom they bragged they had impounded, or else to fight; and therefore with the best of their horse charged the English, and made them at first to shrink a little. But the English foot coming on, the Scots were put to flight; and the flight of the horse hindered the foot from engaging; who therefore fled, as did also the rest of their horse. Thus the folly of the Scottish commanders brought all their odds to an even lay between two small and equal parties; wherein fortune gave the victory to the English, who were not many more in number than those that were killed and taken prisoners of the Scots; and the Church lost their cannon, bag and baggage, with 10,000 arms, and almost their whole army. The rest were got together by Lesley[14] to Stirling.

B. This victory happened well for the King. For had the Scots been victors, the Presbyterians, both there and here, would have domineered again, and the King been in the same condition his father was in at Newcastle, in the hands of the Scottish army. For in pursuit of this victory, the English at last brought the Scots to a pretty good habit of obedience for the King, whensoever he should recover his right.

A. In pursuit of this victory the English marched to Edinburgh (quitted by the Scots), fortified Leith, and took in all the strength and castles they thought fit on this side the Frith, which now was become the bound betwixt the two nations. And the Scotch ecclesiastics began to know themselves

14 David Leslie, 1st Lord Newark (1600 – 1682). —Ed.

better; and resolved in their new army, which they meant to raise, to admit some of the royalists into command. Cromwell from Edinburgh marched towards Stirling, to provoke the enemy to fight, but finding danger in it returned to Edinburgh, and besieged the castle. In the meantime he sent a party into the west of Scotland to suppress Strachan and Kerr, two great Presbyterians that were there levying of forces for their new army. And in the same time the Scots crowned the King at Scone.

The rest of this year was spent in Scotland, on Cromwell's part, in taking of Edinburgh Castle and in attempts to pass the Frith, or any other ways to get over to the Scottish forces; and on the Scots' part, in hastening their levies from the North.

B. What did the Rump at home during this time?

A. They voted liberty of conscience to the sectaries; that is, they plucked out the sting of Presbytery, which consisted in a severe imposing of odd opinions upon the people, impertinent to religion, but conducing to the advancement of the power of the Presbyterian ministers. Also they levied more soldiers, and gave the command of them to Harrison,[15] now made major-general, a Fifth-monarchy-man; and of these soldiers two regiments of horse and one of foot were raised by the Fifth-monarchy-men and other sectaries, in thankfulness for this their liberty from the Presbyterian tyranny. Also they pulled down the late King's statue in the Exchange, and in the niche where it stood, caused

15 Thomas Harrison (1606 – 1660). —Ed.

to be written these words: *Exit tyrannus, Regum ultimus, etc.*

B. What good did that do them, and why did they not pull down the statues of all the rest of the Kings?

A. What account can be given of actions that proceed not from reason, but spite and such-like passions? Besides this, they received ambassadors from Portugal and from Spain, acknowledging their power. And in the very end of the year they prepared ambassadors to the Netherlands to offer them friendship. All they did besides, was persecuting and executing of royalists.

In the beginning of the year 1651 General Dean[16] arrived in Scotland; and on the 11th of April the Scottish Parliament assembled, and made certain acts in order to a better uniting of themselves, and better obedience to the King, who was now at Stirling with the Scottish forces he had, expecting more now in levying. Cromwell from Edinburgh went divers times towards Stirling to provoke the Scots to fight. There was no ford there to pass over his men; at last boats being come from London and Newcastle, Colonel Overton[17] (though it were long first, for it was now July) transported 1,400 foot of his own, besides another regiment of foot and four troops of horse, and entrenched himself at Northferry on the other side; and before any help could come from Stirling, Major-Gener-

16 Richard Deane (1610 – 1653). —Ed.

17 Robert Overton (about 1609–1678). —Ed.

al Lambert[18] also was got over with as many more. By this time Sir John Browne was come to oppose them with 4,500 men, whom the English there defeated, killing about 2,000 and taking prisoners 1,600. This done, and as much more of the army transported as was thought fit, Cromwell comes before St. Johnstone's (from whence the Scottish Parliament, upon the news of his passing the Frith, was removed to Dundee) and summons it; and the same day had news brought him, that the King was marching from Stirling towards England; which was true. But notwithstanding the King was three days' march before him, he resolved to have the town before he followed him; and accordingly had it the next day by surrender.

B. What hopes had the King in coming into England, having before and behind him none, at least none armed, but his enemies?

A. Yes; there was before him the city of London, which generally hated the Rump, and might reasonably be reckoned for 20,000 well-armed soldiers; and most men believed they would take his part, had he come near to the city.

B. What probability was there of that? Do you think the Rump was not sure of the service of the mayor, and those that had command of the city *militia*? And if they had been really the King's friends, what need had they to stay for his coming up to London? They might have seized the Rump, if they had pleased, which had no possibility of defending

18 John Lambert (1619 – 1684). —Ed.

themselves; at least they might have turned them out of the House.

A. This they did not; but, on the contrary, permitted the recruiting of Cromwell's army, and the raising of men to keep the country from coming in to the King. The King began his march from Stirling the last of July, and August the 22nd came to Worcester by way of Carlisle with a weary army of about 13,000, whom Cromwell followed, and joining with the new levies environed Worcester with 40,000, and on the 3rd of September utterly defeated the King's army. Here Duke Hamilton, brother of him that was beheaded, was slain.

B. What became of the King?

A. Night coming on, before the city was quite taken he left it; it being dark, and none of the enemy's horse within the town to follow him, the plundering foot having kept the gates shut, lest the horse should enter and have a share of the booty. The King before morning got into Warwickshire, twenty-five miles from Worcester, and there lay disguised awhile, and afterwards went up and down in great danger of being discovered, till at last he got over into France, from Bright-Hempsted in Sussex.

B. When Cromwell was gone, what was further done in Scotland?

A. Lieutenant-General Monk,[19] whom Cromwell left there with 7,000, took Stirling August 14th by surrender, and Dundee the 3rd of September, by

19 George Monck, 1st Duke of Albemarle (1608 – 1670). —Ed.

storm, because it resisted. This the soldiers plundered, and had good booty, because the Scots for safety had sent thither their most precious goods from Edinburgh and St. Johnstone's. He took likewise by surrender Aberdeen and (the place where the Scottish ministers first learned to play the fools) St. Andrew's. Also in the Highlands, Colonel Alured[20] took a knot of lords and gentlemen, *viz.*, four earls and four lords and above twenty knights and gentlemen, whom he sent prisoners into England. So that there was nothing more to be feared from Scotland: all the trouble of the Rump being to resolve what they should do with it. At last they resolved to unite and incorporate it into one commonwealth with England and Ireland. And to that end sent thither St. Johns,[21] Vane,[22] and other commissioners, to offer them this union by public declaration, and to warn them to choose their deputies of shires and burgesses of towns, and send them to Westminster.

B. This was a very great favour.

A. I think so: and yet it was by many of the Scots, especially by the ministers and other Presbyterians, refused. The ministers had given way to the levying of money for the payment of the English soldiers; but to comply with the declaration of the English commissioners they absolutely forbad.

B. Methinks, this contributing to the pay of their

20 John Alured (1607 – 1651). —Ed.

21 Sir Oliver St John (c. 1598 – 1673). —Ed.

22 Sir Henry Vane the Younger (1613 – 1662). —Ed.

conquerors was some mark of servitude; whereas entering into the union made them free, and gave them equal privilege with the English.

A. The cause why they refused the union, rendered by the Presbyterian *ministers* themselves, was this: that it drew with it a subordination of the Church to the civil state in the things of Christ.

B. This is a downright declaration to all kings and commonwealths in general: that a Presbyterian minister will be a true subject to none of them in the things of Christ; which things what they are, they will be judges themselves. What have we then gotten by our deliverance from the Pope's tyranny, if these petty men succeed in the place of it, that have nothing in them that can be beneficial to the public, except their silence? For their learning, it amounts to no more than an imperfect knowledge of Greek and Latin, and an acquired readiness in the Scripture language, with a gesture and tone suitable thereunto; but of justice and charity (the marrow of religion)[23] they have neither knowledge nor practice, as is manifest by the stories I have already told you. Nor do they distinguish between the godly and the ungodly but by conformity of design in men of judgment, or by repetition of their sermons in the common sort of people.

A. But this sullenness of the Scots was to no purpose. For they at Westminster enacted the union of the two nations and the abolition of monarchy in Scotland, and ordained punishment for those

23 and charity, the manners of religion.

that should transgress that act.

B. What other business did the Rump this year?

A. They sent St. Johns and Strickland[24] ambassadors to the Hague, to offer to the United Provinces; who had audience March the 3rd; St. Johns in a speech showed those states what advantage they might have by this league in their trade and navigations, by the use of the English ports and harbours. The Dutch, though they showed no great forwardness in the business, yet appointed commissioners to treat with them about it. But the people were generally against it, calling the ambassadors and their followers (as they were) traitors and murderers, and made such tumults about their house that their followers durst not go abroad till the States had quieted them. The Rump advertised hereof, presently recalled them. The compliment which St. Johns gave to the commissioners at their taking leave, is worth your hearing. You have, said he, an eye upon the event of the affairs of Scotland, and therefore do refuse the friendship we have offered. Now I can assure you, many in the Parliament were of opinion that we should not have sent any ambassadors to you till we had separated those matters between them and that king, and then expected your ambassadors to us. I now perceive our error, and that those gentlemen were in the right. In a short time you shall see that business ended; and then you will come and seek what we have freely offered, when it shall perplex you

24 Walter Strickland (1598? – 1671). —Ed.

that you have refused our proffer.

B. St. Johns was not sure that the Scottish business would end as it did. For though the Scots were beaten at Dunbar, he could not be sure of the event of their entering England, which happened afterward.

A. But he guessed well: for within a month after the battle at Worcester, an act passed forbidding the importing of merchandize in other than English ships. The English also molested their fishing upon our coast. They also many times searched their ships (upon occasion of our war with France), and made some of them prize. And then the Dutch sent their ambassadors hither to desire what they before refused; but partly also to inform themselves what naval forces the English had ready, and how the people here were contented with the government.

B. How sped they?

A. The Rump showed now as little desire of agreement as the Dutch did then; standing upon terms never likely to be granted. First, for the fishing on the English coast, that they should not have it without paying for it. Secondly, that the English should have free trade from Middleburgh to Antwerp, as they had before their rebellion against the King of Spain. Thirdly, they demanded amends for the old (but never to be forgotten) business of Amboyna. So that the war was already certain, though the season kept them from action till the spring following. The true quarrel, on the

English part, was that their proffered friendship was scorned, and their ambassadors affronted; on the Dutch part, was the greediness to engross all traffic, and a false estimate of our and their own strength.

Whilst these things were doing, the relics of the war, both in Ireland and Scotland, were not neglected, though those nations were not fully pacified till two years after. The persecution also of royalists was continued, amongst whom was beheaded one Mr. Love,[25] for holding correspondence with the King.

B. I had thought a Presbyterian minister, whilst he was such, could not be a royalist, because they think their assembly have the supreme power in the things of Christ; and by consequence they are in England (by a statute) traitors.

A. You may think so still: for though I called Mr. Love a royalist, I meant it only for that one act for which he was condemned. It was he who during the treaty at Uxbridge, preaching before the commissioners there, said: it was as possible for heaven and hell, as for the King and Parliament, to agree. Both he and the rest of the Presbyterians are and were enemies to the King's enemies, Cromwell and his fanatics, for their own, not for the King's sake. Their loyalty was like that of Sir John Hotham's, that kept the King out of Hull, and afterwards would have betrayed the same to the Marquis of Newcastle. These Presbyterians therefore cannot be rightly called loy-

25 Christopher Love (1618 – 1651). —Ed.

al, but rather doubly perfidious, unless you think that as two negatives make an affirmative, so two treasons make loyalty.

This year also were reduced to the obedience of the Rump the islands of Scilly and Man, and the Barbadoes, and St. Christopher's. One thing fell out that they liked not, which was, that Cromwell gave them warning to determine their sitting, according to the bill for triennial Parliaments.

B. That I think indeed was harsh.

A. In the year 1652, May the 14th, began the Dutch war, in this manner. Three Dutch men-of-war, with divers merchants from the straights, being discovered by one Captain Young,[26] who commanded some English frigates, the said Young sent to their admiral to bid him strike his flag (a thing usually done in acknowledgment of the English dominion in the narrow seas); which accordingly he did. Then came up the vice-admiral, and being called to (as the other was) to take down his flag, he answered plainly he would not: but after the exchange of four or five broadsides, and mischief done on either part, he took it down. But Captain Young demanded also, either the vice-admiral himself, or his ship, to make good the damage already sustained; to which the vice-admiral answered that he had taken in his flag, but would defend himself and his ship. Whereupon Captain Young consulting with the captains of his other ships, lest the beginning of the war in this time of

26 Anthony Young. —Ed.

treaty should be charged upon himself, and night also coming on, thought fit to proceed no further.

B. The war certainly began at this time. But who began it?

A. The dominion of the seas belonging to the English, there can be no question but the Dutch began it: and that the said dominion belonged to the English, it was confessed, at first by the admiral himself peaceably, and at last by the vice-admiral, taking in their flags.

About a fortnight after there happened another fight, upon the like occasion. Van Tromp,[27] with forty-two men-of-war, came to the back of Goodwin Sands (Major Bourne[28] being then with a few of the Parliaments ships in the Downs, and Blake[29] with the rest further westward), and sent two captains of his to Bourne, to excuse his coming thither. To whom Bourne returned this answer, that the message was civil, but that it might appear real, he ought to depart. So Tromp departed, meaning (now Bourne was satisfied) to sail towards Blake, and he did so; but so did also Bourne, for fear of the worst. When Tromp and Blake were near one another, Blake made a shot over Tromp's ship, as a warning to him to take in his flag. This he did

27 Marten van Tromp (1598 – 1653), Lieutenant-Admiral and *de facto* supreme commander of the Dutch navy. —Ed.

28 Nehemiah Bourne (c.1611 – 1690). —Ed.

29 By this time, Blake had been appointed General at Sea, a rank that combined the roles of Admiral and Commissioner of the Navy. Admiral was not used in the Parliamentary navy. —Ed.

thrice, and then Tromp gave him a broadside; and so began the fight (at the beginning whereof Bourne came in), and lasted from two o'clock till night, the English having the better, and the flag, as before, making the quarrel.

B. What needs there, when both nations were heartily resolved to fight, to stand so much upon this compliment of who should begin? For as to the gaining of friends and confederates thereby, I think it was in vain; seeing princes and states in such occasions look not much upon the justice of their neighbours, but upon their own concernment in the event.

A. It is commonly so; but in this case, the Dutch knowing the dominion of the narrow seas to be a gallant title, and envied by all the nations that reach the shore, and consequently that they were likely to oppose it, did wisely enough in making this point the state of the quarrel.—After this fight the Dutch ambassadors residing in England sent a paper to the council of state, wherein they styled this last encounter *a rash action*, and affirmed it was done without the knowledge and against the will of their lords the States-general, and desired them that nothing might be done upon it in heat, which might become irreparable. The Parliament hereupon voted: 1. That the States-general should pay the charges they were at, and for the damages they sustained upon this occasion. 2. That this being paid, there should be a cessation of all acts of hostility, and a mutual restitution of all ships and goods taken. 3. And both these agreed to, that there should be made a league between the two commonwealths. These votes were sent to the Dutch ambassadors in answer of their said paper; but with a preamble setting forth the former kindnesses of England to the Netherlands, and taking notice of their new fleet of 150 men-of-war, without any other apparent design than the destruction of the English fleet.

B. What answer made the Dutch to this?

A. None. Tromp sailed presently to Zealand, and Blake with seventy men-of-war to the Orkney Islands, to seize their busses, and to wait for five Dutch ships from the East Indies. And Sir George Askew,[30] newly returned from the Barbadoes, came into the Downs with fifteen men-of-war, where he was commanded to stay for a recruit out of the Thames.

Van Tromp being recruited now to 120 sail, made account to get in between Sir George Askew and the mouth of the river, but was hindered so long by contrary winds, that the merchants calling for his convoy he could stay no longer; and so he went back into Holland, and thence to Orkney, where he met with the said five East India ships and sent them home. And then he endeavoured to engage with Blake, but a sudden storm forced him to sea, and so dissipated his fleet that only forty-two came home in body, the rest singly as well as they could. Blake also came home, but went first

30 Sir George Ayescue (1616 – 1671). —Ed.

to the coast of Holland with 900 prisoners and six men-of-war taken, which were part of twelve which he found and took guarding their busses. This was the first bout after the war declared.

In August following there happened a fight between De Ruyter,[31] the admiral of Zealand with fifty men-of-war, and Sir George Askew, near Plymouth, with forty, wherein Sir George had the better, and might have got an entire victory had the whole fleet engaged. Whatsoever was the matter, the Rump (though they rewarded him), never more employed him after his return in their service at sea: but voted for the year to come three generals, Blake that was one already, and Dean, and Monk.

About this time the Archduke Leopold[32] besieging Dunkirk, and the French sending a fleet to relieve it, General Blake lighting on the French at Calais, and taking seven of their ships, was cause of the town's surrender.

In September they fought again, De Witt and De Ruyter commanding the Dutch, and Blake the English; and the Dutch were again worsted.

Again, in the end of November, Van Tromp with eighty men-of-war showed himself at the back of Goodwin Sands; where Blake, though he had with him but forty, adventured to fight with him, and had much the worst, and (night parting the fray) retired into the river of Thames; whilst Van Tromp

31 Michiel Adriaenszoon de Ruyter (1607 – 1676). —Ed.

32 Archduke Leopold Wilhelm of Austria (1614 – 1662), the Governor of the Spanish Netherlands from 1647 to 1656. —Ed.

keeping the sea, took some inconsiderable vessels from the English, and thereupon (as it was said) with a childish vanity hung out a broom from his main-top-mast, signifying he meant to sweep the seas of all English shipping.

After this, in February, the Dutch with Van Tromp were encountered by the English under Blake and Dean near Portsmouth, and had the worst. And these were all the encounters between them in this year in the narrow seas. They fought also once at Leghorn, where the Dutch had the better.

B. I see no great odds yet on either side; if there were any, the English had it.

A. Nor did either of them ere the more incline to peace. For the Hollanders, after they had sent ambassadors into Denmark, Sweden, Poland, and the Hanse Towns (whence tar and cordage are usually had), to signify the declaration of the war, and to get them to their party, recalled their ambassadors from England. And the Rump without delay gave them their parting audience, without abating a syllable of their former severe propositions; and presently, to maintain the war for the next year, laid a tax upon the people of 120,000*l. per mensem.*

B. What was done in the mean time at home?

A. Cromwell was now quarrelling (the last and greatest obstacle to his design) the Rump. And to that end there came out daily from the army petitions, addresses, remonstrances, and other such papers; some of them urging the Rump to dissolve themselves and make way for another Parliament.

To which the Rump, unwilling to yield and not daring to refuse, determined for the end of their sitting the 5th of November 1654. But Cromwell meant not to stay so long.

In the meantime the army in Ireland was taking submissions, and granting transportations of the Irish, and condemning whom they pleased in a High Court of Justice erected there for that purpose. Amongst those that were executed, was hanged Sir Phelim O'Neale, who first began the rebellion. In Scotland the English built some citadels for the bridling that stubborn nation. And thus ended the year 1652.[33]

B. Come we then to the year 1653.

A. Cromwell wanted now but one step to the end of his ambition, and that was to set his foot upon the neck of this Long Parliament; which he did April the 23rd of this present year 1653, a time very seasonable. For though the Dutch were not mastered yet, they were much weakened; and what with prizes from the enemy and squeezing the royal party, the treasury was pretty full, and the tax of 120,000*l*. a month began *now* to come in; all which was his own in right of the army.

Therefore, without more ado, attended by the Major-Generals Lambert and Harrison, and some other officers, and as many soldiers as he thought fit, he went to the Parliament House, and dissolved them, turning them out, and locked up the doors. And for this action he was more applauded by the

33 Sir Phelim MacShane O'Neill was executed in August 1653. —Ed.

people than for any of his victories in the war, and the Parliament men as much scorned and derided.

B. Now that there was no Parliament, who had the supreme power?

A. If by power you mean the right to govern, nobody *here* had it. If you mean the supreme strength, it was clearly in Cromwell, who was obeyed as general of all the forces in England, Scotland, and Ireland.

B. Did he pretend that for title?

A. No: but presently after he invented a title, which was this: that he was necessitated for the defence of the cause, for which at first the Parliament had taken up arms (that is to say, rebelled), to have recourse to extraordinary actions. You know the pretence of the Long Parliament's rebellion was *salus populi*, the safety of the nation against a dangerous conspiracy of Papists and a malignant party at home; and that every man is bound, as far as his power extends, to procure the safety of the whole nation (which none but the army were able to do, and the Parliament had hitherto neglected); was it not then the general's duty to do it? Had he not therefore right? For that law of *salus populi* is directed only to those that have power enough to defend the people; that is, to them that have the supreme power.

B. Yes, certainly, he had as good a title as the Long Parliament. But the Long Parliament did represent the people; and it seems to me that the sovereign power is essentially annexed to the representative of the people.

A. Yes, if he that makes a representative, that is (in the present case) the King, do call them together to receive the sovereign power, and he divest himself thereof; otherwise not. Nor was ever the Lower House of Parliament the representative of the whole nation, but of the commons only; nor had that House the power to oblige, by their acts or ordinances, any lord or any priest.

B. Did Cromwell come in upon the only title of *salus populi*?

A. No. For this is a title that very few men understand. His way was to get the supreme power conferred upon him by Parliament. Therefore he called a Parliament, and gave it the supreme power, with condition that they should give it to him.[34] Was not this witty? First, therefore, he published a declaration of the causes why he dissolved the Parliament. The sum whereof was: that instead of endeavouring to promote the good of God's people, they endeavoured, by a bill then ready to pass, to recruit the House and perpetuate their own power. Next he constituted a council of state of his own creatures, to be the supreme authority of England; but no longer than till the next Parliament should be called and met. Thirdly, he summoned 142 persons, such as he himself or his trusty officers made choice of; the greatest part of whom were instructed what to do; obscure persons, and most of them fanatics, though styled by Cromwell men of ap-

34 power, to the end . . . to him again.

proved fidelity and honesty. To these the council of state surrendered the supreme authority, and not long after these men surrendered it to Cromwell. July the 4th this Parliament met, and chose for their Speaker one Mr. Rous,[35] and called themselves from that time forward the Parliament of England. But Cromwell, for the more surety, constituted also a council of state: not of such petty fellows as most of these were, but of himself and his principal officers. These did all the business, both public and private; making ordinances, and giving audiences to foreign ambassadors. But he had now more enemies than before. Harrison, who was the head of the Fifth-monarchy-men, laying down his commission, did nothing but animate his party against him; for which afterwards he was imprisoned. This little Parliament in the meantime were making of acts so ridiculous and displeasing to the people, that it was thought he chose them on purpose to bring all ruling Parliaments into contempt, and monarchy again into credit.

B. What acts were those?

A. One of them was, that all marriages should be made by a justice of peace, and the banns asked three several days in the next market: none were forbidden to be married by a minister, but with-

35 Francis Rous (1579 – 1659), a leading Puritan, then elected for Devon. He had opened the debate on the legality of William Laud's new canons in 1640, presented articles of impeachment for John Cousins in 1641, and taken the Solemn League and Covenant in 1643. —Ed.

out a justice of peace the marriage was to be void: so that divers wary couples (to be sure of one another, howsoever they might repent it afterwards) were married both ways. Also they abrogated the engagement, whereby no man was admitted to sue in any court of law that had not taken it, that is, that had not acknowledged the late Rump.

B. Neither of these did any hurt to Cromwell.

A. They were also in hand with an act to cancel all the present laws and law-books, and to make a new code more suitable to the humour of the Fifth-monarchy-men; of whom there were many in this Parliament. Their tenet being, that there ought none to be sovereign but King Jesus, nor any to govern under him but the saints. But their authority ended before the act passed.

B. What was this to Cromwell?

A. Nothing yet. But they were likewise upon an act, now almost ready for the question, that Parliaments henceforward, one upon the end of another, should be perpetual.

B. I understand not this; unless Parliaments can beget one another like animals, or like the phœnix.

A. Why not like the phœnix? Cannot a Parliament at the day of their expiration send out writs for a new one?

B. Do you think they would not rather summon themselves anew; and to save the labour of coming again to Westminster, sit still where they were? Or if they summon the country to make new elections, and then dissolve themselves, by what authority shall the people meet in their county courts, there being no supreme authority standing?

A. All they did was absurd, though they knew not that; no nor *that this would offend Cromwell,* whose design upon the sovereignty[36] the contriver of this act (it seems) perceived not, but Cromwell's party in the House saw it well enough. And therefore (as it was laid) there stood up one of the members and made a motion, that since the commonwealth was like to receive little benefit by their sitting, they should dissolve themselves. Harrison and they of his sect were troubled hereat, and made speeches against it; but Cromwell's party, of whom the speaker was one, left the House, and with the mace before them went to Whitehall, and surrendered their power to Cromwell that had given it to them. And so he got the sovereignty by an act of Parliament; and within four days after, December the 16th, was installed Protector of the three nations, and took his oath to observe certain rules of governing, engrossed in parchment and read before him. This writing was called the instrument.

B. What were the rules which he swore to?

A. One was, to call a Parliament every third year, of which the first was to begin September the 3rd following.

B. I believe he was a little superstitious in the choice of September the 3rd, because it was lucky to him in 1650 and 1651, at Dunbar and Worcester.

A. But he knew not how lucky the same would

---

36 No, nor this, whose design was upon the sovereignty.

be to the whole nation in 1658 at Whitehall.

Another was, that no Parliament should be dissolved till it had sitten five months; and that those bills which they presented to him, should be passed by him within twenty days, or else they should pass without him.

A third, that he should have a council of state of not above twenty-one, nor under thirteen; and that upon the Protector's death this council should meet, and before they parted choose a new Protector. There were many more besides, but not necessary to be inserted.

B. How went on the war against the Dutch?

A. The generals for the English were Blake, and Dean, and Monk; and Van Tromp for the Dutch; between whom was a battle fought the 2nd of June (which was a month before the beginning of this little Parliament), wherein the English had the victory, and drove the enemies into their harbours, but with the loss of General Dean, slain by a cannon-shot. This victory was great enough to make the Dutch send over ambassadors into England, in order to a treaty; but in the meantime they prepared and put to sea another fleet, which likewise, in the end of July, was defeated by General Monk, who got now a greater victory than before; and this made the Dutch descend so far as to buy their peace with the payment of the charge of the war, and with the acknowledgment, amongst other articles, that the English had the right of the flag.

This peace was concluded in March, being the

end of this year, but not proclaimed till April; the money, it seems, being not paid till then.

The Dutch war being now ended, the Protector sent his youngest son Henry into Ireland, whom also some time after he made lieutenant there; and sent Monk lieutenant-general into Scotland, to keep those nations in obedience. Nothing else worth remembering was done this year at home; saving the discovery of a plot of royalists, as was said, upon the life of the Protector, who all this while had intelligence of the King's designs from a traitor in his court, who afterwards was taken in the manner and killed.

B. How came he into so much trust with the King?

A. He was the son of a colonel that was slain in the wars on the late King's side. Besides, he pretended employment from the King's loyal and loving subjects here, to convey to his Majesty such moneys as they from time to time should send him; and to make this credible, Cromwell himself caused money to be sent him.

The following year, 1654, had nothing *in it* of war, but was spent in civil ordinances, in appointing of judges, preventing of plots (for usurpers are jealous), and in executing the King's friends and selling their lands. The 3rd of September, according to the instrument, the Parliament met; in which there was no House of Lords, and the House of Commons was made, as formerly, of knights and burgesses; but not as formerly, of two burgesses for a borough and two knights for a county; for boroughs for the most part had but one burgess, and some counties six or seven knights. Besides, there were twenty members for Scotland, and as many for Ireland. So that Cromwell had now nothing else to do but to show his art of government upon six coach-horses newly presented him, which, being as rebellious as himself, threw him out of the coach-box and almost killed him.

B. This Parliament, which had seen how Cromwell had handled the two former, the long one and the short one, had surely learned the wit to behave themselves better to him than those had done?

A. Yes, especially now that Cromwell in his speech at their first meeting had expressly forbidden them to meddle either with the government by a single person and Parliament, or with the *militia*, or with perpetuating of Parliaments, or taking away liberty of conscience; and told them also that every member of the House, before they sat, must take a recognition of his power in divers points. Whereupon, of above 400 there appeared not above 200 at first; though afterwards (some relenting) there sat above 300. Again, just at their sitting down he published some ordinances of his own, bearing date before their meeting; that they might see he took his own acts to be as valid as theirs. But all this could not make them know themselves. They proceeded to the debate of every article of the recognition.

B. They should have debated that before they had taken it.

A. But then they had never been suffered to sit. Cromwell being informed of their stubborn proceedings, and out of hope of any supply from them, dissolved them.

All that passed besides in this year was the exercise of the High Court of Justice upon some royalists for plots.

In the year 1655 the English, to the number of near 10,000, landed in Hispaniola, in hope of the plunder of the gold and silver, whereof they thought there was great abundance in the town of Santo Domingo; but were well beaten by a few Spaniards, and with the loss of near 1,000 men, went off to Jamaica and possessed it.

This year also the royal party made another attempt in the west; and proclaimed there King Charles the Second; but few joining with them, and some falling off, they were soon suppressed, and many of the principal persons executed.

B. In these many insurrections, the royalists, though they meant well, yet they did but disservice to the King by their impatience. What hope had they to prevail against so great an army as the Protector had ready? What cause was there to despair of seeing the King's business done better by the dissension and ambition of the great commanders in that army, whereof many had the favour to be as well esteemed amongst them as Cromwell himself?

A. That was somewhat uncertain. The Protector, being frustrated of his hope of money at Santo Domingo, resolved to take from the royalists the tenth part yearly of their estates. And to this end chiefly, he divided England into eleven major-generalships, with commission to every major-general to make a roll of the names of all suspected persons of the King's party,[37] and of their estates within his precinct; as also to take caution from them, not to act against the state, and to reveal all plots that should come to their knowledge; and to make them engage the like for their servants. They had commission also to forbid horse-races and concourse of people, and to receive and account for *the money rising from* this decimation.

B. By this the usurper might easily inform himself of the value of all the estates in England, and of the behaviour and affection of every person of quality; which has heretofore been taken for very great tyranny.

A. The year 1656 was a Parliament-year by the instrument. Between the beginning of this year and the day of the Parliament's sitting, which was September 17, these major-generals, resided in several provinces, behaving themselves most tyrannically. Amongst other of their tyrannies was the awing of elections, and making themselves and whom they pleased to be returned members for the Parliament; which was also thought a part of Cromwell's design in their constitution: for he had need of a giving Parliament, having lately, upon a peace made with the French, drawn upon himself

37 party, and to receive the tenth part of.

a war with Spain.

This year it was that Captain Stainer[38] set upon the Spanish Plate-fleet, being eight in number, near Cadiz; whereof he sunk two, and took two, there being in one of them two millions of pieces of eight, which amounts to 400,000*l.* sterling.

This year also it was that James Naylor[39] appeared at Bristol, and would be taken for Jesus Christ. He wore his beard forked, and his hair composed to the likeness of that in the Volto Santo; and being questioned, would sometimes answer, Thou sayest it. He had also his disciples, that would go by his horse side, to the mid-leg in dirt. Being sent for by the Parliament he was sentenced to stand on the pillory, to have his tongue bored through, and to be marked on the forehead with the letter B, for blasphemy, and to remain in Bridewell. Lambert, a great favourite of the army, endeavoured to save him, partly because he had been his soldier, and partly to curry favour with the sectaries of the army; for he was now no more in the Protector's favour, but meditating how he might succeed him in his power.

About two years before this, there appeared

---

38 Sir Richard Stayner (1625 – 1662). —Ed.

39 James Naylor (1616 – 1660), originally from Yorkshire, had joined the Parliamentary army in 1642 and served, until 1650, as quartermaster under John Lambert. He had later had a religious experience and, after meeting George Fox, the Quaker leader, he had joined the movement, becoming one of the most prominent ambulant Quaker evangelist known as the Valiant Sixty, preaching against enclosure and the slave trade. —Ed.

in Cornwall a prophetess, much famed for her dreams and visions, and hearkened to by many, whereof some were eminent officers. But she and some of her accomplices being imprisoned, we heard no more of her.

B. I have heard of another, one Lilly,[40] that prophesied all the time of the Long Parliament. What did they to him?

A. His prophecies were of another kind; he was a writer of almanacs, and a pretender to a pretended art of judicial astrology; a mere cozener, to get maintenance from a multitude of ignorant people; and no doubt had been called in question, if his prophecies had been any way disadvantageous to that Parliament.

B. I understand not how the dreams and prognostications of madmen (for such I take to be all those that foretell future contingencies) can be of any great disadvantage to the commonwealth.

A. Yes. You know[41] there is nothing that renders human counsels difficult, but the uncertainty of future time; nor that so well directs men in their deliberations, as the foresight of the sequels of their actions; prophecy being many times the principal cause of the event foretold. If, upon some prediction, the people should have been made confident that Oliver Cromwell and his army should be, upon a day to come, utterly defeated; would not every one have endeavoured to assist, and to deserve well

40 William Lilly (1602 – 1681). —Ed.

41 Yes, yes: know.

of the party that should give him that defeat? Upon this account it was that fortune-tellers and astrologers were so often banished out of Rome.

The last memorable thing this year, was a motion made by a member of the House, an alderman of London, that the Protector might be petitioned and advised by the House to leave the title of Protector, and take upon him that of King.

B. That was indeed a bold motion, and which would, if prosperous, have put an end to *a great* many men's ambition, and to the licentiousness of the whole army. I think the motion was made on purpose to ruin both the Protector himself and his ambitious officers.

A. It may be so. In the year 1657 the first thing the Parliament did, was the drawing up of this petition to the Protector, to take upon him the government of the three nations, with the title of King. As of other former Parliaments, so of this, the greatest part had been either kept out of the House by force, or else themselves had forborne to sit and become guilty of setting up this King Oer. But those few that sat, presented their petition to the Protector, April the 9th, in the Banqueting-house at Whitehall; where Sir Thomas Widdrington,[42] the Speaker, used the first arguments, and the Protec-

42 A barrister by profession, Sir Thomas Widdrington SL (d. 1664), had been chosen as Speaker in September 1656. He'd represented Berwick in Parliament in 1640 and was chosen a member of the Council of State in 1651. In 1656 he was representing the constituency of Northumberland. —Ed.

tor desired some time to seek God, the business being weighty. The next day they sent a committee to him to receive his answer; which answer being not very clear, they pressed him again for a resolution; to which he made answer in a long speech, that ended in a peremptory refusal. And so retaining still the title of Protector, he took upon him the government according to certain articles contained in the said petition.

B. What made him refuse the title of King?

A. Because he durst not take it at that time; the army being addicted to their great officers, and amongst their great officers many hoping to succeed him, and, the succession having been promised to Major-General Lambert, would have mutinied against him. He was therefore forced to stay for a more propitious conjuncture.

B. What were those articles?

A. The most important of them were: 1. That he would exercise the office of chief-magistrate of England, Scotland, and Ireland, under the title of Protector, and govern the same according to the said petition and advice: and that he would in his life-time name his successor.

B. I believe the Scots, when they first rebelled, never thought of being governed absolutely, as they were by Oliver Cromwell.

A. 2. That he should call a Parliament every three years at farthest. 3. That those persons which were legally chosen members, should not be secluded without consent of the House. In allowing this clause, the Protector observed not that the secluded members of this same Parliament, are thereby re-admitted. 4. The members were qualified. 5. The power of the Other House was defined. 6. That no law should be made but by Act of Parliament. 7. That a constant yearly revenue of a million of pounds should be settled for the maintenance of the army and navy; and 300,000*l.* for the support of the government, besides other temporary supplies as the House of Commons should think fit. 8. That all the officers of state should be chosen by the Parliament. 9. That the Protector should encourage the ministry. Lastly, that he should cause a profession of religion to be agreed on and published. There are divers others of less importance. Having signed the articles, he was presently with great ceremony installed anew.

B. What needed that, seeing he was still but Protector?

A. But the articles of this petition were not all the same with those of his former instrument. For now there was to be another House; and whereas before, his council was to name his successor, he had power now to do it himself; so that he was an absolute monarch, and might leave the succession to his son if he would, and so successively, or transfer it to whom he pleased.

The ceremony being ended, the Parliament adjourned to the 20th of January following; and then the Other House also sat; *and the secluded members according to an article of the petition sat* with their fellows.

The House of Commons being now full, took little notice of the Other House, wherein there were not of sixty persons above nine lords; but fell a questioning all that their fellows had done, during the time of their seclusion; whence had followed the avoidance of the power newly placed in the Protector. Therefore, going to the House, he made a speech to them, ending in these words: By the living God, I must, and do dissolve you.

In this year, the English gave the Spaniard another great blow at Santa Cruz, not much less than that they had given him the year before in the bay of Cadiz.

About the time of the dissolving of this Parliament, the royalists had another design against the Protector; which was, to make an insurrection in England, the King being *then* in Flanders ready to second them with an army thence. But this also was discovered by treachery, and came to nothing but the ruin of those who were engaged in it; whereof many in the beginning of the next year were by a High Court of Justice imprisoned, and some executed.

This year also was Major-General Lambert put out of all employment, a man second to none but Oliver in the favour of the army. But because he expected by that favour, or by promise from the Protector, to be his successor in the supreme power, it would have been dangerous to let him have command in the army; the Protector having designed for his successor his eldest son Richard.

In the year 1658, September the 3rd, the Protector died at Whitehall; having ever since his last establishment been perplexed with fears of being killed by some desperate attempt of the royalists.

Being importuned in his sickness by his privy-council to name his successor, he named his son Richard; who, encouraged thereunto, not by his own ambition, but by Fleetwood,[43] Desborough,[44] Thurlow,[45] and other of his council, was content to take it upon him; and presently addresses were made to him from the armies in England, Scotland, and Ireland. His first business was the chargeable and splendid funeral of his father.

Thus was Richard Cromwell seated on the imperial throne of England, Ireland, and Scotland, successor to his father; lifted up to it by the officers of the army then in town, and congratulated by all the parts of the army throughout the three nations; scarce any garrison omitting their particular flattering addresses to him.

B. Seeing the army approved of him, how came

---

43 Charles Fleetwood (c. 1618 – 1692), who had been until 1655 Lord Deputy of Ireland. —Ed.

44 John Desborough (1608 – 1680) had been made a member of the Protector's Privy Council the year prior and accepted in 1658, a seat in Cromwell's Other House (the Upper House), established, under the terms of the Humble Petition and Advice, to serve as a bulwark against the Lower House, which, during the Naylor case, which was also during the Rule of the Major-Generals, had proven difficult to control. —Ed.

45 John Thurloe (1616 – 1668), then Postmaster General. —Ed.

he so soon cast off?

A. The army was inconstant; he himself irresolute, and without any military glory. And though the two principal officers had a near relation to him; yet neither of them, but Lambert, was the great favourite of the army; and by courting Fleetwood to take upon him the Protectorship, and by tampering with the soldiers, had gotten again to be a colonel. He and the rest of the officers had a council at Wallingford House (where Fleetwood dwelt) for the dispossessing of Richard; though they had not yet considered how the nations should be governed afterwards. For from the beginning of the rebellion, the method of ambition was constantly this: first to destroy, and then to consider what they should set up.

B. Could not the Protector, who kept his court at Whitehall, discover what the business of the officers was at Wallingford House, so near him?

A. Yes, he was by divers of his friends informed of it; and counselled by some of them, who would have done it, to kill the chief of them; but he had not courage enough to give them such a commission. He took, therefore, the counsel of some milder persons, which was to call a Parliament. Whereupon writs were presently sent to those, that in the last Parliament were the Other House, and other writs to the sheriffs for the election of knights and burgesses, to assemble on the 27th of January following. Elections were made according to the ancient manner, and a House of Commons now of the right English temper, and about four hundred in number, including twenty for Scotland, and as many for Ireland. Being met, they take themselves, without the Protector and Other House, to be a Parlialiament, and to have the supreme power of the three nations.

For their first business, they intended *to question* the power of that Other House: but because the Protector had recommended to them for their first business an act (already drawn up) for the recognition of his Protectoral power, they began with that; and voted (after a fortnight's deliberation) that an act should be made whereof this act of recognition should be part; and that another part should be for the bounding of the Protector's power, and for the securing the privileges of Parliament and liberties of the subject; and that all should pass together.

B. Why did these men obey the Protector at first, in meeting upon his only summons? Was not that as full a recognition of his power as was needful? Why by this example did they teach the people that he was to be obeyed, and then by putting laws upon him, teach them the contrary? Was it not the Protector that made the Parliament? Why did they not acknowledge their maker?

A. I believe it is the desire of most men to bear rule; but few of them know what title one has to it more than another, besides the right of the sword.

B. If they acknowledged the right of the sword, they were neither just nor wise to oppose the present government, set up and approved by all the forces of the three kingdoms. The principles of this House of Commons were, no doubt, the very same with theirs who began the rebellion; and would, if they could have raised a sufficient army, have done the same against the Protector; and the general of their army would, in like manner, have reduced them to a Rump. For they that keep an army, and cannot master it, must be subject to it as much as he that keeps a lion in his house. The temper of all the Parliaments, since the time of Queen Elizabeth, has been the same with the temper of this Parliament; and shall always be such, as long as the Presbyterians and men of democratical principles have the like influence upon the elections.

A. After *this* they resolved concerning the Other House, that during this Parliament they would transact with it, but without intrenching upon the right of the peers, to have writs sent to them in all future Parliaments. These votes being passed, they proceed to another, wherein they assume to themselves the power of the *militia*. Also to show their supreme power, they delivered out of prison some of those that had been (they said) illegally committed by the former Protector. Other points concerning civil rights and concerning religion, very pleasing to the people, were now also under their consideration. So that in the end of this year the Protector was no less jealous of the Parliament, than of the council of officers at Wallingford House.

B. Thus it is when ignorant men will undertake reformation. Here are three parties, the Protector, the Parliament, and the Army. The Protector against Parliament and army, the Parliament against army and Protector, and the army against Protector and Parliament.

A. In the beginning of 1659 the Parliament passed divers other acts. One was, to forbid the meetings in council of the army-officers without order from the Protector and both the Houses; another, that no man shall have any command or *place of* trust in the army, who did not first, under his hand, engage himself never to interrupt any of the members, but that they might freely meet and debate in the House. And to please the soldiers, they voted to take presently into consideration the means of paying them their arrears. But whilst they were considering this, the Protector (according to the first of those acts) forbad the meeting of officers at Wallingford House. This made the government, which by the disagreement of the Protector and army was already loose, to fall in pieces. For the officers from Wallingford House, with soldiers enough, came over to Whitehall, and brought with them a commission ready drawn (giving power to Desborough to dissolve the Parliament) for the Protector to sign; which also, his heart and his party failing him, he signed. The Parliament nevertheless continued sitting; but at the end of the week the House adjourned till the Monday after, being April the 25th. At their coming on Monday morning, they found the door of the House shut up, and the passages to it filled with soldiers, who plainly told them they must sit no longer. Richard's authority and business in town being thus at an end, he retired into the country; where within a few days (upon promise of the payment of his debts, which his father's funeral had made great) he signed a resignation of his Protectorship.

B. To whom?

A. To nobody. But after ten days' cessation of the sovereign power, some of the Rumpers that were in town, together with the old Speaker, Mr. William Lenthal,[46] resolved amongst themselves, and with Lambert, Hazlerig, and other officers, who were also Rumpers, in all forty-two, to go into the House; which they did, and were by the army declared to be the Parliament.

There were also in Westminster Hall at that time, about their private business, some few of those whom the army had secluded in 1648, and were called the secluded members. These knowing themselves to have been elected by the same authority, and to have the same right to sit, attempted to get into the House, but were kept out by the soldiers. The first vote of the Rump reseated was, *that such persons as, heretofore members of this Parliament, have not sitten in this Parliament, since the year* 1648, *shall not sit in this House*

46 William Lenthall (1591 – 1662) was Speaker of the House from 1640 until 1647; from 1647 until 1653; from 1654 until 1655; and finally from 1659 until 1660. —Ed.

till further order of the Parliament. And thus the Rump recovered their authority May the 7th 1659, which they lost in April 1653.

B. Seeing there had been so many shiftings of the supreme authority, I pray you, for memory's sake, repeat them briefly in times and order.

A. First, from 1640 to 1648, when the King was murdered, the sovereignty was disputed between King Charles I. and the Presbyterian Parliament. Secondly, from 1648 to 1653, the power was in that part of the Parliament which voted the trial of the King, and declared themselves, without King or House of Lords, to have the first and supreme authority of England and Ireland. For there were in the Long Parliament two factions, Presbyterian and Independent; the former whereof sought only the subjection of the King, not his destruction directly; the latter sought directly his destruction; and this part is it, which is called the Rump. Thirdly, from April the 20th to July the 4th, the supreme power was in the hands of a council of state constituted by Cromwell. Fourthly, from July the 4th to December the 12th of the same year, it was in the hands of men called unto it by Cromwell, whom he termed men of fidelity and integrity, and made them a Parliament; which was called, in contempt of one of the members, Barebone's Parliament. Fifthly, from December the 12th 1653 to September the 3rd 1658, it was in the hands of Oliver Cromwell, with the title of Protector. Sixthly, from September the 3rd 1658 to April the 25th

1659, Richard Cromwell had it as successor to his father. Seventhly, from April the 25th 1659 to May the 7th of the same year, it was nowhere. Eighthly, from May the 7th 1659, the Rump, which was turned out of doors in 1653, recovered it again; and shall lose it again to a committee of safety, and again recover it, and again lose it to the right owner.

B. By whom, and by what art, came the Rump to be turned out the second time?

A. One would think them safe enough. The army in Scotland, which when it was in London had helped Oliver to put down the Rump, submitted now, begged pardon, and promised obedience. The soldiers in town had their pay mended, and the commanders everywhere took the old engagement, whereby they had acknowledged their authority heretofore. They also received their commissions in the House itself from the speaker, who was generalissimo. Fleetwood was made lieutenant-general, with such and so many limitations as were thought necessary by the Rump, that remembered how they had been served by the general, Oliver. Also Henry Cromwell, lord-lieutenant of Ireland, having resigned his commission by command, returned into England.

But Lambert, to whom (as was said) Oliver had promised the succession, and who as well as the Rump knew the way to the Protectorship by Oliver's own footsteps, was resolved to proceed in it upon the first opportunity; which presented itself presently after. Besides some plots of royalists, whom after the old fashion they again persecuted, there was an insurrection made against them by Presbyterians in Cheshire, headed by Sir George Booth,[47] one of the secluded members. They were in number about 3,000, and their pretence was for a free Parliament. There was a great talk of another rising, or endeavour to rise, in Devonshire and Cornwall at the same time. To suppress Sir George Booth, the Rump sent down more than a sufficient army under Lambert; which quickly defeated the Cheshire party, and recovered Chester, Liverpool, and all the other places they had seized. Divers also of their commanders in and after the battle were taken prisoners, whereof Sir George Booth himself was one.

This exploit done, Lambert, before his return, caressed his soldiers with an entertainment at his own house in Yorkshire, and got their consent to a petition to be made to the House, that a general might be set up in the army; as being unfit that the army should be judged by any power extrinsic to itself.

B. I do not see that unfitness.

A. Nor I. But it was (as I have heard) an axiom of Sir Henry Vane's. But it so much displeased the

47 Although he sided with the Parlamentarians during the war, and held various offices during the Protectorate, including military commissioner for Cheshire and treasurer at war, George Booth, 1st Baron Delamer (1622 – 1684) had since come to be regarded by Royalists as a well-wisher to their cause, and had eventually become leader in an effort by new Royalists and Cavaliers to effect a Restoration. —Ed.

Rump, that they voted, that the having of more generals in the army than were already settled, was unnecessary, burthensome, and dangerous to the commonwealth.

B. This was not Oliver's method; for though this Cheshire victory had been as glorious as that of Oliver at Dunbar, yet it was not the victory that made Oliver general, but the resignation of Fairfax, and the proffer of it to Cromwell by the Parliament.

A. But Lambert thought so well of himself, as to expect it. Therefore, at his return to London, he and other of the officers assembling at Wallingford House, drew their petition into form, and called it a representation; wherein the chief point was to have a general, but many others of less importance were added; and this they represented to the House, October the 4th, by Major-General Desborough. And this so far forth awed them, as to teach them so much good manners as to promise to take it presently into debate. Which they did; and October the 12th, having recovered their spirits, voted: that the commissions of Lambert, Desborough, and others of the council at Wallingford House, should be void: item, that the army should be governed by a commission to Fleetwood, Monk, Hazlerig, Walton,[48] Morley,[49] and Overton, till February the 12th following. And to make this good against the force they expected from Lambert, they ordered Hazlerig and Morley to issue warrants to such officers as

48 Valentine Walton (1594 – 1661). —Ed.

49 Herbert Morley (c. 1616 – 1667). —Ed.

they could trust, to bring their soldiers next morning into Westminster; which was done somewhat too late. For Lambert had first brought his soldiers thither, and beset the House, and turned back the Speaker, which was then coming to it; but Hazlerig's forces marching about St. James's park-wall, came into St. Margaret's churchyard; and so both parties looked all day one upon another, like enemies, but offered not to fight: whereby the Rump was put out of possession of the House; and the officers continued their meeting as before, at Wallingford House.

There they chose from among themselves, with some few of the city, a committee, which they called the committee of safety, whereof the chief were Lambert and Vane; who, with the advice of a general council of officers, had power to call delinquents to trial, to suppress rebellions, to treat with foreign states, &c. You see now the Rump cut off, and the supreme power (which is charged with *salus populi*) transferred to a Council of Officers. And yet Lambert hopes for it in the end. But one of their limitations was, that they should within six weeks present to the army a new model of the government. If they had done so, do you think they would have preferred Lambert or any other to the supreme authority therein, rather than themselves?

B. I think not. When the Rump had put into commission, amongst a few others, for the government of the army, that is to say, for the government of the three nations, General Monk, already commander-in-chief of the army in Scotland, and that had done much greater things in this war than Lambert, how durst they leave him out of this committee of safety? Or how could Lambert think that General Monk would forgive it, and not endeavour to fasten the Rump again?

A. They thought not of him; his gallantry had been shown on remote stages, Ireland and Scotland. His ambition had not appeared here in their contentions for the government, but he had complied both with Richard and the Rump. After General Monk had signified by letter his dislike of the proceedings of Lambert and his fellows, they were much surprised, and began to think him more considerable than they had done; but it was too late.

B. Why? His army was very small for so great an enterprise.

A. The general knew very well his own and their forces, both what they were then, and how they might be augmented, and what generally city and country wished for, which was the restitution of the King: which to bring about, there needed no more but to come with his army (though not very great) to London; to the doing whereof, there was no obstacle but the army with Lambert. What could he do in this case? If he had declared presently for the King or for a free Parliament, all the armies in England would have joined against him, and assuming the title of a Parliament would have furnished themselves with money.

General Monk, after he had thus quarrelled by his letter with the Council of Officers, secured first those officers of his own army which were Anabaptists and therefore not to be trusted, and put others into their places; then drawing his forces together, marched to Berwick. Being there, he indicted a convention of the Scots, of whom he desired that they would take order for the security of that nation in his absence, and raise some maintenance for his army in their march. The convention promised for the security of the nation their best endeavour, and raised him a sum of money, not great, but enough for this purpose, excusing themselves upon their present wants. On the other side, the committee of safety with the greatest and best part of their army sent Lambert to oppose him; but at the same time, by divers messages and mediators urged him to a treaty; which he consented to, and sent three officers to London to treat with as many of theirs. These six suddenly concluded (without power from the general) upon these articles: that the King be excluded; a free state settled; the ministry and universities encouraged; with divers others. Which the general liked not, and imprisoned one of his commissioners for exceeding his commission. Whereupon another treaty was agreed on, of five to five. But whilst these treaties were in hand, Hazlerig, a member of the Rump, seized on Portsmouth, and the soldiers sent by the committee of safety to reduce it, instead of that, entered into the town and joined with Hazlerig. Secondly, the city renewed their tumults for a free Parliament. Thirdly, the Lord Fairfax, a member also of the Rump, and greatly favoured in Yorkshire, was raising forces there behind Lambert, who being now between two armies, his enemies would gladly have fought with the general. Fourthly, there came news that Devonshire and Cornwall were listing of soldiers. Lastly, Lambert's army wanting money, and sure they should not be furnished from the Council of Officers, which had neither authority nor strength to levy money, grew discontented, and (for their free quarter) were odious to the northern countries.

B. I wonder why the Scots were so ready to furnish General Monk with money; for they were no friends to the Rump.

A. I know not; but I believe the Scots would have parted with a greater sum, rather than the English should not have gone together by the ears amongst themselves. The Council of Officers being now beset with so many enemies, produced speedily their model of government; which was to have a free Parliament, which should meet December the 15th, but with such qualifications of no King, no House of Lords, as made the city more angry than before. To send s into the west to suppress those that were rising there, they durst not, for fear of the city; nor could they raise another for want of money. There remained nothing but to break, and quitting Wallingford House to shift for themselves. This coming to the knowledge of their army in the north, they deserted Lambert; and the Rump, the 26th of December, re-possessed the House.

B. Seeing the Rump was now reseated, the business pretended by General Monk for his marching to London, was at an end.

A. The Rump, though seated, was not well settled, but (in the midst of so many tumults for a free Parliament) had as much need of the general's coming up now as before. He therefore sent them word, that because he thought them not yet secure enough, he would come up to London with his army; which they not only accepted, but also intreated him to do, and voted him for his services 1,000*l.* a year.

The general marching towards London, the country everywhere petitioned him for a free Parliament. The Rump, to make room in London for his army, dislodged their own. The general for all that, had not let fall a word in all this time that could be taken for a declaration of his final design.

B. How did the Rump revenge themselves on Lambert?

A. They never troubled him; nor do I know any cause of so gentle dealing with him: but certainly Lambert was the ablest of any officer they had to do them service, when they should have means and need to employ him. After the general was come to London, the Rump sent to the city for their part of a tax of 100,000*l.* a month, for six months, according to an act which the Rump had made formerly before their disseisin by the committee of safety. But the city, who were adverse to the Rump, and keen upon a free Parliament, could not be brought to give their money to their enemies and to purposes repugnant to their own. Hereupon the Rump sent order to the general to break down the city gates and their portcullises, and to imprison certain obstinate citizens. This he performed, and it was the last service he did them.

About this time the commission, by which General Monk with others had the government of the army put into their hands by the Rump before the usurpation of the Council of Officers, came to expire; which the present Rump renewed.

B. He was thereby the sixth part of the general of the whole forces of the commonwealth. If I had been as the Rump, he should have been sole general. In such cases as this, there cannot be a greater vice than pinching. Ambition should be liberal.

A. After the pulling down of the city gates, the general sent a letter to the Rump, to let them know that that service was *very* much against his nature, and to put them in mind how well the city had served the Parliament throughout the whole war.

B. Yes. But for the city the Parliament never could have made the war, nor the Rump ever have murdered the King.

A. The Rump considered not the merit of the city, nor the good-nature of the general. They were busy. They were giving out commissions, making of acts for abjuration of the King and his line, and for the old engagement, and conferring with the city to get money. The general also desired to hear conference between some of the Rump and some of the secluded members, concerning the justice of their seclusion, and of the hurt that could follow from their readmission: and it was granted. After long conference, the general finding the Rump's pretences unreasonable and ambitious, declared himself (with the city) for a free Parliament, and came to Westminster with the secluded members (whom he had appointed to meet and stay for him at Whitehall), and replaced them in the House amongst the Rumpers; so that now the same cattle that were in the House of Commons 1640, except those that were dead, and those that went from them to the late King at Oxford, are all there again.

B. But this (methinks) was no good service to the King, unless they had learned better principles.

A. They had learned nothing. The major part was now again Presbyterian. It is true they were so grateful to General Monk as to make him general of all the forces in the three nations. They did well also to make void the engagement; but it was because those acts were made to the prejudice of their party; but recalled nothing of their own rebellious ordinances, nor did anything in order to the good of the present King; but on the contrary, they declared by a vote: that the late King began the war against his two Houses.

B. The two Houses considered as two persons, were they not two of the King's subjects? If a king raise an army against his subject, is it lawful for that subject to resist with force, when (as in this case) he might have had peace upon his submission?

A. They knew they had acted vilely and sottishly; but because they had always pretended to greater than ordinary wisdom and godliness, they were loath to confess it. The Presbyterians now saw their time to make a Confession of their Faith, and presented it to the House of Commons;[50] which the Commons, to show they had not changed their principles (after six readings in the House) voted to be printed, and once a year to be read publicly in every church.

B. I say again, this re-establishing of the Long Parliament was no good service to the King.

A. Have a little patience. They were re-established with two conditions, one: to determine their sitting before the end of March, another: to send out writs before their rising for new elections.

B. That qualifies.

A. That brought in the King: for few of this Long Parliament (the country having felt the smart of their former service) could get themselves chosen again. This New Parliament began to sit April the 25th 1660. How soon these called in the King; with what joy and triumph he was received; how earnestly his Majesty pressed the Parliament for the act of oblivion, and how few were excepted out of it; you know as well as I.

50 . . . House of Commons, to show . . . principles; which, after . . . House, was voted to be, &c.

B. But I have not yet observed in the Presbyterians any oblivion of their former principles. We are but returned to the state we were in at the beginning of the sedition.

A. Not so: for before that time, though the Kings of England had the right of the *militia* in virtue of the sovereignty, and without dispute, and without any particular act of Parliament directly to that purpose; yet now, after this bloody dispute, the next (which is the present) Parliament, in proper and express terms hath declared the same to be the right of the King only, without either of his Houses of Parliament; which act is more instructive to the people, than any arguments drawn from the title of sovereign, and consequently fitter to disarm the ambition of all seditious haranguers for the time to come.

B. I pray God it prove so. Howsoever, I must confess that this Parliament has done all that a Parliament can do for the security of our peace: which I think also would be enough, if preachers would take heed of instilling evil principles into their auditory. I have seen in this revolution a circular motion of the sovereign power through two usurpers, *father and son*, from the late King to this his son. For (leaving out the power of the Council of Officers, which was but temporary, and no otherwise owned by them but in trust) it moved from King Charles I. to the Long Parliament; from thence to the Rump; from the Rump to Oliver Cromwell; and then back again from Richard Cromwell to the

Rump; thence to the Long Parliament; and thence to King Charles II., where long may it remain.

A. Amen. And may he have as often as there shall be need such a general.

B. You have told me little of the general till now in the end: but truly, I think the bringing of his little army entire out of Scotland up to London, was the greatest stratagem that is extant in history.

Appendix I

List of MPs Elected to the Short Parliament (April 1640)

Bedfordshire	
Bedfordshire	Thomas Wentworth, 5th Baron Wentworth Sir Oliver Luke
Bedford	Sir Beauchamp St John Samuel Luke
Berkshire	
Berkshire	John Fettiplace Henry Marten
Windsor	Sir Arthur Ingram Sir Richard Harrison
Reading	Edward Herbert Sir John Berkeley
Wallingford	Edmund Dunch Unton Croke
Abingdon	Sir George Stonhouse Bt
Buckinghamshire	
Buckinghamshire	John Hampden Arthur Goodwin

Buckingham	Sir Peter Temple Sir Alexander Denton
Wycombe	Sir Edmund Verney Thomas Lane
Aylesbury	Sir John Pakington, Bt Ralph Verney
Amersham	William Drake Edmund Waller
Wendover	Robert Croke Sir Walter Pye
Marlow	John Borlase Sir William Hicks
CAMBRIDGESHIRE	
Cambridgeshire	Sir Dudley North Sir John Cutts
Cambridge University	Thomas Eden Henry Lucas
Cambridge	Oliver Cromwell Thomas Meautys
CHESHIRE	
Cheshire	Sir William Brereton, Bt Thomas Aston
City of Chester	Sir Thomas Smith Robert Brerewood
CORNWALL	
Cornwall	William Godolphin Richard Buller
Launceston	Bevil Grenville Ambrose Manaton
Liskeard	John Harris George Kekewich

Lostwithiel	Nicholas Kendall Richard Arundell
Truro	John Rolle Francis Rous
Bodmin	Richard Prideaux Sir Richard Wynn Bt
Helston	William Godolphin Sidney Godolphin
Saltash	George Buller (MP) Francis Buller
Camelford	Piers Edgecumbe Edward Reade
Grampound	John Trevanion William Coryton Warwick Mohun
Eastlow	William Scawen William Code
Westlow	Anthony Mildmay George Potter
Penryn	Joseph Hall Richard Vyvyan
Tregoney	John St Aubyn Sir John Arundell
Bossiney	Edward Herle Anthony Nichols
St Ives	William Dell Sir Henry Marten
Fowey	Jonathan Rashleigh Edwin Rich
St Germans	William Scawen John Eliot
Mitchel	Peter Courtney William Chadwell

Newport	Nicholas Trefusis John Maynard
St Mawes	Dr George Parry James Lord Sheffield
Callington	Sir Samuel Rolle Thomas Gardiner
CUMBERLAND	
Cumberland	Sir George Dalston Sir Patricius Curwen
Carlisle	Sir William Dalston Bt Richard Barwis
DERBYSHIRE	
Derbyshire	Sir John Curzon Bt John Manners
Derby	William Allestry Nathaniel Hallowes
DEVON	
Devon	Edward Seymour Thomas Wise
Exeter	Robert Walker Jacob Tucker
Totnes	Oliver St John John Maynard
Plymouth	Robert Trelawney John Waddon
Barnstaple	George Peard Thomas Matthew
Plympton Erle	Sir Richard Strode Sir Nicholas Slanning Thomas Hele Bt
Tavistock	William Lord Russell John Pym

Clifton Dartmouth Hardness	John Upton Andrew Voysey
Bere Alston	John Harris William Strode
Tiverton	Peter Ball Peter Sainthill
Dorset	
Dorset	Richard Rogers George Lord Digby
Poole	John Pyne William Constantine
Dorchester	Denzil Holles Denis Bond
Lyme Regis	Sir Walter Erle Edmund Prideaux Richard Rose
Weymouth	Sir John Strangways Thomas Gyard
Melcombe	Giles Strangways Richard King
Bridport	Thomas Trenchard Sir John Meller
Shaftesbury	William Whitaker Edward Hyde
Wareham	John Trenchard Gilbert Jones
Corfe Castle	Henry Jermyn Thomas Jermyn
Essex	
Essex	Sir Thomas Barrington Bt Harbottle Grimston (senior)
Colchester	Sir William Masham Bt Harbottle Grimston (junior)

Maldon	Sir Henry Mildmay John Porter
Harwich	Sir Thomas Cheek Sir John Jacob
GLOUCESTERSHIRE	
Gloucestershire	Sir Robert Tracy Sir Robert Cooke
Gloucester	William Singleton Henry Brett
Cirencester	Henry Poole John George
Tewksury	Sir Anthony Ashley Cooper Sir Edward Alford
HAMPSHIRE	
Hampshire	Sir Henry Wallop Richard Whitehead
Winchester	John Lisle Sir William Ogle
Southampton	Sir John Mill, 1st Baronet Thomas Levington
Portsmouth	William Hamilton Hon. Henry Percy
Peterfield	Sir William Lewis William Uvedale
Yarmouth	William Oglander John Bulkeley
Newport	Lucius Viscount Falkland Henry Worsley
Stockbridge	William Heveningham William Jephson
Newtown	Nicholas Weston Sir John Meux, 1st Baronet

Lymington	John Doddington John Kempe
Christchurch	Arnold Herbert Henry Tulse
Whitchurch	Sir Thomas Jervoise Richard Jervoise
Andover	Robert Wallop Sir Richard Wynn, 2nd Baronet
HEREFORDSHIRE	
Herefordshire	Sir Robert Harley Sir Walter Pye
Hereford	Richard Weaver Richard Seaborne
Weobley	William Tomkins Thomas Tomkins
Leominster	William Smallman Walter Kyrle
HERTFORDSHIRE	
Hertfordshire	Sir William Lytton Arthur Capel
St Albans	Sir John Jennings Richard Coningsby
Hertford	Viscount Cranborne Sir Thomas Fanshawe
HUNTINGDONSHIRE	
Huntingdonshire	Thomas Cotton Sir Capel Bedel
Huntingdon	Robert Bernard William Montagu
KENT	
Kent	Sir Roger Twysden Norton Knatchbull

Canterbury	Edward Masters John Nutt
Rochester	Sir Thomas Walsingham John Clerke
Maidstone	Sir George Fane Francis Barnham
Queensborough	Sir Edward Hales John Wolstenholme
LANCASHIRE	
Lancashire	Sir Gilbert Hoghton, 2nd Baronet William Farrington
Preston	Richard Shuttleworth Thomas Standish
Lancaster	Roger Kirkby John Harrison
Newton	Sir Richard Wynn, 2nd Baronet William Sherman
Wigan	Orlando Bridgeman Alexander Rigby
Clitheroe	Sir Ralph Assheton Richard Shuttleworth
Liverpool	James Lord Cranfield John Holcroft
LEICESTERSHIRE	
Leicestershire	Sir Arthur Hesilrige Hon. Lord Grey of Ruthyn
Leicester	Simon Every Thomas Coke
LINCOLNSHIRE	
Lincolnshire	Sir John Wray Sir Edward Hussey

Lincoln	John Farmery Thomas Grantham
Boston	Sir Anthony Irby William Ellis
Grimsby	Christopher Wray Sir Gervase Holles
Stamford	Thomas Hatton Thomas Hatcher
Grantham	Sir Edward Bashe Henry Pelham
MIDDLESEX	
Middesex	Sir Gilbert Gerard, Bt Sir John Franklyn
Westminster	Sir John Glynne William Bell
City of London	Thomas Soame Isaac Penington Matthew Cradock Samuel Vassall
MONMOUTHSHIRE	
Monmouthshire	William Morgan Walter Rumsey
Monmouth Boroughs	Charles Jones
NORFOLK	
Norfolk	Sir John Holland, Bt Sir Edmund Moundeford
Norwich	Thomas Atkins Thomas Tooley
King's Lynn	William Doughty Thomas Gurling (Alderman)
Yarmouth	Miles Corbet Edward Owner

Thetford	Sir Thomas Wodehouse Framlingham Gawdy
Castle Rising	Thomas Talbot Nicholas Harman
NORTHAMPTONSHIRE	
Northamptonshire	John Crew Sir Gilbert Pickering, Bt
Peterborough	David Cecil William FitzWilliam, 2nd Baron FitzWilliam
Northampton	Zouch Tate Richard Knightley
Brackley	Sir Thomas Wenman Sir Martin Lister
Higham Ferrers	Sir Christopher Hatton
NORTHUMBERLAND	
Northumberland	Sir John Fenwick Sir William Widdrington
Newcastle	Sir Peter Riddel Thomas Liddell
Morpeth	Sir Philip Mainwaring Thomas Witherings
Berwick on Tweed	Sir Thomas Widdrington Hugh Potter
NOTTINGHAMSHIRE	
Nottinghamshire	Sir Thomas Hutchinson Robert Sutton
Nottingham	Sir Charles Cavendish Gilbert Boone
East Retford	Sir Gervase Clifton Francis Pierrepont
OXFORDSHIRE	

Oxfordshire	Hon. James Fiennes Sir Francis Wenman
Oxford University	Sir Francis Windebanke John Danvers
Oxford	Charles Lord Howard Viscount Andover Thomas Cooper
Woodstock	William Lenthall William Fleetwood
Banbury	Nathaniel Fiennes
RUTLAND	
Rutland	Hon. Baptist Noel Sir Guy Palmes
SALOP	
Shropshire	William Pierrepont Sir Vincent Corbet, 1st Baronet
Shrewsbury	Francis Newport Thomas Owen
Bridgnorth	(Sir) Thomas Whitmore Edward Acton
Ludlow	Charles Baldwin Ralph Goodwin
Wenlock	Sir Thomas Littleton, Bt Richard Cresset
Bishops Castle	Robert Howard Richard Moor
SOMERSET	
	Sir Ralph Hopton Thomas Smith
	John Glanville Humphrey Hooke

	Sir Charles Berkley Alexander Popham
	Sir Edward Rodney John Baber
	Sir William Portman Roger Hill
	Edmund Wyndham General Robert Brooke
	Francis Wyndham Alexander Popham
	Sir Henry Berkeley Edward Phelips
	Edward Kyrton Thomas Earl
STAFFORDSHIRE	
Staffordshire	Sir Edward Littleton Sir William Bowyer
Lichfield	Sir Walter Devereux Sir Richard Dyott
Stafford	Ralph Sneyd Richard Weston
Newcastle under Lyme	Sir John Merrick Richard Lloyd
Tamworth	George Abbot Sir Simon Archer
SUFFOLK	
Suffolk	Sir Nathaniel Barnardiston Sir Philip Parker
Ipswich	John Gurdon William Cage
Dunwich	Henry Coke Anthony Bedingfield

Orford	Sir Charles le Grosse Sir Edward Duke
Eye	Sir Frederick Cornwallis Sir Roger North
Aldeburgh	William Rainsborough Squire Bence
Sudbury	Sir Robert Crane, 1st Baronet Richard Pepys
Bury St Edmunds	Sir Thomas Jermyn John Godbolt
Surrey	
Surrey	Sir Richard Onslow Sir Ambrose Browne
Southwark	Robert Holborne Richard Tuffnell
Bletchingley	Edward Bysshe Edmund Hoskins
Reigate	Edward Thurland Sir Thomas Bludder
Guildford	Sir Robert Parkhurst George Abbotts
Gatton	Sir Samuel Owfield Edward Sanders
Haslemere	Sir John Jacques William Eliot
Sussex	
Sussex	Sir Thomas Pelham Bt Anthony Stapley
Chichester	Christopher Lewknor Edward Dowse
Horsham	Thomas Middleton Hall Ravenscroft

Midhurst	Thomas May Robert Long
Lewes	Anthony Stapley James Rivers
New Shoreham	John Alford William Marlott
Bramber	Sir John Suckling Sir Thomas Bowyer
Steyning	Thomas Leedes Sir Thomas Farnefold
East Grinstead	Sir Henry Compton Robert Goodwin
Arundel	Henry Garton Henry Goring
WARWICKSHIRE	
Warwickshire	Sir Thomas Lucy William Combe
Coventry	William Jesson Simon Norton
Warwick	William Purefoy Godfrey Bosvile
WESTMORLAND	
Westmorland	Sir Philip Musgrave Sir Henry Bellingham
Appleby	Richard Viscount Dungarvon Richard Lowther
WILTSHIRE	
Wiltshire	Philip Lord Herbert Sir Francis Seymour
Salisbury	Robert Hyde Michael Oldisworth

Wilton	Sir Henry Vane (the elder) Sir Benjamin Rudyerd
Downton	Sir Edward Griffin William Eyre
Hindon	Sir Miles Fleetwood George Garrett
Heytesbury	Sir John Berkeley Thomas Moore
Westbury	Sir Thomas Penyston, 1st Baronet John Ashe
Calne	William Maynard Walter Norborne
Devizes	Edward Bayntun Henry Danvers
Chippenham	Sir Edward Baynton Edward Hungerford
Malmesbury	Sir Neville Poole Sir Anthony Hungerford
Cricklade	Robert Jenner Thomas Hodges
Great Bedwyn	Richard Hardinge Charles Seymour
Ludgershall	William Ashburnham Sir John Evelyn
Old Sarum	Edward Herbert Sir William Howard
Wootton Bassett	Thomas Windebanke Edward Hyde
Malborough	Sir William Carnaby Francis Baskerville
WORCESTERSHIRE	
Worcestershire	Sir Thomas Lyttelton Sir John Pakington

Worcester	John Coucher John Nash
Droitwich	John Wilde Samuel Sandys
Evesham	William Sandys William Morton
Bewdley	Sir Henry Herbert
YORKSHIRE	
Yorkshire	Henry Belasyse Sir William Savile, 3rd Baronet
York	Sir Edward Osborne, 1st Baronet Sir Roger Jaques
Kingston upon Hull	Sir John Lister Sir Henry Vane, junior
Knaresborough	Sir Henry Slingsby Henry Benson
Scarborough	Sir Hugh Cholmeley John Hotham
Ripon	William Mallory Sir Paul Neille
Richmond	Sir William Pennyman, 1st Baronet Maulger Norton
Hedon	Sir Philip Stapleton John Alured
Boroughbridge	Ferdinando, Lord Fairfax Francis Neville
Thirsk	John Belasyse William Frankland
Aldborough	Richard Aldborough Brian Palmes
Beverley	Sir John Hotham Bt Michael Warton

Pontefract	Sir John Ramsden Sir George Wentworth of Woolley
CINQUE PORTS	
Hastings	Sir John Baker Robert Reed
Romney	Thomas Godfrey William Steele
Hythe	Henry Heyman John Wandesford
Dover	Sir Edward Boys Sir Peter Heyman
Sandwich	Sir John Manwood Nathaniel Finch
Rye	Sir John Colepepper John White
Winchelsea	Nicholas Crisp John Finch
WALES	
Anglesey	John Bodvel
Beaumaris	Charles Jones
Brecknockshire	William Morgan
Brecknock	Herbert Price
Cardiganshire	James Lewis
Cardigan	John Vaughan
Carmarthenshire	Henry Vaughan
Carmarthen	Francis Lloyd
Carnarvonshire	Thomas Glynn
Carnarvon	John Glynn
Denbighshire	Sir Thomas Salusbury, 2nd Baronet

Denbigh Boroughs	John Salusbury
Flitshire	John Mostyn
Flint	Sir Thomas Hanmer, 2nd Baronet
Glamorgan	Sir Edward Stradling
Cardiff	William Herbert
Merioneth	Henry Wynn
Montgomeryshire	Richard Herbert
Montgomery	Sir Edward Lloyd
Pembrokeshire	John Wogan
Pembroke	Sir John Stepney, 3rd Baronet
Haverford West	Hugh Owen
Radnorshire	Charles Price
Radnor	Richard Jones

Appendix II

List of MPs Elected to the Long Parliament (November 1640)

Bedfordshire	
Bedfordshire	Thomas Wentworth, 5th Baron Wentworth Sir Oliver Luke
Bedford	Sir Beauchamp St John Samuel Luke
Berkshire	
Berkshire	John Fettiplace Henry Marten
Windsor	Cornelius Holland William Taylor
Reading	Sir Francis Knollys (Senior) Sir Francis Knollys (Junior)
Wallingford	Edmund Dunch Thomas Howard
Abingdon	Sir George Stonhouse Bt
Buckinghamshire	
Buckinghamshire	John Hampden Arthur Goodwin

Buckingham	Sir Peter Temple Sir Alexander Denton
Wycombe	Sir Edmund Verney Thomas Lane
Aylesbury	Sir John Pakington, Bt Ralph Verney
Amersham	William Cheyney William Drake
Wendover	Robert Croke Thomas Fountaine
Marlow	John Borlase Gabriel Hippesley
Cambridgeshire	
Cambridgeshire	Sir Dudley North Bt. Thomas Chicheley
Cambridge University	Thomas Eden Henry Lucas
Cambridge	Oliver Cromwell John Lowry
Cheshire	
Cheshire	Peter Venables Sir William Brereton, Bt
City of Chester	Sir Thomas Smith Francis Gamull
Cornwall	
Cornwall	Alexander Carew Sir Bevil Grenville
Launceston	Ambrose Manaton William Coryton
Liskeard	John Harris Joseph Jane

Lostwithiel	John Trevanion Richard Arundell
Truro	John Rolle Francis Rous
Bodmin	John Arundell Anthony Nichols
Helston	William Godolphin Sidney Godolphin
Saltash	George Buller Edward Hyde
Camelford	Piers Edgecumbe William Glanville
Grampound	William Coryton James Campbell
Eastlow	Francis Buller Thomas Lower
Westlow	Thomas Arundell Henry Killigrew
Penryn	John Bampfylde Sir Nicholas Slanning
Tregoney	Richard Vyvyan John Polwhele
Bossiney	Sir Christopher Yelverton Sir John Clotworthy
St Ives	Francis Godolphin Viscount L'Isle
Fowey	Jonathan Rashleigh Sir Richard Buller
St Germans	Benjamin Valentine John Moyle (Junior)
Mitchel	William Chadwell John Arundell

Newport	Richard Edgecumbe John Maynard
St Mawes	Dr George Parry Richard Erisey
Callington	Sir Arthur Ingram George Fane
CUMBERLAND	
Cumberland	Sir George Dalston Sir Patricius Curwen, Bt
Carlisle	Sir William Dalston Bt Richard Barwis
Cockermouth	Sir John Hippisley Sir John Fenwick
DERBYSHIRE	
Derbyshire	Sir John Curzon Bt Sir John Coke
Derby	William Allestry Nathaniel Hallowes
DEVON	
Devon	Edward Seymour Thomas Wise
Exeter	Robert Walker Simon Snow
Totnes	Oliver St John John Maynard
Plymouth	Robert Trelawney John Waddon
Barnstaple	George Peard Richard Ferris
Plympton Erle	Michael Oldisworth Sir Nicholas Slanning

Tavistock	John Pym Lord William Russell
Clifton Dartmouth Hardness	John Upton Roger Matthew
Bere Alston	William Strode Sir Francis Cheeke
Tiverton	Peter Sainthill George Hartnall
Ashburton	Sir John Northcote Sir Edmund Fowell
Honiston	William Poole Walter Yonge
Okehampton	Edward Thomas Lawrence Whitaker
Dorset	
Dorset	Richard Rogers George Lord Digby
Poole	John Pyne William Constantine
Dorchester	Denzil Holles Denis Bond
Lyme Regis	Edmund Prideaux Richard Rose
Weymouth	Sir John Strangways Sir Walter Erle
Melcombe	Gerrard Napier Richard King
Bridport	Giles Strangways Roger Hill
Shaftesbury	William Whitaker Samuel Turner
Wareham	John Trenchard Thomas Erle

Corfe Castle	Sir Francis Windebank Giles Green
ESSEX	
Essex	Lord Rich Sir William Masham Bt
Colchester	Harbottle Grimston (Junior) Sir Thomas Barrington Bt
Maldon	Sir Henry Mildmay Sir John Clotworthy
Harwich	Harbottle Grimston (Senior) Sir Thomas Cheek
GLOUCESTERSHIRE	
Gloucestershire	John Dutton Nathaniel Stephens
Gloucester	Thomas Pury Henry Brett
Cirencester	Sir Theobald Gorges John George
Tewksbury	Sir Robert Cooke Edward Stephens
HAMPSHIRE	
Hampshire	Sir Henry Wallop Richard Whitehead
Winchester	John Lisle Sir William Ogle
Southampton	George Gallop Edward Exton
Portsmouth	George Goring Edward Dowse
Yarmouth	Viscount L'Isle Sir John Leigh

Petersfield	Sir William Lewis William Uvedale
Newport alias Medina	Lucius Viscount Falkland Henry Worsley
Stockbridge	William Heveningham William Jephson
Newtown	Sir John Meux, 1st Baronet Sir John Barrington Bt.
Christchurch	Henry Tulse Matthew Davis
Whitchurch	Sir Thomas Jervoise Richard Jervoise
Lymington	John Button Henry Campion
Andover	Robert Wallop Henry Vernon
HEREFORDSHIRE	
Herefordshire	Sir Rorbert Harley Fitzwilliam Coningsby
Hereford	Richard Weaver Richard Seaborne
Weobley	Arthuer Jones Lord Ranelagh Thomas Tomkins
Leominster	Sampson Eure Walter Kyrle
HERTFORDSHIRE	
Hertfordshire	Sir William Lytton Arthur Capel
St Albans	Sir John Jennings Edward Wingate
Hertford	Charles Cecil Sir Thomas Fanshawe

HUNTINGDONSHIRE	
Huntingdonshire	Sir Sidney Montagu Valentine Walton
Huntingdon	George Montagu Edward Montagu
KENT	
Kent	Sir Edward Dering Sir John Colepepper
Canterbury	Sir Edward Masters John Nutt
Rochester	Sir Thomas Walsingham Richard Lee
Maidstone	Francis Barnham Sir Humfrey Tufton
Queensborough	Sir Edward Hales William Harrison
LANCASHIRE	
Lanchashire	Ralph Ashton Roger Kirkby
Lancaster	John Harrison Thomas Fanshawe
Preston	Richard Shuttleworth Thomas Standish
Newton	William Ashurst Peter Legh
Wigan	Orlando Bridgeman Alexander Rigby
Clitheroe	Sir Ralph Assheton Richard Shuttleworth (Junior)
Liverpool	Sir Richard Wynn, 2nd Baronet John Moore

LEICESTERSHIRE	
Leicestershire	Sir Arthur Hesilrige Henry de Grey, Lord Ruthin
Leicester	Thomas Grey Lord Grey of Groby Thomas Coke
LINCOLNSHIRE	
Lincolnshire	Sir John Wray Sir Edward Ayscough
Lincoln	Thomas Grantham John Broxholme
Boston	Sir Anthony Irby William Ellis
Grimsby	Christopher Wray Sir Gervase Holles
Stamford	Geoffrey Palmer Thomas Hatcher
Grantham	Thomas Hussey Henry Pelham
MIDDLESEX	
Middlesex	Sir Gilbert Gerard Sir John Franklyn
Westminster	John Glynne William Bell
City of London	Sir Thomas Soame Isaac Penington Samuel Vassall Matthew Cradock
MONMOUTHSHIRE	
Monmouthshire	Sir Charles Williams William Herbert
Monmouth	Thomas Trevor

NORFOLK	
Norfolk	Sir John Potts Sir Edmund Moundeford
Norwich	Richard Harman Richard Catelyn
King's Lynn	John Perceval Thomas Toll
Yarmouth	Miles Corbet Edward Owner (Recorder)
Thetford	Sir Thomas Wodehouse Framlingham Gawdy
Castle Rising	Sir John Holland, Bt Sir Christopher Hatton
NORTHAMPTONSHIRE	
Northamptonshire	Sir Gilbert Pickering, Bt John Dryden, Bt
Peterborough	William Fitzwilliam Sir Robert Napier, 2nd Baronet
Northampton	Zouch Tate Richard Knightley
Brackley	John Crew Sir Martin Lister
Higham Ferrars	Sir Christopher Hatton
NORTHUMBERLAND	
Northumberland	Sir William Widdrington Henry Percy
Newcastle	Sir John Melton John Blakiston
Berwick upon Tweed	Sir Thomas Widdrington Sir Edward Osborne
Morpeth	John Fenwick Sir William Carnaby

Nottinghamshire	
Nottinghamshire	Sir Thomas Hutchinson Robert Sutton
Nottingham	Francis Pierrepoint William Stanhope
East Retford	Sir Gervase Clifton Charles Cavendish
Oxfordshire	
Oxfordshire	Thomas Wenman, 2nd Viscoutn Wenman James Fiennes
Oxford University	Sir Thomas Roe John Selden
Oxford	John Whistler John Smith
Woodstock	William Lenthall Sir Robert Pye
Banbury	Nathaniel Fiennes
Rutland	
Rutland	Sir Guy Palmes Baptist Noel
Salop	
Shropshire	Sir Richard Lee, 2nd Baronet Sir Richard Newport
Shrewsbury	Francis Newport William Spurstow
Bridgnorth	Sir Thomas Whitmore Edward Acton
Ludlow	Charles Baldwin Ralph Goodwin
Wenlock	William Pierrepont Sir Thomas Littleton, Bt

Bishops Castle	Robert Howard Richard Moor
SOMERSET	
Somerset	Sir John Poulett Sir John Stawell
Bristol	Humphrey Hooke Richard Longe
Bath	William Bassett Alexander Popham
Wells	Sir Ralph Hopton Sir Edward Rodney
Taunton	Sir William Portham George Searle
Bridgwater	Peter Wroth Edmund Wyndham
Minehead	Sir Francis Popham Alexander Luttrell
Ilchester	Edward Phelips Robert Hunt
Milborne Port	Edward Kyrton John Digby
STAFFORDSHIRE	
Staffordshire	Sir Edward Littleton Hervey Bagot
Stafford	Ralph Sneyd Richard Weston
Newcastle under Lyme	Sir Richard Leveson Sir John Merrick
Lichfield	Sir Richard Cave Michael Noble
Tamworth	Ferdinando Stanhope Henry Wilmot

Suffolk	
Suffolk	Sir Nathaniel Barnardiston Sir Philip Parker
Ipswich	John Gurdon William Cage
Dunwich	Henry Coke Anthony Bedingfield
Orford	Sir William Playters, 2nd Baronet Sir Charles le Grosse
Aldeburgh	Squire Bence William Rainsborough
Sudbury	Sir Simonds d'Ewes Sir Robert Crane
Eye	Sir Frederick Cornwallis Sir Roger North
Bury St Edmunds	Thomas Jermyn Sir Thomas Barnardiston
Surrey	
Surrey	Sir Richard Onslow Sir Ambrose Browne
Southwark	Edward Bagshawe John White
Bletchingly	John Evelyn (Senior) Edward Bysshe (Junior)
Reigate	William Monson Sir Thomas Bludder
Guildford	Sir Robert Parkhurst George Abbotts
Gatton	Sir Samuel Owfield Thomas Sandys
Haslemere	John Goodwin Poynings More

SUSSEX	
Sussex	Sir Thomas Pelham, Bt Anthony Stapley
Chichester	Christopher Lewknor Sir William Morley
Horsham	Thomas Middleton Hall Ravenscroft
Midhurst	Thomas May William Cawley
Lewes	Herbert Morley James Rivers
New Shoreham	John Alford William Marlott
Bramber	Sir Thomas Bowyer Arthur Onslow
Steyning	Thomas Leedes Sir Thomas Farnefold
East Grinstead	Lord Buckhurst Robert Goodwin
Arundel	Henry Garton Sir Edward Alford
WARWICKSHIRE	
Warwickshire	Richard Shuckburgh James Compton
Coventry	John Barker Simon Norton
Warwick	William Purefoy Sir Thomas Lucy
WESTMORLAND	
Westmorland	Sir Philip Musgrave Sir Henry Bellingham

Appleby	Viscount Dungarvan Sir John Brooke
Wiltshire	
Wiltshire	Sir James Thynne Sir Henry Ludlow
Salisbury	Robert Hyde Michael Oldisworth
Wilton	Sir Henry Vane (the elder) Sir Benjamin Rudyerd
Downton	Sir Edward Griffin Sir Anthony Ashley Cooper
Hindon	Robert Reynolds Miles Fleetwood
Heytesbury	Thomas Moore Edward Ashe
Westbury	William Wheler John Ashe
Calne	George Lowe Hugh Rogers
Devizes	Edward Bayntun Robert Nicholas
Chippenham	Sir Edward Hungerford Sir Edward Bayntun
Malmesbury	Sir Neville Poole Sir Anthony Hungerford
Cricklade	Robert Jenner Thomas Hodges
Great Bedwyn	Sir Walter Smith Richard Hardinge
Ludgershall	William Ashburnham Sir John Evelyn
Old Sarum	Robert Cecil Edward Herbert

Wootton Bassett	Edward Poole William Pleydell
Marlborough	John Francklyn Sir Francis Seymour
WORCESTERSHIRE	
Worcestershire	John Wilde Humphrey Salwey
Worcester	John Coucher John Nash
Droitwich	Endymion Porter Samuel Sandys
Evesham	Richard Cresheld William Sandys
Bewdley	Sir Henry Herbert
YORKSHIRE	
Yorkshire	Ferdinando Fairfax, Lord Fairfax of Cameron Henry Belasyse
York	Sir William Allanson Thomas Hoyle (Alderman)
Kingston upon Hull	Sir Henry Vane, junior Sir John Lister
Knaresborough	Sir Henry Slingsby Henry Benson
Scarborough	Sir Hugh Cholmeley John Hotham
Ripon	William Mallory John Mallory
Richmond	Sir William Pennyman, Bt. Sir Thomas Danby
Hedon	Sir William Strickland John Alured

Boroughbridge	Sir Philip Stapylton Sir Thomas Mallaverer Bt
Thirsk	John Belasyse Sir Thomas Ingram
Aldborough	Richard Aldborough Robert Strickland
Beverley	Sir John Hotham Bt Michael Warton
Pontefract	Sir George Wentworth of Woolley Sir George Wentworth of Wentworth Woodhouse
Malton	Thomas Hebblethwaite John Wastell
Northallerton	Sir Henry Cholmley Sir John Ramsden
CINQUE PORTS	
Hastings	John Ashburnham Thomas Eversfield
Romney	Sir Norton Knatchbull Thomas Webb
Hythe	Henry Heyman John Harvey
Dover	Sir Edward Boys Sir Peter Heyman
Sandwich	Sir Thomas Peyton Sir Edward Partridge
Seaford	Sir Thomas Parker Francis Gerard
Rye	John White Sir John Jacob, 1st Baronet
Winchelsea	John Finch Nicholas Crisp

WALES	
Anglesey	John Bodvel
Newburgh	John Griffith
Brecknockshire	William Morgan
Brecknock	Herbert Price
Cardiganshire	Walter Lloyd
Cardigan	John Vaughan
Carmarthenshire	Henry Vaughan
Carmarthen	Francis Lloyd
Carnarvonshire	John Griffith (Junior)
Carnarvon	William Thomas
Denbighshire	Thomas Middleton
Denbigh Boroughs	Simon Thelwall
Flintshire	John Mostyn
Flint	John Salusbury
Glamorgan	Philip Herbert, 5th Earl of Pembroke
Cardiff	William Herbert
Merioneth	William Price
Montgomeryshire	Sir John Pryce, 1st Baronet
Montgomery	Richard Herbert
Pembrokeshire	John Wogan
Pembroke	Hugh Owen
Naverford West	Sir John Stepney, 3rd Baronet
Radnorshire	Charles Price
Radnor	Philip Warwick

Appendix III

The Regicides

ifty-nine Commissioners (judges) signed the death warrant for Charles I. They are listed below in the order in which they appear, along with the fate that befell them following Restoration. An additional seventeen Commissioners sat one or more days at the trial, but did not sign the warrant. On the other hand, fourteen individuals, who were not Commissioners, were deemed regicides and an additional two were excepted from the Indemnity and Oblivion Act and found guilty of high treason.

The Signatories

JOHN BRADSHAW (1602 – 1659), as President of the Court that tried Charles I, was posthumostly executed. On 30 January 1661, his body was exhumed and hung with chains at Tylburn, from morning until four o'clock in the afternoon, when it was decapitated. The body was thrown into a pit, along with Oliver Cromwell's and Henry Ireton's, and the head placed on a 20-foot pike outside of Westminster Hall, facing the direction of the spot where Charles I had been executed.

THOMAS GREY, LORD GREY OF GROBY (1623 – 1657) became disillusioned with Oliver Cromwell and joined the Fifth Monarchists. Arrested on suspicion by instruction of the Lord Protector, he was taken prisoner to Windsor Castle. He successfully applied to Cromwell for his release, which he was granted in 1655. He remained politically inactive until his death.

OLIVER CROMWELL (1599 – 1658) was posthumostly executed. On 30 January 1661, his body was exhumed and hung with chains at Tylburn, from morning until four o'clock in the afternoon, when it was finally decapitated. The body was thrown into a pit, along with John Bradshaw's and Henry Ireton's, and the head placed on a 20-foot pike outside of Westminster Hall, facing the direction of the spot where Charles I had been executed, until 1685, following which, it was privately owned, going from hand to hand, until it was re-buried beneath the floor of the antechapel at Sidney Sussex College, Cambridge, in 1960. The body was exhumed and reburied a number of times to evade the wrath of Royalists; its whereabouts is uncertain.

EDWARD WALLEY (1607 – 1675) deemed the Restoration his cue to leave England. With his son-in-law, Major-General William Goffe, he set sail to North America, landing in Boston on 27 July 1660, where he was warmly received by Governor John Endecott. Walley and Goffe established themselves in Cambridge, during which period the Indemnity and Oblivion Act 1660 was passed by Parliament in England, which pardoned all the regicides except him and a number of others. Hitherto able to go about their business openly, the arrival of orders for their arrest forced them to go into hiding, relocating to New Haven, Connecticut, where regicide John Drixwell (see below) was already living. For the next fourteen years they managed to avoid capture, going from place to place, at times hiding in a cave, shielded by sympathisers and supported by their wives in England. He was thought to have died in Switzerland.

SIR MICHAEL LIVESEY (b. 1614) fled to the Netherlands after being denounced as a regicide.

The circumstances of his death are unknown.

JOHN OKEY (1606 – 1662) not desiring to wait until the final list of those included in the pardon of the Indemnity and Oblivion Act was known, fled to Germany, along with regicide John Barkstead. By this they forfeited their right to trial and were declared outlaws. From there they went to the Netherlands, where they were arrested by the English Ambassador to the Dutch court. Back in England, their being outlaws made their execution for high treason just a matter of establishing their identity. They received the standard sentence for their case, and were hung, drawn, and quartered on 16 April 1662.

SIR JOHN D'ANVERS (1585 – 1655) died, according to Mark Noble, 'neglected and in contempt with all parties'. He was excepted from the Indemnity and Oblivion Act and thus all the property he had accumulated, being confiscated by the Crown, was lost to his heir.

SIR JOHN BOURCHIER (c. 1595 – 1660) was too ill to be tried for regicide at the Restoration, and died a few months later.

HENRY IRETON (1611 – 1651) was posthumostly executed. On 30 January 1661, his body was exhumed and hung with chains at Tylburn, from morning until four o'clock in the afternoon, when it was finally decapitated. The body was thrown into a pit, along with Oliver Cromwell's and John Bradshaw's, and the head placed on a 20-foot pike outside of Westminster Hall, facing the direction of the spot where Charles I had been executed.

SIR THOMAS MAULEVERER, 1ST BARONET (1599 – 1655)'s son an heir fought for the Royalists, so at Restoration he was allowed to succeed to the Baronetcy.

SIR HARDRESS WALLER (1604 – 1666) fled to France at Restoration, but soon surrendered to the authorities. Brought to England, he pleaded guilty at trial and condemned to death. However, intervention by his friends saved him and he was allowed to live, albeit in prison. Mont Orgueil, in Jersey, was his final destination.

JOHN BLAKISTON (1603 – 1649)'s estate was, at Restoration, confiscated by the Sheriff of Durham.

JOHN HUTCHINSON (1615–1664) was expelled from Parliament as a regicide on 9 June 1660. Through expression of genuine contrition and repentance for his involvement in the regicide, and thanks to the intervention of high-placed relatives, he was spared. This, however, precipitated a crisis of conscience, and he would have offered himself as a sacrifice had his wife not persuaded him otherwise. All the same, in 1663 he was arrested on suspicion of involvement in the Farnley Wood Plot and promptly imprisoned, despite inconclusive evidence. Relieved at last, he spent the rest of his days in captivity, refusing to purchase his release and dying in a cell in the ruinous and insalubrious Sandown Castle.

WILLIAM GOFFE (1605?–1679?). *See* EDWARD WALLEY.

THOMAS PRIDE (d. 1658) was posthumously sentenced to execution. It is said, however, that when his body was exhumed on 30 January 1661, it was too far decayed for the sentence to be carried out. The Royalists then attempted to hang his son, who had also been an active member in the New Model Army, but he managed to escape.

PETER TEMPLE (1599 – 1663) was excepted from the Indemnity and Oblivion Act 1660. At Restoration, his estate was confiscated and the balance of his life he spent a prisoner in the Tower of London.

THOMAS HARRISON (1606 – 1660) remained at home at Restoration, calmly awaiting his fate. In his case, it was arrest. At his trial, he manfully admitted his part in the regicide, refusing to apologise and defending his actions as having been motivated by principle. The prosecution, however, was clear on the outcome, for the verdict of guilty was arrived without allowing Harrison leisure to go into his defence (he was frequently interrupted). He was the first of the regicides to be executed (by being hung, drawn, and quartered). At the moment of execution, the hangman asked for his forgiveness, to which Harrison replied 'I do forgive thee with all my heart . . . Alas poor man, thou doith it ignorantly, the Lord grant that this sin may be not laid to thy charge'. Harrison then transferred all the money remaining in his pocket into the executioner's hands and submitted to the proceedings, in the belief that in the matter of Charles I he had acted righteously and that a day would come when men would think better of the regicides.

JOHN HEWSON (d. 1662) interpreted the Restoration as his cue to flee to Amsterdam, and then possibly Rouen, in either of which cities he remained until his death.

HENRY SMITH (1620 – 1668) was brought to trial at Restoration. Found guilty, his death sentence was commuted to life imprisonment upon appeal. He was held in the Tower of London until 1664, and in Mont Orgueil Castle, in Jersey, thereafter.

SIR PEREGRINE PELHAM (d. 1650), being dead long before Restoration, had his estate confiscated by the Crown.

RICHARD DEANE (1610 – 1653) was disinterred at Restoration and reburied in a communal pit.

SIR ROBERT TICHBORNE (1604 – 1682) surrendered in obedience to King Charles II's proclamation of 4 June 1660 at Restoration. All the land he had accummulated during the war and the confiscation of crown lands were sequestrated. At his trial, he pleaded not guilty, alleging ignorance, but was found otherwise. His original sentence was death, but he obtained a reprieve. His surrender counted in his favour and prevented execution, according to the terms of the Indemnity and Oblivion Act; also in his favour was the claim that he had helped save a number of Royalists during the Protectorate. Moreover, having been called to the bar, the House of Lords heard his defence. He was then sentenced to life imprisonment, much to the joy of the Royalist pamphleteers, and sent to Holy Island. From there he was sent, on account of illness, to Dover Castle, where his family were allowed to live with him, and finally to the Tower of London, where he died.

HUMPHREY EDWARDS (1582 – 1658) died intestate and his estate went to his sister, Lady Ottley. However, as he was expected from the Indemnity and Oblivion Act, the estate was later confiscated by the crown.

DANIEL BLAGRAVE (1603 – 1668) saw Restoration as his cue to flee to the Continent. He settled in Aachen, where he remained until his death.

OWEN ROWE (1592 – 1661) was brought to trial and sentenced to death, but he died in the Tower of London while awaiting execution.

WILLIAM PUREFOY (1580 – 1659)'s estate passed on to his married daughters, but it was later confiscated by the Crown for his part in the regicide.

ADRIAN SCROPE (1601 – 1660) surrendered in obedience to the King's proclamation of 4 June 1660 and the House of Commons voted that he should benefit from the Indemnity and Oblivion Act and was released on parole. However, the Lords remained firm and Scrope was excepted. At trial Richard Browne, late Major-General for Parliament and now Lord Mayor elect of London, betrayed a private conversation in which Scrope had refused to condemn the regicide. Scrope claimed to have no memory of uttering the words alleged, but to no avail: he was sentenced to be hung, drawn, and quartered. He was executed at Charing Cross.

JAMES TEMPLE (1606 – 1680) was excluded from the Indemnity and Oblivion Act and was captured while attempting to flee to Ireland under his first wife's maiden name. At his trial, he claimed that he had only acted as judge in the trial of Charles I in order to obtain information for the Royalists, and that he had begged Cromwell to spare the King's life. He avoided execution, but was sentenced to life in prison. He was held at the Tower of London, then to Mont Orgueil, in Jersey, and finally to Elizabeth Castle, located in a tidal island in Saint Helier, also in Jersey. In his *Loyall Martyrology*, William Winstanley described him as 'not so much famous for his valour as his villainy, being remarkable for nothing but this horrible business of the king's murther, for which he came into the pack to have a share in the spoyle'.

AUGUSTINE GARLAND (1603 – 1677) was brought to trial at Restoration. He pleaded not guilty, and denied knowing he was near the King when accused of being the one who spat on His Majesty's face. His death sentence was commuted to transportation to Tangier, where he was to serve life in prison. However, there is no evidence the sentence was carried out.

EDMUND LUDLOW (1617 – 1692) had been elected to Parliament as member for Hindon, but his election was annulled after Parliament ruled that all regicides should be arrested. He went into hiding, but then surrendered to the Speaker after the King's proclamation. Upon seeing this would not guarantee his life, he escaped, going to France and then Switzerland, settling in Vevey and obtaining permission to live there. Throughout this period he used an assumed name. The year after the Glorious Revolution of 1688 he returned to England, but, being remembered only as a regicide, and calls being made for his arrest, he fled again, ending up once again in Vevey, where he remained until his death.

HENRY MARTEN (1602 – 1680) surrendered to the authorities after the King's proclamation. He was found guilty, but, through the inaction of the House of Lords, he escaped execution, and was sentenced to internal exile to the far north of England. From there he was transferred to Windsor Castle until the King, who thought him 'an ugly rascal and whore-master' desired him moved away from his person, leading Marten to be sent to Chepstow, in Wales, where he was, nevertheless, allowed to live in a suite of rooms, attended by his common-law wife (his legitimate wife lived apart) and with freedom to travel occasionally, until he choked to death while enjoying dinner.

VINCENT POTTER (1614 – 1661) was arraigned at the Sessions House of the Lord Mayor and Sheriffs of the City of London and Middlesex on 16 October 1660. He pleaded not guilty. At trial he requested a postponement on account of being ill and in great pain (he might have been suffering from kidney stones), but to no avail: the trial went ahead, he was found guilty of high treason, and he was sentenced to death. He died in the Tower of London while awaiting execution.

SIR WILLIAM CONSTABLE, 1ST BARONET (1590 – 1655) was dug out at Restoration and reburied in a communal pit.

SIR RICHARD INGOLDSBY (1617 – 1685) was pardoned, firstly because of his activities in support of General George Monck, who had been key in the Restoration of the monarchy, and because of his claim to have been physically forced by his cousin, Oliver Cromwell, to sign Charles I's death warrant, Cromwell putting

Ingoldsby's hand into his own and scribbling the signature in this manner. He was created a Knight of the Bath at Charles II's coronation and, elected to Parliament for Aylesbury, remained a Member until his death.

WILLIAM CAWLEY (1602 – 1667) was excepted from pardon after Restoration. He fled to the Netherlands and then to Switzerland, where he joined Edmund Ludlow and Nicholas Love, a judge at Charles I's trial who had not signed the death warrant. He died in Vevey.

JOHN BARKSTEAD. *See* JOHN OKEY.

ISAAC EWER (d. c. 1650)'s estate was confiscated by the Crown after Restoration.

JOHN DIXWELL (1607 – 1689) was condemned to death for regicide, but he escaped to New Haven Connecticut, where he lived under the assumed name of John Davids. In 1664 he was reunited with the newly arrived Edward Walley and William Goffe (see above). Unlike the latter, he was not subject to warrants for his arrest, since in England he was believed dead and in the colony he was only known by his assumed name. His true identity was only revealed while on his deathbed.

VALENTINE WALTON (1594 – 1661) saw the writing on the wall concerning the imminent Restoration, and fled to Haunau, in the Electorate of Hesse. Knowledge of his being hated by the Royal family prompted him to flee to Flanders, where he hid in the garb of a gardner. Meanwhile, in England, he was excepted from the Indemnity and Oblivion Act, and his estate was confiscated, a great part of what he had acquired belonging to the Queen as part of her dower. A death sentence would have been inevitable.

SIMON MAYNE (1612 – 1661) after Restoration he was tried and sentenced to death. He was held in the Tower of London while he appealed, but he died before the appeal could be heard in court.

THOMAS HORTON (1603 – 1649)'s estate was confiscated by the Crown after Restoration.

JOHN JONES, OF MAES-Y-GARNEDD (1597 – 1660), was walking in Finsbury when he was arrested, apparently unaware of the danger he was in after Restoration. Expecting no mercy, at trial he made no effort to plead a point of law and was sentenced to death. He was hung, drawn, and quartered along with Adrian Scroop.

JOHN MOORE (1599 – 1650).

GILBERT MILLINGTON (1598 – 1666) was tried at Restoration and found guilty of high treason, but his death sentence was commuted to life imprisonment on appeal.

GEORGE FLEETWOOD (1623 – 1672) surrendered in obedience to the King's proclamation and pleaded guilty a trial, where he said he wished he could express his sorrow and wept. Found a traitor, he heard the court awarding the following judgment along with another: 'That you be led back to the place whence you came, and from thence to be drawn upon a hurdle to the place of execution, and there you shall be hanged by the neck, and being alive shall be cut down, and your privy members shall be cut off, your entrails to be taken out of your bodies, and (you living) the same to be burnt before your eyes, and your heads to be cut off, your bodies to be divided into quarters, and heads and quarters disposed of at the pleasure of the king's majesty, and the Lord have mercy upon your souls'. This, however, he avoided thanks to a saving clause in the Indemnity and Oblivion Act, which suspended execution for those who benefited from the King's proclamation. In his petition to Parliament, Fleetwood claimed he had been coerced by Cromwell into signing Charles' death warrant, his name having been added without his knowledge, and, he being young at the time, Cromwell's power, commands, and threats having then frightened him into court. He also presented certificates of services to Monck and Ashley in the effort to restore the monarchy. In consideration of this, his sentence was commuted to transportation to Tangiers, where he remained until death, but his estate was confiscated all the same and given to the Duke of York.

JOHN ALURED (1607 – 1651) was excepted from the Indemnity and Oblivion Act and his estate, then held by his heirs, was confiscated by the Crown.

ROBERT LIBURNE (1613 – 1665) was arrested soon after Restoration and found guilty of high treason. He was sentenced to death, but the sentence was later commuted to life imprisonment. He died a prisoner in Drake's Island, in Plymouth Sound.

WILLIAM SAY (1604 – 1666) fled to the Continent and then plotted with the Dutch government, at war with England at the time, to send him there with an army to overthrow the monarchy a second time. He asked Edmond Ludlow to join him in this cause, but Ludlow was circumspect and rejected Say's repeated and ebullient offers. The Dutch made peace with the English, and Say died in obscurity, his whereabouts unknown.

ANTHONY STAPLEY (1590 – 1655) was excepted from the Indemnity and Oblivion Act, and his estate, then was subject by confiscation by the Crown. His son, Sir John, along with the latter's brother, however, actively supported Restoration, thus winning the King's favour and leading him to be created baronet in 1660.

SIR GREGORY NORTON, 1ST BARONET (1603 – 1652) disinherited his son Henry when the latter opposed the execution of Charles I. Upon his death, however, Henry inherited his estate.

THOMAS CHALONER (1595 – 1661) fled to the Netherlands after Restoration, and died in Middelburgh the following year.

THOMAS WOGAN (b. 1620) surrendered in obedience to the King's proclamation, albeit after the time period allowed. His surrender was accepted, and therefore, as per the Indemnity and Oblivion Act, his execution was suspended pending a future act of Parliament. His estate, forfeited, was given to Robert Werden. In 1664, he escaped from Cliffort Tower, in York Castle, and fled to the Netherlands. The was seen in Rotterdam and the last known reference to him comes from Aphra Behn, who in 1666 wrote that he was 'in Utrecht, plotting'.

JOHN VENN (1586 – 1650) would have been subject to the utmost penalties of the law, but, being dead, his estate was confiscated by the Crown.

GREGORY CLEMENT (1594 – 1660) was arrested shortly after Restoration, tried, found guilty of high treason, and sentenced to death. He was hung, drawn, and quartered at Charing Cross.

JOHN DOWNES (1609 – 1666) was arrested soon after Restoration. He was tried for Regicide, found guilty of high treason, and condemned to death. However, because he had intervened on behalf of Charles I and had only signed the latter's death warrant after being intimidated by other commissioners, his sentence was commuted to life in prison. He died in the Tower of London.

THOMAS WAITE (d. 1688) surrendered in obedience to the King's proclamation, but was then proved troublesome in court, refusing to plead and prevaricating. He was found guilty of treason, but his sentence was commuted to life imprisonment because Cromwell had forced him to sign Charles death warrant, Cromwell taking Waite's hand into his own and using it to sign Waite's name on the document. He died a prisoner in Mont Orgueil Castle, in Jersey.

THOMAS SCOT (d. 1660) initially fled to Flanders, but then surrendered in Brussels. At trial, he was found guilty of high treason and condemned to death. Unrepentant, he was hung, drawn, and quartered at Charing Cross.

JOHN CAREW (1622 – 1660) fled England, but was unable to evade arrest. At trial he was found guilty of high treason and condemned to death. He was hung, drawn, and quartered at Charing Cross.

MILES CORBET (1595 – 1662) fled to the Netherlands, but was arrested by the English ambassador to the Dutch court, along with John Okey and John Barkstead. Brought back to England under guard, he was tried, found guilty of high treason, and condemned to death.

OTHER REGICIDES

DANIEL AXTELL (1622 – 1660), an Officer of the Guard, was arraigned for treason. He initially tried to justify his actions by saying he had only been following orders, but witnesses refuted this by testifying that he had been rude to the King and encouraged others to jeer and mock. He was found guilty and told that even if he had been simply obeying the orders of a superior officer, the latter was a traitor and therefore the orders traitorous, making him also a traitor. At execution he showed his true colours, stating, 'If I had a thousand lives, I could lay them all down for the Cause'. He was hung, drawn, and quarted and his head displayed on a pike at Westminster Hall.

ANDREW BROUGHTON (1602/3 – 1687) learnt of his being exempted from the Indemnity and Oblivion Act and, together with John Phelps, who had also been excepted, fled to the Continent. It seems they were initially in Hamburg, but then went to Switzerland, where he was reunited with other regicides, including Edmund Ludlow and Nicholas Love. He and Phelps died in Vevey.

JOHN COOK (1608 – 1660), the Clerk at the Court, was tried and found guilty of treason. He was hung, drawn, and quartered at Charing Cross.

EDWARD DENDY (1613 – 1674), the Serjeant-at-Arms, fled to the Continent at Restoration. While in Rotterdam, the English Ambassador sought a warrant for his arrest, but Dendy escaped before it could be obtained, ending up in Switzerland, where he was reunited with other regicides.

ISAAC DORISLAUS (1595 – 1649), the University of Cambridge's first ever professor of History and a republican, had prepared the charge of high treason against Charles I. A man of all seasons, he had earlier made peace with and worked for the court, despite a history of republican propagandising. He was sent to the Dutch Republic to negotiate for the Commonwealth and was murdered in The Hague by Royalist refugees for his role in the regicide.

FRANCIS HACKER (d. 1660), another Officer of the Guard, was executed at Tyburn after being found guilty of treason. Instead of being quarted, his body was handed over to his family for burial. His property was forfeited to the Crown and given to the Duke of York.

WILLIAM HEWLETT, a Captain in the Guard, was tried along with Francis Hacker and Daniel Axtell, but avoided execution.

CORNELIUS HOLLAND (1599 – 1671), a Member of the Council of State, and said to be the main hand that drew the charges against Charles I. At Restoration he fled to Switzerland.

HERCULES HUNCKS (d. 1660), an Officer of the Guard, had refused to sign the order to the executioners of Charles I, causing Cromwell to mock him as a 'peevish fellow'. Francis Hacker signed in his place. Huncks was pardoned after testifying against him and Daniel Axtell.

ROBERT PHAYRE (1619? – 1682), an Officer of the Guard, refused to sign the order to the executioners. He was arrested and imprisoned in the Tower of London, but avoided execution after his father-in-law, Sir Thomas Herbert, and Bishop Clancarty pleaded for him. All his estates were sequestrated, but afterward his Irish estates were released. He regained his liberty by degress and was free to go anywhere by May 1662.

JOHN PHELPS (c. 1619 – 1666). See ANDREW BROUGHTON.

MATTHEW TOMLINSON (1617 – 1681), an Officer of the Guard, never sat at the trial of Charles I, though he had been appointed a Commissioner. At Restoration he obtained a pardon by testifying against Daniel Axtell and Francis Hacker, and by corroboration of his claim to have shown courtesy to the King. Charles II and other Royalists thought he ought to have allowed the King to escape and were unhappy about his impunity.

HUGH PETERS (1598 – 1660), a radical Protestant preacher, was arrested at Restoration. In his defence to the House of Lords he denied having had any part in the regicide, even though, through his preaching and addresses to Parliament on Cromwell's behalf, he had made a name for himself as a leading Puritan opponent of the House of Stuart. Moreover, circumstantial evidence pointed to his having been one of the two heavily disguised executioners at the King's execution. He was found guilty and hung, drawn, and quartered at Charing Cross.

RICHARD BRANDON (d. 1649), a London hangman at the time, is often named as the executioner of Charles I. He is said to have refused the job, but may have accepted under duress, and received, according to a posthumous pamphlet purporting to be his confession, £30 to do the deed, 'all in half crowns'.

ALSO EXCEPTED FROM THE INDEMNITY AND OBLIVION ACT

JOHN LAMBERT (1619 – 1684), a Parliamentary general, was initially exempted from prosecution, but the Cavalier Parliament voted in 1662 to charge him with high treason, of which he was found guilty at trial. He was removed to Guernsey, pending further instructions, but avoided execution and was allowed to dwell there and later in Drake Island, as a prisoner, for the remainder of his days.

SIR HENRY VANE THE YOUNGER (1613 – 1662) was excepted from the Indemnity and Oblivion Act, but was, all the same, arrested and taken to the Tower of London. Parliament petitioned clemency, which was granted, but he remained a prisoner. Later, Parliament petitioned the King to have him brought to trial, where he was found guilty of high treason against Charles II. A commoner would have normally been hung, drawn, and quarterd, but he was granted a gentleman's death by beheading. At his execution he delivered a long and heated speech of self-justification.

Appendix IV

List of MPs in the Rump Parliament (1648)

Bedfordshire	
Bedfordshire	Sir Roger Burgoyne, 2nd Baronet
Bedford	Sir Beauchamp St John Samuel Luke
Berkshire	
Berkshire	Philip Herbert, 4th Earl of Pembroke Henry Marten
Windsor	Cornelius Holland
Reading	Tanfield Vachel Daniel Blagrave
Wallingford	Edmund Dunch
Abingdon	Henry Neville
Buckinghamshire	
Buckinghamshire	George Fleetwood Edmund West
Buckingham	Sir Peter Temple John Dormer

Wycombe	Richard Browne
Aylesbury	Thomas Scot Simon Mayne
Amersham	Sir William Drake, 1st Baronet
Wendover	Richard Ingoldsby Thomas Harrison
Marlow	Bulstrode Whitelocke
CAMBRIDGESHIRE	
Cambridgeshire	Francis Russell
Cambridge University	Henry Lucas Nathaniel Bacon
Cambridge	Oliver Cromwell John Lowry
CHESHIRE	
Cheshire	Sir William Brereton George Booth
City of Chester	John Ratcliffe
CORNWALL	
Cornwall	Hugh Boscawen Nicholas Trefusis
Launceston	
Liskeard	George Kekewich
Lostwithiel	John Maynard
Truro	Francis Rous
Bodmin	Anthony Nichols
Helston	John Penrose
Saltash	Henry Wills
Camelford	William Say Gregory Clement
Grampound	Sir John Trevor

Eastlow	John Moyle
Westlow	John Arundell
Penryn	Sir John Bampfylde, 1st Baronet
Tregoney	John Carew
Bossiney	Sir Christopher Yelverton
St Ives	John Feilder Henry Rainsford
Fowey	John Upton
St Germans	Benjamin Valentine
Mitchel	Charles Lord Rochester
Newport	
St Mawes	Richard Erisey
Callington	Thomas Dacres Lord Clinton
Cumberland	
Cumberland	William Airmine Richard Tolson
Carlisle	Thomas Cholmley Edward Howard, 1st Baron Howard of Escrick
Cockermouth	Sir John Hippisley Francis Allen
Derbyshire	
Derbyshire	Sir John Coke
Derby	Nathaniel Hallowes
Devon	
Devon	William Morice
Exeter	Samuel Clark

Totnes	Oliver St John John Maynard
Plymouth	Sir John Yonge, 1st Baronet
Barnstaple	Philip Skippon John Dodderidge
Plympton Erle	Christopher Martyn Sir Richard Strode
Tavistock	Edmund Fowell Elisha Crimes
Clifton Dartmouth Hardness	Thomas Boone
Bere Alston	Francis Drake
Tiverton	John Elford Robert Shapcote
Ashburton	Sir Edmund Fowell Sir John Northcote Bt
Honiton	Walter Yonge
Okehampton	Lawrence Whitaker
DORSET	
Dorset	John Browne Sir Thomas Trenchard
Poole	John Pyne
Dorchester	Denis Bond
Lyme Regis	Edmund Prideaux Richard Rose
Weymouth	
Melcombe	William Sydenham John Bond
Bridport	Roger Hill Thomas Ceeley
Shaftesbury	John Fry John Bingham

Wareham	John Trenchard
Corfe Castle	Francis Chettel
Essex	
Essex	Sir William Masham Bt
Colchester	John Sayer
Maldon	Sir Henry Mildmay
Harwich	Sir Thomas Cheek
Gloucestershire	
Gloucestershire	Nathaniel Stephens
Gloucester	Thomas Pury John Lenthall
Cirencester	Sir Thomas Fairfax Nathaniel Rich
Tewkesbury	John Stephens
Hampshire	
Hampshire	Richard Whitehead Richard Norton
Winchester	John Lisle Nicholas Love
Southampton	George Gallop Edward Exton
Portsmouth	Richard Cromwell
Yarmouth	Viscount L'Isle Sir John Leigh
Petersfield	
Newport alias Medina	Sir Henry Worsley, 2nd Baronet William Stephens LLD
Stockbridge	William Hevingham William Jephson

Newtown	Sir John Barrington John Bulkeley
Christchurch	John Kempe Richard Edwards
Whitchurch	Sir Thomas Jervoise Thomas Hussey
Lymington	John Button Henry Campion
Andover	Robert Wallop
HEREFORDSHIRE	
Herefordshire	
Hereford	Edmund Weaver Bennet Hoskyns
Weobley	Robert Andrews William Crowther
Leominster	
HERTFORDSHIRE	
Hertfordshire	
St Albans	
Hertford	Viscount Cranborne William Leman
HUNTINGDONSHIRE	
Huntingdonshire	Valentine Walton Edward Montagu, 1st Earl of Sandwich
Huntingdon	Abraham Burrell
KENT	
Kent	Augustine Skinner John Boys
Canterbury	Sir Edward Masters John Nutt

Rochester	Richard Lee Sir Thomas Walsingham
Maidstone	Thomas Twisden
Queensborough	Sir Michael Livesey Augustine Garland
LANCASHIRE	
Lancashire	Ralph Assheton Sir Richard Hoghton, 3rd Baronet
Lancaster	Sir Robert Bindlosse Thomas Fell
Preston	William Langton
Newton	William Ashurst
Wigan	Alexander Rigby
Clitheroe	Richard Shuttleworth
Liverpool	John Moore Thomas Birch
LEICESTERSHIRE	
Leicestershire	Sir Arthur Hesilrige Henry Smith
Leicester	Lord Grey of Groby Peter Temple
LINCOLNSHIRE	
Lincolnshire	Sir John Wray, 2nd Baronet
Lincoln	Thomas Grantham Thomas Lister
Boston	
Grimsby	William Wray Edward Rossiter
Stamford	Thomas Hatcher John Weaver

Grantham	Sir William Airmine
MIDDLESEX	
Middlesex	Sir Edward Spencer
Westminster	John Glynne William Bell
City of London	Isaac Penington John Venn
MONMOUTHSHIRE	
Monmouthshire	John Herbert Henry Herbert
Monmouth	Thomas Pury (Junior)
NORFOLK	
Norfolk	
Norwich	Thomas Atkins Erasmus Erle
King's Lynn	William Cecil, 2nd Earl of Salisbury Thomas Toll
Yarmouth	Miles Corbet Edward Owner
Thetford	Sir Thomas Wodehouse
Castle Rising	Sir John Holland, 1st Baronet
NORTHAMPTONSHIRE	
Northamptonshire	Sir Gilbert Pickering, Bt John Dryden Bt.
Peterborough	
Northampton	Zouch Tate
Brackley	
Higham Ferrars	Edward Harvey
NORTHUMBERLAND	

Northumberland	William Fenwick
Newcastle	John Blakiston Robert Ellison
Berwick upon Tweed	Sir Thomas Widdrington Robert Scawen
Morpeth	John Fiennes George Fenwick
NOTTINGHAMSHIRE	
Nottinghamshire	John Hutchinson Gervase Pigot
Nottingham	Gilbert Millington Francis Pierrepoint
East Retford	Edward Nevill
OXFORDSHIRE	
Oxfordshire	James Fiennes
Oxford University	John Selden
Oxford	John Doyley John Nixon
Woodstock	William Lenthall
Banbury	
RUTLAND	
Rutland	Thomas Waite James Harrington
SALOP	
Shropshire	Humphrey Edwards
Shrewsbury	Thomas Hunt William Masham
Bridgnorth	Robert Clive Robert Charlton
Ludlow	Thomas Mackworth Thomas Moor

Wenlock	William Pierrepont Sir Humphrey Bridges
Bishops Castle	Isaiah Thomas John Corbet
SOMERSET	
Somerset	John Harrington
Bristol	Richard Aldworth Luke Hodges
Bath	James Ashe Alexander Popham
Wells	Lislebone Long
Taunton	Robert Blake George Searle
Bridgwater	Sir Thomas Wroth John Palmer
Minehead	Edward Popham Walter Strickland
Ilchester	William Strode Thomas Hodges
Milborne Port	William Carent
STAFFORDSHIRE	
Staffordshire	John Bowyer Thomas Crompton
Stafford	
Newcastle under Lyme	Sir John Merrick
Lichfield	Michael Noble
Tamworth	George Abbot Sir Peter Wentworth
SUFFOLK	
Suffolk	Sir Nathaniel Barnardiston

Ipswich	John Gurdon Francis Bacon
Dunwich	Robert Brewster
Orford	Sir Charles Legross
Aldeburgh	Squire Bence Alexander Bence
Sudbury	Brampton Gurdon
Eye	
Bury St Edmunds	Sir Thomas Barnardiston
Surrey	
Surrey	
Southwark	George Thomson George Snelling
Bletchingly	John Evelyn (Senior) Edward Bysshe
Reigate	William Monson, 1st Viscount Monson George Evelyn
Guildford	
Gatton	
Haslemere	John Goodwin Carew Raleigh
Sussex	
Sussex	Anthony Stapley
Chichester	
Horsham	Hall Ravenscroft
Midhurst	William Cawley Sir Gregory Norton, Bt.
Lewes	Herbert Morley Henry Shelley
New Shoreham	Herbert Springet

Bramber	James Temple
Steyning	Edward Apsley
East Grinstead	Robert Goodwin John Baker
Arundel	John Downes
WARWICKSHIRE	
Warwickshire	
Coventry	John Barker
Warwick	William Purefoy Godfrey Bosvile
WESTMORLAND	
Westmoreland	James Bellingham Henry Lawrence
Appleby	Richard Salway Henry Ireton
WILTSHIRE	
Wiltshire	 Edmund Ludlow
Salisbury	Michael Oldisworth John Dove
Wilton	Sir Henry Vane (the elder)
Downton	Alexander Thistlewaite
Hindon	Robert Reynolds Edmund Ludlow
Heytesbury	Thomas Moore Edward Ashe
Westbury	John Ashe
Calne	Hugh Rogers Rowland Wilson
Devizes	Sir Edward Bayntun Robert Nicholas

Chippenham	William Eyre of Neston Sir Edward Bayntun
Malmesbury	Sir John Danvers
Cricklade	
Great Bedwyn	Edmund Harvey
Ludgershall	
Old Sarum	Hon. Robert Cecil Sir Richard Lucy
Wootton Bassett	
Marlborough	Charles Fleetwood Philip Smith
WORCESTERSHIRE	
Worcestershire	John Wilde Humphrey Salwey
Worcester	John Coucher
Droitwich	George Wylde Edmund Wylde
Evesham	Richard Cresheld
Bewdley	Nicholas Lechmere
YORKSHIRE	
Yorkshire	
York	Sir William Allanson Thomas Hoyle (Alderman)
Kingston upon Hull	Sir Henry Vane (Junior) Peregrine Pelham
Knaresborough	Sir William Constable, Bt. Thomas Stockdale
Scarborough	John Anlaby Luke Robinson
Ripon	Sir Charles Egerton Sir John Bourchier

Richmond	Thomas Chaloner Francis Thorpe
Hedon	Sir William Strickland John Alured
Boroughbridge	Sir Thomas Maulaverer, Bt Henry Stapylton
Thirsk	Thomas Lascelles William Ayscough
Aldborough	Brian Stapylton James Chaloner
Beverley	James Nelthorpe
Pontefract	Henry Arthington William White
Malton	Henry Darley John Wastell
Northallerton	Richard Darley
CINQUE PORTS	
Hastings	Roger Gratwick
Romney	
Hythe	Henry Heyman Thomas Westrow
Dover	John Dixwell Benjamin Weston
Sandwich	
Seaford	
Rye	William Hay John Fagg
Winchelsea	Samuel Gott
WALES	
Anglesey	
Newburgh	

Appendix IV

Brecknockshire	Philip Jones
Brecknock	Ludovic Lewis
Cardiganshire	Sir Richard Pryse, 1st Baronet
Cardigan	Thomas Wogan
Carmarthenshire	
Carmarthen	
Carnarvon	
Carnarvonshire	
Denbighshire	
Denbigh	
Flintshire	John Trevor
Flint	
Glamorgan	Philip, Lord Herbert
Cardiff	Algernon Sidney
Merioneth	John Jones
Montgomeryshire	
Montgomery	George Devereux
Pembrokeshire	
Pembroke	Sir Hugh Owen, 1st Baronet
Haverford West	
Radnorshire	Arthur Annesley
Radnor	

Appendix V

Cromwell Speech Dissolving Parliament 20 April 1653

It is high time for me to put an end to your sitting in this place, which you have dishonored by your contempt of all virtue, and defiled by your practice of every vice; ye are a factious crew, and enemies to all good government; ye are a pack of mercenary wretches, and would like Esau sell your country for a mess of pottage, and like Judas betray your God for a few pieces of money.

Is there a single virtue now remaining amongst you? Is there one vice you do not possess? Ye have no more religion than my horse; gold is your God; which of you have not barter'd your conscience for bribes? Is there a man amongst you that has the least care for the good of the Commonwealth?

Ye sordid prostitutes have you not defil'd this sacred place, and turn'd the Lord's temple into a den of thieves, by your immoral principles and wicked practices? Ye are grown intolerably odious to the whole nation; you were deputed here by the people to get grievances redress'd, are yourselves gone! So! Take away that shining bauble there, and lock up the doors.

In the name of God, go!

Appendix VI

List of Members Elected to the Barebones Parliament

Bedfordshire	Nathaniel Taylor Edward Cater
Berkshire	Samuel Dunch Vincent Goddard Thomas Wood.[
Buckinghamshire	George Fleetwood George Baldwin.
Cambridgeshire	John Sadler Thomas French Robert Castle Samuel Warner
Cheshire	Robert Duckenfield Henry Birkenhead
Cornwall	Robert Bennet Francis Langdon Anthony Rous John Bawden
Cumberland	Robert Fenwick
Derbyshire	Gervase Bennet Nathaniel Barton

Devon	General-at-sea George Monck John Carew Thomas Saunders Christopher Martyn James Erisey Francis Rous Richard Sweet
Dorset	William Sydenham John Bingham
Durham	Henry Dawson
Essex	Joachim Matthews Henry Barrington John Brewster Christopher Earl Dudley Templer
Gloucestershire	John Crofts William Neast Robert Holmes
Hampshire (*See* Southampton below)	
Herefordshire	Wroth Rogers John Herring
Hertfordshire	Henry Lawrence William Reeve
Huntingdonshire	Edward Montagu Stephen Pheasant
Kent	Viscount Lisle Thomas Blount William Kenrick William Cullen Andrew Broughton
Lancashire	William West John Sawry Robert Cunliffe

Leicestershire	Henry Danvers Edward Smith John Prat
Lincolnshire	Sir William Brownlow Richard Cust Barnaby Bowtel Humphrey Walcot William Thompson
Middlesex	Sir William Roberts Augustine Wingfield Arthur Squib
City of London	Robert Tichborne John Ireton Samuel Moyer John Langley John Stone Henry Barton Praise-God Barebone
Monmouthshire	Philip Jones
Norfolk	Robert Jermy Tobias Frere Ralph Wolmer Henry King William Burton
Northamptonshire	Sir Gilbert Pickering, Bt Thomas Brooke
Northumberland	Henry Ogle
Nottinghamshire	John Oddingsels Edward Cludd
Oxfordshire	Sir Charles Wolseley William Draper Dr Jonathan Goddard
Rutland	Edward Horseman
Shropshire	William Bottrell Thomas Baker

Somerset	General-at-sea Robert Blake John Pine Dennis Hollister Henry Henley
County of Southampton	Richard Norton Richard Major John Hildesley
Staffordshire	George Bellot John Chetwood
Suffolk	Jacob Caley Francis Brewster Robert Dunken John Clarke Edward Plumstead
Surrey	Samuel Highland Laurence March
Sussex	Anthony Stapley William Spence Nathaniel Studeley
Warwickshire	John St Nicholas Richard Lucy
Westmorland	Major-General Charles Howard
Wiltshire	Sir Anthony Ashley Cooper Nicholas Green Thomas Eyre
Worcestershire	Richard Salwey John James
Yorkshire	Lord Eure Walter Strickland Francis Lascelles John Anlaby Thomas Dickenson Thomas St. Nicholas Roger Coats Edward Gill

APPENDIX VI

Wales	Bussy Mansell James Philipps John Williams Hugh Courtenay Richard Price John Brown
Scotland	Sir James Hope Alexander Brodie (nominated but did not take his seat) John Swinton William Lockhart Alexander Jaffrays
Ireland	Sir Robert King Colonel John Hewson Colonel Henry Cromwell Colonel John Clark Daniel Hutchinson (Alderman) Vincent Gookin
Nominated	Lord General Oliver Cromwell Major-General Lambert Major-General Harrison Major-General Desborough Colonel Matthew Tomlinson

Index

B

C

D

E

F

G

H

I

J

K

L

M

N

O

P

Q

R

S

T

U

V

W

Y

Z

www.ingramcontent.com/pod-product-compliance
Lightning Source LLC
Chambersburg PA
CBHW030359100426
42812CB00028B/2766/J

* 9 7 8 1 9 1 0 8 9 3 0 0 5 *